Lua Game Development Cookbook

Over 70 recipes that will help you master the elements
and best practices required to build a modern game
engine using Lua

Mário Kašuba

[PACKT] open source *
PUBLISHING   community experience distilled

BIRMINGHAM - MUMBAI

Lua Game Development Cookbook

First published: July 2015

Production reference: 1200715

Published by Packt Publishing Ltd.
Livery Place
35 Livery Street
Birmingham B3 2PB, UK.

ISBN 978-1-84951-550-4

www.packtpub.com

Credits

Author
Mário Kašuba

Reviewers
Victor Andrade de Oliveira

Anthony Zhang

Commissioning Editor
Sarah Cullington

Acquisition Editor
Kevin Colaco

Content Development Editor
Govindan K

Technical Editor
Vivek Arora

Copy Editors
Merilyn Pereira

Laxmi Subramanian

Project Coordinator
Sanjeet Rao

Proofreader
Safis Editing

Indexer
Rekha Nair

Graphics
Jason Monteiro

Abhinash Sahu

Production Coordinator
Manu Joseph

Cover Work
Manu Joseph

About the Author

Mário Kašuba achieved a master's degree in applied informatics at Slovak Technical University in Bratislava, where he used the Lua language in 3D robotics simulations and developed various multimedia applications along with a few computer games.

Currently, he is the co-owner and chief information officer of an IT Academy company, while he also leads courses on C/C++, PHP, Linux, Databases, Typo3, Silverstripe CMS, VMware virtualization, and the Microsoft Windows Server operating system.

He also works as the head web developer and system administrator for the web portal `http://www.rodinka.sk/`.

I would like to acknowledge the support provided by my family, friends, and colleagues. I am particularly grateful to the members of the Lua users community who helped me with the reviewing process. I would also like to thank the staff at Packt Publishing for their guidance and valuable support.

About the Reviewer

Victor Andrade de Oliveira is a Brazilian computer engineer who graduated from the Institute for Higher Studies of the Amazon (IESAM) with a vast knowledge of the Lua language and has worked for more than 5 years in the development of interactive and embedded applications for Ginga—the middleware of the Japanese-Brazilian Digital TV System (ISDB-TB) and ITU-T Recommendation for IPTV services.

Anthony Zhang is a programmer, electronics hobbyist, and digital artist who has an unhealthy obsession with robotics. If you want to hear him talk for hours on end, ask him something about AI, physical computing, obscure processor functionality, and computer graphics. These days, you'll find him working on video games, doing ridiculous things with microcontrollers, and attempting to add LEDs where they don't belong.

www.PacktPub.com

Support files, eBooks, discount offers, and more

For support files and downloads related to your book, please visit www.PacktPub.com.

Did you know that Packt offers eBook versions of every book published, with PDF and ePub files available? You can upgrade to the eBook version at www.PacktPub.com and as a print book customer, you are entitled to a discount on the eBook copy. Get in touch with us at service@packtpub.com for more details.

At www.PacktPub.com, you can also read a collection of free technical articles, sign up for a range of free newsletters and receive exclusive discounts and offers on Packt books and eBooks.

https://www2.packtpub.com/books/subscription/packtlib

Do you need instant solutions to your IT questions? PacktLib is Packt's online digital book library. Here, you can search, access, and read Packt's entire library of books.

Why Subscribe?

- ▸ Fully searchable across every book published by Packt
- ▸ Copy and paste, print, and bookmark content
- ▸ On demand and accessible via a web browser

Free Access for Packt account holders

If you have an account with Packt at www.PacktPub.com, you can use this to access PacktLib today and view 9 entirely free books. Simply use your login credentials for immediate access.

Table of Contents

Preface

Game development is one of the most complex processes in the world as it requires a wide set of skills such as programming, math, physics, art, sound engineering, management, marketing, and many more. Even with modern technologies, it may take from a few hours to several years to create a game. This depends on the game complexity and tools available.

Computer games are usually based on a mix of simple concepts, which are turned into an enjoyable experience. The first step in making a good game is a game prototype. These can be made with the help of various game engines. However, learning how to use a game engine to the full extent may require you to study how it actually works. This way you have to rely on the available documentation and features that the game engine provides. Many game engines today provide a scripting language as a tool to implement certain game mechanics or to extend the game engine itself with new features.

The Lua programming language is gaining popularity in the game industry mainly due to its simplicity and efficiency. Most of the time, it's used only for simple tasks such as NPC dialogs, user interface, or custom game events. However, with additional Lua modules, you can create your own full-fledged game engine that can use almost all the capabilities of the modern computer hardware.

In this book, you'll find a set of recipes with solutions to the most common problems you may encounter while creating games with the Lua language.

The best way to learn something is to play with it. Therefore, each recipe is paired with simple demo applications that will help you understand the topic covered. You may even use these demo samples to create your own game prototype in no time.

All sample applications are available in the digital content of this book.

What this book covers

Chapter 1, Basics of the Game Engine, covers important algorithms and the basic design of a game engine written in the Lua programming language, as well as LuaSDL multimedia module preparation, which is the main part of all the recipes in this book.

Chapter 2, Events, deals with handling input events that are an important part of any game engine.

Chapter 3, Graphics – Common Methods, contains basic concepts used in computer graphics. You'll learn how to initialize the graphics mode, use basic OpenGL functions, load images, create textures, and draw text on the screen.

Chapter 4, Graphics – Legacy Method with OpenGL 1.x-2.1, explains how to use the intermediate mode of OpenGL, which is intended for use on older GPUs. Even when this mode is currently deprecated, it holds important information that is vital when using modern versions of OpenGL. It may be used as a precursor to more advanced topics in *Chapter 5, Graphics – Modern Method with OpenGL 3.0+*.

Chapter 5, Graphics – Modern Method with OpenGL 3.0+, covers the basics of using the GLSL shading language with the Lua language to draw various scenes. You'll also learn how to use per-pixel lighting, render into textures and apply surface effects with normal maps.

Chapter 6, The User Interface, covers the implementation of the custom user interface from simple windows to window controls.

Chapter 7, Physics and Game Mechanics, explains how to prepare and use the LuaBox2D module with the Lua language for physics simulation. The Box2D library is quite popular in modern side-scrolling games mainly because it offers great flexibility.

Chapter 8, Artificial Intelligence, deals with pathfinding algorithms and fuzzy logic. You'll learn how pathfinding works in games with simple maze or even tiled environments. More advanced topics cover decision making with fuzzy logic. In combination with pathfinding algorithms, you can create intelligent game opponents that won't jump into a lava lake at the first opportunity.

Chapter 9, Sounds and Networking, covers how to initialize the sound card, play sounds, and music. The second part covers network communication with the high-performance ZeroMQ library. It contains many improvements over traditional socket communication and it's used by companies such as AT&T, Cisco, EA, Zynga, Spotify, NASA, Microsoft, and CERN.

What you need for this book

Sample demonstrations for recipes require the Microsofts Windows or Linux operating systems. Unfortunately, Mac OS is not currently supported.

If you intend to build binary Lua modules from this book, you'll need the C/C++ compiler along with the recent version of the CMake building system. Additionally, Linux users will need to install development packages for the XOrg display server in order to include the graphical output.

However, it's not necessary to do so as binary Lua modules are included in code files for this book.

The recipes in *Chapter 5, Graphics – Modern Method with OpenGL 3.0+*, require a graphic card released after 2010 with support for OpenGL 3.3.

Who this book is for

This book is for all programmers and game enthusiasts who want to stop dreaming about creating a game, and actually create one from scratch.

The reader should know the basics of programming and using the Lua language. Knowledge of the C/C++ programming language is not necessary, but it's strongly recommended in order to write custom Lua modules extending game engine capabilities or to rewrite parts of the Lua code into a more efficient form.

Algebra and matrix operations are required in order to understand advanced topics in *Chapter 4, Graphics – Legacy Method with OpenGL 1.x-2.1* and *Chapter 5, Graphics – Modern Method with OpenGL 3.0+*.

Sample demonstrations are coupled with binary libraries for Windows and Linux operating systems for convenience.

Sections

In this book, you will find several headings that appear frequently (Getting ready, How to do it, How it works, There's more, and See also).

To give clear instructions on how to complete a recipe, we use these sections as follows:

Getting ready

This section tells you what to expect in the recipe, and describes how to set up any software or any preliminary settings required for the recipe.

How to do it...

This section contains the steps required to follow the recipe.

How it works...

This section usually consists of a detailed explanation of what happened in the previous section.

There's more...

This section consists of additional information about the recipe in order to make the reader more knowledgeable about the recipe.

See also

This section provides helpful links to other useful information for the recipe.

Conventions

In this book, you will find a number of text styles that distinguish between different kinds of information. Here are some examples of these styles and an explanation of their meaning.

Code words in text, database table names, folder names, filenames, file extensions, pathnames, dummy URLs, user input, and Twitter handles are shown as follows: "We can include other contexts through the use of the `include` directive."

A block of code is set as follows:

```
local sum_of_numbers = 0
local iterations = 3
for i=1,iterations do
  sum_of_numbers = sum_of_numbers + 1/iterations
  print(("%f"):format(sum_of_numbers))
end
-- is the result equal to 1?
print("Sum equals to 1?", sum_of_numbers == 1)
```

When we wish to draw your attention to a particular part of a code block, the relevant lines or items are set in bold:

```
gl.Begin(gl_enum.GL_LINES)
    -- A
    gl.Color4f(1, 0, 0, 1)
    gl.Vertex3f(-0.5, -0.5, 0)
    -- B
    gl.Color4f(0, 1, 0, 1)
    gl.Vertex3f(0.5, -0.5, 0)
    -- C
    gl.Color4f(0, 0, 1, 1)
    gl.Vertex3f(0.5, 0.5, 0)
    -- D
    gl.Color4f(1, 1, 0, 1)
    gl.Vertex3f(-0.5, 0.5, 0)
gl.End()
```

Any command-line input or output is written as follows:

```
mkdir luagl/build
cd luagl/build
cmake ..
```

New terms and **important words** are shown in bold. Words that you see on the screen, for example, in menus or dialog boxes, appear in the text like this: "You can validate settings by pressing the **Configure** button"

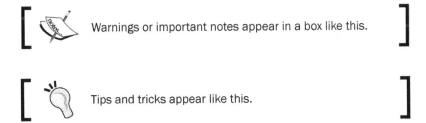

Warnings or important notes appear in a box like this.

Tips and tricks appear like this.

Reader feedback

Feedback from our readers is always welcome. Let us know what you think about this book—what you liked or disliked. Reader feedback is important for us as it helps us develop titles that you will really get the most out of.

To send us general feedback, simply e-mail feedback@packtpub.com, and mention the book's title in the subject of your message.

If there is a topic that you have expertise in and you are interested in either writing or contributing to a book, see our author guide at www.packtpub.com/authors.

Customer support

Now that you are the proud owner of a Packt book, we have a number of things to help you to get the most from your purchase.

Downloading the example code

You can download the example code files from your account at http://www.packtpub.com for all the Packt Publishing books you have purchased. If you purchased this book elsewhere, you can visit http://www.packtpub.com/support and register to have the files e-mailed directly to you.

Errata

Although we have taken every care to ensure the accuracy of our content, mistakes do happen. If you find a mistake in one of our books—maybe a mistake in the text or the code—we would be grateful if you could report this to us. By doing so, you can save other readers from frustration and help us improve subsequent versions of this book. If you find any errata, please report them by visiting http://www.packtpub.com/submit-errata, selecting your book, clicking on the **Errata Submission Form** link, and entering the details of your errata. Once your errata are verified, your submission will be accepted and the errata will be uploaded to our website or added to any list of existing errata under the Errata section of that title.

To view the previously submitted errata, go to https://www.packtpub.com/books/content/support and enter the name of the book in the search field. The required information will appear under the **Errata** section.

Piracy

Piracy of copyrighted material on the Internet is an ongoing problem across all media. At Packt, we take the protection of our copyright and licenses very seriously. If you come across any illegal copies of our works in any form on the Internet, please provide us with the location address or website name immediately so that we can pursue a remedy.

Please contact us at copyright@packtpub.com with a link to the suspected pirated material.

We appreciate your help in protecting our authors and our ability to bring you valuable content.

Questions

If you have a problem with any aspect of this book, you can contact us at
questions@packtpub.com, and we will do our best to address the problem.

1
Basics of the Game Engine

In this chapter, we will cover the following recipes:

- ▸ Preparing a basic file structure for the game engine
- ▸ Making a stack
- ▸ Making a queue
- ▸ Making a prioritized queue
- ▸ Extending ipairs for use in sparse arrays
- ▸ Creating Lua modules
- ▸ Handling errors with pcall, xpcall, and assert
- ▸ Using Lua with existing projects written in C/C++
- ▸ Getting LuaSDL for libSDL 1.2
- ▸ Designing the main application loop with LuaSDL

Introduction

Almost every game uses a game engine to help developers in video game production. It is usually used as a base platform for the game and manages all important functions from 2D/3D graphics, physics, sound effects, and network communication to artificial intelligence, scripting, and support for various software/hardware platforms. Using the scripting language in games has gained a lot of attention in the last decade mainly because it allows you to create game prototypes faster, easier, and it's an important part of the so-called **modding** support for the game community.

For instance, you can look at *Quake* game from the id software company, which uses its own scripting language Quake C and is one of the reasons why there are so many mods for this game. However, the source code for this language must be compiled before using. Depending on the project size this means a significant amount of time spent between feature implementation and testing. The Lua language can be used without prior compilation, which allows developers to test out their code right away.

The first game that used the Lua language for scripting was *Grim Fandango* from the company LucasArts. It was successfully used in further major game titles and today it can be commonly found in many multiplatform and mobile games.

Modern game engines are one of the most complex applications that are used. This leads to the situation where game developers use game engine as a black box without knowing how it actually works. For certain game titles, this might work out quite well. However, if you want to make a quick game prototype with certain features that are not present in the game engine, you'll most probably have to write your own game engine extension or find a workaround.

Lua language is fast and mature enough to be used as a game engine base language. Time-critical portions of a code can be written in C or C++ language and accessed via a Lua/C language interface. With this approach, you can view the Lua language as a high-level glue for the game engine process design.

This book will use Lua 5.1 version mainly because it's well supported and the existing code can be ported into a newer version with minor changes. Another reason behind this choice is that Lua 5.1 API is used in LuaJIT which is Just-In-Time implementation of Lua language. It's generally regarded as a faster version of the Lua language, which gives you speed comparable to compiled C code.

Lua language itself doesn't provide access to graphical output, sound devices or even input devices except basic I/O file interface. This shortcoming can be overcome with the use of LuaSDL binding to libSDL multimedia library that gives us the power to access all the devices needed to create a game with graphics and sounds. Installation and use of this library binding will be contained in this chapter.

It's always good practice to maintain a consistent file structure in any project. The Lua language doesn't formally specify modular structure and it's often the case when each module uses its own style of module specification. This results in namespace conflicts and unpredictable behavior.

The first part of this chapter will cover the preparation of a modular file structure for your application, implementation of the most common data structures, and error handling.

The second half of this chapter will deal with more advanced stuff such as writing and using the Lua modules and using libSDL multimedia library to develop interactive applications in Lua.

Preparing a basic file structure for the game engine

When programming a larger project, it's always important to keep it maintainable. One of the common practices is to keep a modular structure. Modular structure can be achieved by keeping files separated in certain directories.

Lua language uses a `require` function to include modules in your script files. This function uses a default list of paths where it tries to find the module file. The Lua modules can be written as plain Lua scripts or use a form of binary library, which is OS and CPU architecture dependent. This is especially troublesome if want to include binary libraries for all supported operating systems and CPU architectures in one project.

A default set of paths might not always be appropriate for your project, mainly if you bundle many third-party modules with it.

This recipe shows how to set up the Lua interpreter so that it can find correct files in a systematic and user-definable way. This recipe should be used at the beginning of your main Lua script file so that further calls to the `require` function in Lua will use your file path structure.

Getting ready

You can use a directory structure as shown in the following diagram. If you intend to implement your application for multiple platforms, always divide platform-specific files into separate directories.

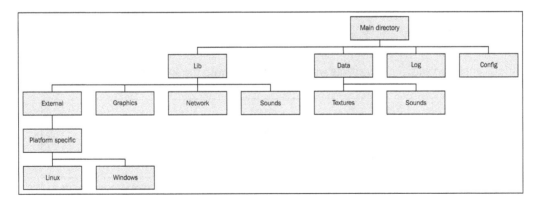

The Lib directory contains all the Lua module files and binary libraries.

However, each operating system uses its own file naming convention for binary libraries. The Lua language doesn't have an easy way to obtain the OS name. For this purpose, you can download and use the Lua script module `os_name.lua` from `https://gist.github.com/soulik/82e9d02a818ce12498d1`.

You should copy this file into your project directory so that the Lua interpreter can find it.

How to do it...

The `require` function in the Lua language uses a set of default paths defined in `package.path` and `package.cpath` string variables. With your new directory structure, you'd have to change those two variables manually for each operating system, which could be cumbersome.

Instead, you can define a Lua script to build up these two string variables from a generic list of paths for both Lua script files and binary libraries.

In the first step, you need to create a list of directories:

```
-- A list of paths to lua script modules
local paths = {
  '{root}/{module}',
  '{root}/lib/{module}',
  '{root}/lib/external/{module}',
  '{root}/lib/external/platform-specific/{platform}/{module}',
}
-- A list of paths to binary Lua modules
local module_paths = {
  '?.{extension}',
  '?/init.{extension}',
  '?/core.{extension}',
}
```

Strings enclosed with curly brackets will be substituted with the following values:

Name	Value
root	This is the application's root directory
platform	This is the current platform
module	This is the module's file path
extension	This is the module's filename extension, which is platform dependent

Binary module filename extensions that are platform dependent are also set in a table:

```
-- List of supported OS paired with binary file extension name
local extensions = {
  Windows = 'dll',
  Linux = 'so',
  Mac = 'dylib',
}
```

Now, you need to set `root_dir` which is the current working directory of the application and the current platform name as follows:

```
-- os_name is a supplemental module for
-- OS and CPU architecture detection
local os_name = require 'os_name'

-- A dot character represent current working directory
local root_dir = '.'
local current_platform, current_architecture = os_name.getOS()

local cpaths, lpaths = {}, {}
local current_clib_extension = extensions[current_platform]
```

Before you start building the path list, you need to check whether the current platform has defined binary module extensions as follows:

```
if current_clib_extension then
  -- now you can process each defined path for module.
  for _, path in ipairs(paths) do
    local path = path:gsub("{(%w+)}", {
      root = root_dir,
      platform = current_platform,
    })
    -- skip empty path entries
    if #path>0 then
      -- make a substitution for each module file path.
      for _, raw_module_path in ipairs(module_paths) do
        local module_path = path:gsub("{(%w+)}", {
          module = raw_module_path
        })
        -- add path for binary module
        cpaths[#cpaths+1] = module_path:gsub("{(%w+)}", {
          extension = current_clib_extension
        })
        -- add paths for platform independent lua and luac modules
```

```
          lpaths[#lpaths+1] = module_path:gsub("{((%w+)}", {
             extension = 'lua'
          })
          lpaths[#lpaths+1] = module_path:gsub("{((%w+)}", {
             extension = 'luac'
          })
       end
     end
   end
   -- build module path list delimited with semicolon.
   package.path = table.concat(lpaths, ";")
   package.cpath = table.concat(cpaths, ";")
 end
```

With this design, you can easily manage your module paths just by editing `paths` and `module_paths` tables.

Keep in mind that you need to execute this code before any `require` command.

How it works...

This recipe builds content for two variables that are used in the `require` function—`package. path` and `package.cpath`.

Both variables use a semicolon as a delimiter for individual paths. There's also a special character—the question mark which is substituted with the module name. Note that the path order might not be as important in this case as with our default list of paths. The path order might cause problems if you expect to use a module out of the project directory structure. Therefore, a customized set of paths from this recipe should always be used before the default set of paths.

The Lua language allows the use of hierarchical structure of modules. You can specify a submodule with package names delimited by a dot.

```
   require 'main_module.submodule'
```

A dot is always replaced with the correct directory separator.

Making a stack

Stack data structure can be defined in the Lua language as a closure that always returns a new table. This table contains two functions defined by keys, `push` and `pop`. Both operations run in constant time.

Getting ready

Code from this recipe will be probably used more than once in your project so that it can be moved into the Lua module file with similar algorithms. The module file can use the following structure:

```
-- algoritms.lua

-- Placeholder for a stack data structure code

return {
  stack = stack,
}
```

This module structure can be used with algorithms from other recipes as well to keep everything organized.

How to do it...

The following code contains a local definition of the `stack` function. You can remove the `local` statement to make this function global or include it as part of the module:

```lua
local function stack()
  local out = {}
  out.push = function(item)
    out[#out+1] = item
  end
  out.pop = function()
    if #out>0 then
      return table.remove(out, #out)
    end
  end
  out.iterator = function()
    return function()
      return out.pop()
    end
  end
  return out
end
```

This stack data structure can be used in the following way:

```
local s1 = stack()
-- Place a few elements into stack
for _, element in ipairs {'Lorem','ipsum','dolor','sit','amet'} do
  s1.push(element)
end

-- iterator function can be used to pop and process all elements
for element in s1.iterator() do
    print(element)
end
```

How it works...

Calling the `stack` function will create a new empty table with three functions. Push and pop functions use the property of the length operator that returns the integer index of the last element. The `iterator` function returns a closure that can be used in a `for` loop to pop all the elements. The `out` table contains integer indices and no holes (without empty elements). Both the functions are excluded from the total length of the `out` table.

After you call the `push` function, the element is appended at the end of the `out` table. The Pop function removes the last element and returns the removed element.

Making a queue

The queue data structure can be constructed in a similar way as a stack with the `table.insert` and `table.remove` functions. However, this will add unnecessary overhead because each element insertion at the beginning of the list will need to move other elements as well. A better solution is using two indices that indicate the beginning and the end of the list.

Getting ready

The code from this recipe can be placed into the `algorithms.lua` file as in the *Making a stack* recipe.

How to do it...

The queue data structure will consist of a constructor that returns a new table with three functions: a `push`, a `pop`, and an `iterator`. The resulting table uses the modified version of the length operator to get the right length of the queue:

```
local function queue()
```

```lua
    local out = {}
    local first, last = 0, -1
    out.push = function(item)
      last = last + 1
      out[last] = item
    end
    out.pop = function()
      if first <= last then
        local value = out[first]
        out[first] = nil
        first = first + 1
        return value
      end
    end
    out.iterator = function()
      return function()
        return out.pop()
      end
    end
    setmetatable(out, {
      __len = function()
        return (last-first+1)
      end,
    })
    return out
end
```

A new queue data structure can be created by calling the `queue` function:

```lua
local q1 = queue()
-- Place a few elements into queue
for _, element in ipairs {'Lorem','ipsum','dolor','sit','amet'} do
  q1.push(element)
end

-- You can use iterator to process all elements in single for loop
for element in q1.iterator() do
  -- each queue element will be printed onto screen
  print(element)
end
```

How it works...

This algorithm uses a pair of integer indices that represent positions of the first and the last element of the queue. This approach provides element insertion and deletion in constant time. Because the original length operator isn't suitable for this case, a modified one is provided.

The iterator function creates a new closure that is used in a `for` loop. This closure is called repeatedly until the `pop` function returns an empty result.

Making a prioritized queue

A prioritized queue or simple priority queue extends basic queue with the entry sorting feature. Upon entry insertion, you can set what will be the priority of the entry. This data structure is often used in job queuing where the most important (highest priority) jobs must be processed before the jobs with lower priority. Priority queues are often used in artificial intelligence as well.

This version of the prioritized queue allows you to obtain entries with minimal or maximal priority at constant time. Element priority can be updated. However, priority queue insertion, update, and removal might use linear time complexity in worst case scenarios.

There are two rules that should be noted:

▶ Each entry of this queue should be unique
▶ The order of retrieving elements with the same priority is not defined

Getting ready

This recipe will use the following shortcuts:

```
local ti = table.insert
local tr = table.remove

-- removes element from table by its value
local tr2 = function(t, v)
  for i=1,#t do
    if t[i]==v then
      tr(t, i)
      break
    end
  end
end
```

It's recommended to put it all together in one Lua module file.

How to do it...

The priority queue can be defined as in the following code:

```
return function pqueue()
  -- interface table
  local t = {}

  -- a set of elements
  local set = {}
  -- a set of priority bags with a elements
  local r_set = {}
  -- sorted list of priorities
  local keys = {}

  -- add element into storage, set its priority and sort keys
  --   k - element
  --   v - priority
  local function addKV(k, v)
    set[k] = v
    -- create a new list for this priority
    if not r_set[v] then
      ti(keys, v)
      table.sort(keys)
      local k0 = {k}
      r_set[v] = k0
      setmetatable(k0, {
        __mode = 'v'
      })
    -- add element into list for this priority
    else
      ti(r_set[v], k)
    end
  end

  -- remove element from storage and sort keys
  local remove = function(k)
    local v = set[k]
    local prioritySet = r_set[v]
    tr2(prioritySet, k)
    if #prioritySet < 1 then
      tr2(keys, v)
      r_set[v] = nil
```

```lua
          table.sort(keys)
          set[k] = nil
      end
  end; t.remove = remove

  -- returns an element with the lowest priority
  t.min = function()
    local priority = keys[1]
    if priority then
      return r_set[priority][1] or {}
    else
      return {}
    end
  end

  -- returns an element with the highest priority
  t.max = function()
    local priority = keys[#keys]
    if priority then
      return r_set[priority][1] or {}
    else
      return {}
    end
  end

  -- is this queue empty?
  t.empty = function()
    return #keys < 1
  end
  -- simple element iterator, retrieves elements with
  -- the highest priority first
  t.iterate = function()
    return function()
      if not t.empty() then
        local element = t.max()
        t.remove(element)
        return element
      end
    end
  end
  -- setup pqueue behavior
  setmetatable(t, {
    __index = set,
```

```
    __newindex = function(t, k, v)
      if not set[k] then
        -- new item
        addKV(k, v)
      else
        -- existing item
        remove(k)
        addKV(k, v)
      end
    end,
  })
  return t
end
```

How it works...

This priority queue algorithm uses three tables: `set`, `r_set`, and `keys`. These tables help to organize elements into so-called **priority bags**. The first one, `set` contains elements paired with their priorities. It's also used when you try to obtain element priority from the queue. The second one, `r_set` contains priority bags. Each bag represents a priority level. The last one `keys` contains a sorted list of priorities, which is used in the extraction of elements from a minimal or maximal priority bag.

Each element can be inserted in a way similar to the Lua table with the exception that the inserted element is used as a key and `priority` is stored as a value:

```
priority_queue[element] = priority
```

This form of access can be used to update element priority. Elements with minimal or maximal priority can be extracted using the `min` or `max` function respectively;

```
local min_element = priority_queue.min()
local max_element = priority_queue.max()
```

Note that elements remain in the priority queue until you delete them with the `remove` function;

```
priority_queue.remove(element)
```

Priority queue can be queried with the `empty` function that returns true if there's no element in the queue;

```
priority_queue.empty()
```

You can use the iterator function in `for` loop to process all queue elements sorted by their priority:

```
for element in priority_queue.iterator() do
  -- do something with this element
end
```

Extending ipairs for use in sparse arrays

The `ipairs` function in the Lua language is used to iterate over entries in a sequence. This means every entry must be defined by the pair of key and value, where the key is the integer value. The main limitation of the `ipairs` function is that the keys must be consecutive numbers.

You can modify the `ipairs` function so that you can successfully iterate over entries with integer keys that are not consecutive. This is commonly seen in sparse arrays.

Getting ready

In this recipe, you'll need to define our own `iterator` function, which will return every entry of a sparse array in deterministic order. In this case, the iterator function can be included in your code as a global function to accompany `pairs` and `ipairs` functions; or you can put it in a Lua module file not to pollute the global environment space.

How to do it...

This code shows a very simple sparse array iterator without any caching:

```
function ipairs_sparse(t)
  -- tmpIndex will hold sorted indices, otherwise
  -- this iterator would be no different from pairs iterator
  local tmpIndex = {}
  local index, _ = next(t)
  while index do
    tmpIndex[#tmpIndex+1] = index
    index, _ = next(t, index)
  end
  -- sort table indices
  table.sort(tmpIndex)
  local j = 1

  return function()
    -- get index value
    local i = tmpIndex[j]
```

```
      j = j + 1
      if i then
         return i, t[i]
      end
   end
end
```

The following lines of code show the usage example for iteration over a sparse array;

```
-- table below contains unsorted sparse array
local t = {
   [10] = 'a', [2] = 'b', [5] = 'c', [100] = 'd', [99] = 'e',
}
-- iterate over entries
for i, v in ipairs_sparse(t) do
   print(i,v)
end
```

How it works...

The Lua language uses iterator functions in the control structure called the generic `for`. The generic `for` calls the iterator function for each new iteration and stops when the iterator function returns nil. The `ipairs_sparse` function works in the following steps:

1. It builds a new index of keys from the table.

2. It sorts the index table.

3. It returns a closure where each call of the closure returns a consecutive index and a value from the sparse array.

Each call to `ipairs_sparse` prepares a new index table called `index`. The index consists of (integer, entry) pairs.

Creating Lua modules

The Lua language doesn't impose strict policies on what a module should look like. Instead, it encourages programmers to find their own style depending on the situation.

Getting ready

In this recipe, you will create three versions of a module that contains one local variable, one variable accessible from outside the module, one function that returns a simple value, and a function that uses a value from the current module.

How to do it...

There are three types of modules that are commonly used:

- ▶ A module that returns a table as a module interface
- ▶ A module in the form of an object
- ▶ A module in the form of a singleton object

The first case is used mostly with modules that contain an interface to third-party libraries. The second type of module is used less often, but it's useful if you need multiple instances of the same object, for example, a network stack. The last one uses a similar approach as in the previous case, but this time there's always only one instance of the object. Many games use the singleton object for the resource management system.

A module that returns a table as an interface

In this case, the module uses locally defined variables and functions. Every function intended for external use is put into one table. This common table is used as an interface with the outer world and is returned at the end of the module:

```
-- module1.lua
local var1 = 'ipsum'
local function local_function1()
  return 'lorem'
end

local function local_function2(self)
  return var1 .. self.var2
end
-- returns module interface
return {
  lorem = local_function1,
  ipsum = local_function2,
  var2 = 'sit',
}
```

A module in the form of an object

This module type doesn't manipulate the global namespace. Every object you create uses its own local namespace:

```
-- module2.lua
local M = function()
  local instance
  local var1 = 'ipsum'
```

```lua
    instance = {
      var2 = 'sit',
      lorem = function()
        return 'lorem'
      end,
      ipsum = function(self)
        return var1 .. self.var2
      end,
    }
    return instance
  end

  return M
```

A module in the form of a singleton object

This is a special case of object module. There is only one and the same object instance:

```lua
-- module3.lua
local instance

local M = function()
  if not instance then
    local var1 = 'ipsum'
    instance = {
      var2 = 'sit',
      lorem = function()
        return 'lorem'
      end,
      ipsum = function(self)
        return var1 .. self.var2
        end,
    }
  end
  return instance
end

return M
```

How it works...

Modules are used with the `require` function that registers them in the global table `modules.loaded`. This table contains the compiled code of every module used and ensures that each module is loaded only once.

Object modules return a local variable M, which contains an object interface. However, you can use any other name for this variable. Choosing between tables or closure as object contained is mostly a matter of application design.

Variable `var1` is always hidden from the outside world and can be changed only by the exposed function. Variable `var2` is freely accessible and can be modified anytime.

The following lines of code show the usage patterns for all three types of module:

```
local module1 = require 'module1'
local module2 = require 'module2'
local module3 = require 'module3'
-- create two instances of module2
local module2_A = module2()
local module2_B = module2()
-- try to create an instance of module2 twice
local module3_A = module3()
local module3_B = module3()


-- usage of a module with interface table
print('Module 1 - Before:',
   module1:lorem() .. module1:ipsum())
module1.var2 = 'amet'
print('Module 1 - After:',
   module1:lorem() .. module1:ipsum())


-- usage of a module in a form of an object
print('Module 2a - Before:',
   module2_A:lorem() .. module2_A:ipsum())
module2_A.var2 = 'amet'
print('Module 2a - After:',
   module2_A:lorem() .. module2_A:ipsum())
print('Module 2b - After:',
   module2_B:lorem() .. module2_B:ipsum())


-- usage of a module in a form of a singleton object
print('Module 3a - Before:',
   module3_A:lorem() .. module3_A:ipsum())
```

```
module3_A.var2 = 'amet'
print('Module 3a - After:',
  module3_A:lorem() .. module3_A:ipsum())
print('Module 3b - After:',
  module3_B:lorem() .. module3_B:ipsum())
```

Handling errors with pcall, xpcall, and assert

By default, the Lua language uses its internal error function. If an error occurs, Lua will usually abort code execution and put the error message with trace back into the standard error output. You can override the standard behavior with the pcall and xpcall functions. The main difference between these two functions is that pcall will return the status code and error message as the second return value, and xpcall will use the user-defined error function.

This way you can catch nonfatal errors and emulate the try and catch block.

Getting ready

This recipe will show error handling on a simple function that can exit prematurely with the error message:

```
local function f1(a, b)
  assert((a == 1), "The first parameter must be equal to 1")
  print(b)
  return a+1
end
```

How to do it...

Here's how you can catch a nonfatal error with pcall by emulating the try and catch block:

```
function try(fn, catch_fn)
  local status, msg = pcall(fn)
  if not status then
    catch_fn(msg)
  end
end

try(function()
  f1(2, 3) -- this will throw "an exception"
end, function(e)
```

```
      print('An exception occured:', e)
      error('Throw exception')
end)
```

The next recipe shows how to create your own specialized `xpcall2` function that can handle input parameters for a function:

```
local function xpcall2(fn, ...)
   local arg = {...}
   return xpcall(
      -- function wrapper to pass function arguments
      function(...)
         return fn(unpack(arg))
      end,
      -- error function
      function(msg)
         return debug.traceback(msg, 3)
      end
   )
end

print(xpcall2(f1, 2, 'a'))
```

How it works...

The whole principle of the `try` and `catch` block emulation in Lua relies on the `pcall` function that catches the error message and pushes it into the `catch` block function.

The only weakness of this approach is that you can't get more information because you're handling errors outside of the scope of where the error occurred.

This issue can be solved with `xpcall` which handles error before stack unwinding so you can use the debug library to get more information about the error.

Xpcall2 works as a wrapper function that not only passes parameters into protected function calls, but also handles getting the trace back with the `debug.traceback` function and returns results or a status code with an error message.

Using Lua with existing projects written in C/C++

The Lua language provides a set of API functions for communication between C/C++ and the Lua programming language. You can use these functions in your C code after you include the `lua.h` header file or `lua.hpp` for C++ source code. You can rely on this set of functions, but sooner or later you'll see that there are certain usage patterns which can be used to simplify your C/C++ code or just simply make it more readable and error prone. This is especially true if you want to expose C++ objects and structures to the Lua language environment.

Fortunately, there is the Lutok2 library to help you with that. It consists of a set of header files and a freely based previous project called Lutok from Julio Merino.

This chapter will cover how to use Lutok2 library as the C++ API library for the Lua language and as a C++ class wrapper so that you can easily manage making your own extensions in the future. You'll also see that this library is used in many other libraries to cover access to multimedia devices from the Lua language.

Getting ready

The first thing you need to do before starting is to get the Lua binary library and the header files. After this step, you can download the Lutok2 header files and use them in your project.

On Windows:

1. Download the Lua binary files from
   `https://code.google.com/p/luaforwindows/downloads/list`.

2. Download and unzip the Lutok2 source code from `https://github.com/soulik/lutok2/archive/master.zip` or get a clone of the repository with the `git` command:

   ```
   git clone https://github.com/soulik/lutok2.git
   ```

On Linux:

1. Use your package manager to install the Lua developer package or build the Lua binary library from source code at `http://www.lua.org/ftp/lua-5.1.5.tar.gz`.

2. Download and unzip the Lutok2 source code from `https://github.com/soulik/lutok2/archive/master.zip` or get a clone of the repository with the `git` command:

   ```
   git clone https://github.com/soulik/lutok2.git
   ```

In both cases, you'll need the C++ compiler that can handle C++11 version of the standard C++ language. You can use clang or gcc compiler under the Unix-like environment, or the recent version of Microsoft Visual C++.

How to do it...

In the following steps, you'll see most common scenarios of using the Lua language in your C/C++ project. Most of the Lutok2 code samples are paired with equivalent Lua C API code so that you can see what the equivalent C code looks like without using the Lutok2 library.

Initializing the Lua state

This is how you initialize a Lua state with Lutok2:

```
#include <lutok2/lutok2.hpp>

int main(int argc, char ** argv){
  lutok2::State state;
  return 0;
}
```

This is how you do the same with Lua C API:

```
#include <lua.hpp>

int main(int argc, char ** argv){
  lua_State * state = luaL_newstate();
  return 0;
}
```

Creating a Lua module in C/C++

With Lutok2:

```
#include <lutok2/lutok2.hpp>

using namespace lutok2;

    /* A function to be exposed should always use following form:
     * Input argument : A reference to Lutok2 State object
     * Output variable: An integral number of return values
     */
int lua_example_myfunction(State & state){
  // C/C++ code to be invoked
```

```
      return 0;
    }

    extern "C" LUA_API int luaopen_example(lua_State * current_state){
      State * state = State(current_state);
      Module myModule;
      /* Expose lua_example_myfunction function in
       * Lua language environment.
       * Key value represents a function name in Lua.
       * Value should always be a function pointer.
       */
      myModule["myfunction"] = lua_example_myfunction;

      /* This module will return a Lua table
       * that exposes all functions listed in myModule.
       */
      state->stack->newTable();
      state->registerLib(myModule);
      return 1;
    }
```

With Lua C API:

```
    #include <lua.hpp>

    static int lua_example_myfunction(lua_State * L){
      return 0;
    }

    static const struct luaL_Reg module[] = {
      {"myfunction", lua_example_myfunction},
      {NULL, NULL}
    };

    extern "C" LUA_API int luaopen_example(lua_State * L){
      lua_newtable(L);
      luaL_register (L, NULL, module);
      return 1;
    }
```

Passing variables from C/C++ into the Lua environment

With Lutok:

```
int lua_example_myfunction(State & state){
  void * userData = (void*)123456789;
  Stack * stack = state->stack;

  stack->push<bool>(true);
  stack->push<int>(12345);
  stack->push<LUA_NUMBER>(12345.6789);
  stack->push<const std::string &>("A text");
  stack->push<void*>(userData);
  stack->newTable();
    stack.setField<bool>("boolean", false);
    stack.setField<int>("integer", (int)12345);
    stack.setField<LUA_NUMBER>("number", (lua_Number)12345.6789);
    stack.setField<const std::string &>("string", "A text");
    stack.setfield<void *>("userData", userData);
  return 6;
}
```

With Lua C API:

```
static int lua_example_myfunction(lua_State * L){
  void * userData = (void*)123456789;
  lua_pushboolean(L, (int)true);
  lua_pushinteger(L, 12345);
  lua_pushnumber(L, 12345.6789);
  lua_pushstring(L, "A text");
  lua_pushlightuserdata(L, userData);
  lua_newtable(L);
    lua_pushboolean(L, (int)false);
    lua_setfield(L, -2, "boolean");
    lua_pushinteger(L, 12345);
    lua_setfield(L, -2, "integer");
    lua_pushnumber(L, 12345.6789);
    lua_setfield(L, -2, "number");
    lua_pushstring(L, "A text");
    lua_setfield(L, -2, "A text");
    lua_pushlightuserdata(L, userData);
    lua_setfield(L, -2, "userData");
  return 6;
}
```

Passing variables from the Lua environment to C/C++

To get a variable from the Lua environment, you need to call the corresponding Lua C API function `lua_to*`, for example, `lua_tointeger(L, index)`. You can use the corresponding version of the `luaL_check*(L, index)` function to obtain a value with additional checks for the correct data type.

Lutok2 provides a similar mechanism where you can use a template form of the `to` function:

```
state.stack->to<DATA_TYPE_NAME>(index);
```

The part `DATA_TYPE_NAME` presents a name of the target data type and the `index` value is a position of the variable in the registry. The first function parameter is at index 1. The second one is at index 2, and so on.

The example code for Lutok2 C++ API is as follows:

```
int integerValue = state.stack->to<int>(1);
```

The example code for the plain Lua C API is as follows:

```
int integerValue = luaL_checkinteger(L, 1);
```

Making the C++ class accessible from Lua with Lutok2

Let's assume that your class is defined in the `ExampleObject.hpp` header file. In this minimal case, the class contains one numerical property and one member function that returns a string value. The header file will contain the following lines of code:

```
#ifndef EXAMPLE_OBJECT_H
#define EXAMPLE_OBJECT_H

#include <string>

class ExampleObject {
public:
  int x;
  inline const std::string helloWorld(){
    return "Hello world";
  }
};
#endif
```

Now, you'll need to create a class declaration and implementation of the C++ class wrapper. You should always use a reasonable name for the wrapper class so that it is clear what class is actually handled. This example uses the name `LuaExampleObject`.

The header file will be called `LuaExampleObject.hpp` and it will contain a declaration for the `LuaExampleObject` class. This header file contains the following lines:

```
#ifndef LUA_EXAMPLE_OBJECT_H
#define LUA_EXAMPLE_OBJECT_H

#include "ExampleObject.hpp"

class LuaExampleObject : public Object<ExampleObject> {
public:
  explicit LuaExampleObject(State * state) :
    Object<ExampleObject>(state){
    /* Properties handle access to member variables
     * with getter and setter functions
     */
    LUTOK_PROPERTY("x",
      &LuaExampleObject::getX,
      &LuaExampleObject::setX);
    // Methods allow you to call member functions
    LUTOK_METHOD("helloWorld",
      &LuaExampleObject::helloWorld);
  }

  ExampleObject * constructor(State & state, bool & managed);
  void destructor(State & state, ExampleObject * object);
  int getX(State & state, ExampleObject * object);
  int setX(State & state, ExampleObject * object);
  int helloWorld(State & state, ExampleObject * object);
};
#endif
```

The implementation file will be called `LuaExampleObject.cpp` and it will consist of the main code that handles access to member variables and functions:

```
#include <lutok2/lutok2.hpp>
using namespace lutok2;

#include "LuaExampleObject.hpp"

ExampleObject * LuaExampleObject::constructor(State & state, bool
  & managed){
  return new ExampleObject;
}

void LuaExampleObject::destructor(State & state, ExampleObject *
  object){
```

```
   delete object;
}

int LuaExampleObject::getX(State & state, ExampleObject * object){
   state.stack->push<int>(object->x);
   return 1;
}

int LuaExampleObject::setX(State & state, ExampleObject * object){
   if (state.stack->is<LUA_TNUMBER>(1)){
     object->x = state.stack->to<int>(1);
   }
   return 0;
}

int LuaExampleObject::helloWorld(State & state, ExampleObject *
   object){
   state.stack->push<const std::string &>(object->helloWorld());
   return 1;
}
```

Furthermore, to finish while process, you'll need to register a Lua interface. This is usually done during the module initialization routine. The following code sample shows how to prepare a C++ source file with module initialization. This module will return a table that is used in the Lua script as an interface to create an instance of `ExampleObject`. Note that this module doesn't register itself in the global variable space. This is currently the preferred way of using modules in the Lua language.

The main module file will be called `ExampleModule.cpp` and will consist of the following lines:

```
#include <lutok2/lutok2.hpp>
using namespace lutok2;

#include "LuaExampleObject.hpp"

extern "C" LUA_API int luaopen_example(lua_State * current_state){
   // State object is freed automatically after Lua state closes!
   State * state = new State(current_state);
   Stack * stack = state->stack;

   // Prepare main module interface table
   stack->newTable();

   /* Object interface registration always returns Lua function
```

```
    * with object constructor.
    */
    state->registerInterface<LuaExampleObject>(
      "LuaExample_ExampleObject");
    /* A new instance of ExampleObject can be obtained by
     * calling ExampleObject function from main interface table.
     */
    stack->setField("ExampleObject");
    return 1;
}
```

Now, you can include all source code in your C++ project in your favorite IDE and compile them into the binary library.

Don't forget to move the resulting binary library with the module to the working directory with your Lua script or anywhere the Lua interpreter can find it.

Finally, your Lua script will look like this:

```
local exampleModule = require 'Example'

local example_object = exampleModule.ExampleObject()
example_object.x = 5
print(example_object.x)
print(example_object.helloWorld())
```

This will create a new `ExampleObject` instance, sets and gets content of member variable; in the final step, it calls the member function that returns a string value.

How it works...

The Lutok2 library contains most of the commonly used Lua C API functions while sanitizing access to class objects.

The core of this library is divided into two sections:

- ▸ Functions that manage Lua states and Lua modules
- ▸ Functions that manage Lua stack content

All Lutok2 classes are encapsulated in Lutok2 namespace, so there should be no naming conflicts with other libraries. It contains automatic management of the Lua state for these use cases:

- Lua modules
- A standalone application that creates a Lua state during runtime

Class wrapper objects use the template form of `lutok2::Object` as a generic base class that handles most of the work in order to register the class interface in the current Lua environment. The template parameter is mandatory and specifies what class will be wrapped.

```
lutok2::Object<CLASS_NAME>
```

The constructor of the class wrapper must always be present, as it defines what methods or properties will be available in the Lua environment. It's called automatically during interface registration. The body of the constructor usually consists of several macros that specify the class members. There are two macros you can use, which are as follows:

- `LUTOK_METHOD(LUA_NAME, FUNCTION)`
- `LUTOK_PROPERTY(LUA_NAME, FUNCTION, FUNCTION)`

The member functions are defined by their name as a string value and a function pointer. The member variables use a similar notation while using two function pointers. The first one points to the *getter* function that returns a value of the member variable. The second one points to the *setter* function that sets the value of the member variable. If you don't want to allow the member variable modification, you can use the pointer to the `nullMethod` function instead of your own *setter* function. This will effectively block any changes to the member variable from the Lua script.

Another part of the C++ class wrapper is the functions that manage object instance creation and destruction—`constructor` and `destructor`. The constructor method is called when you actually call the object constructor in the Lua environment and it gives you space to actually create a new object instance. There's a reference to the `managed` argument, which you can change to the `false` value if the object instance is managed elsewhere. This will also cause that destructor method won't be called upon garbage collection in the Lua environment:

```
CLASS_NAME * constructor(State & state, bool & managed);
```

The destructor method is called when the object is freed in the Lua environment during garbage collection. This is the place where you can clean up and free up the object's instance:

```
void destructor(State & state, CLASS_NAME * object);
```

Getting LuaSDL for libSDL 1.2

LuaSDL is a binding to the famous libSDL 1.2 multimedia library. LuaSDL provides an interface not only to libSDL itself but also to the SDL_image, SDL_mixer, SDL_net, SDL_ttf, and SDL_gfx libraries.

Getting ready

The LuaSDL module depends on many external libraries. To make the module preparation easier, there's a LuaSDL project repository at GitHub with support for the CMake building system. This project repository contains all the necessary external libraries, which make module building process a breeze.

You'll need to have the following software installed to successfully build the LuaSDL module:

▶ The git version control system is available at `https://git-scm.com/`

▶ The CMake building system version 3.1 or newer is available at `http://www.cmake.org/`

▶ The C/C++ compiler, Microsoft Visual Studio, GCC, and clang are supported

▶ The Netwide Assembler—NASM (optional) used only for CPU-specific optimizations is available at `http://www.nasm.us/`

How to do it...

The building process of LuaSDL is the same on both Windows and Linux operating systems with minor differences:

1. Download the LuaSDL source code with the `git` command:

   ```
   git clone --recursive https://github.com/soulik/LuaSDL.git
   ```

2. You need to create an empty working directory, which will contain the project and binary files:

   ```
   mkdir LuaSDL/build
   cd LuaSDL/build
   ```

3. Now, you can run the `CMake` building tool to prepare the project files or to make further changes to the building configuration:

   ```
   cmake ..
   ```

4. After successful preparation of the building environment, you can either open the project file in your IDE or simply run the make command to start the compilation depending on the compiler of your choice:

  ❑ For Microsoft Visual Studio—use the `luasdl.sln` file

  ❑ For Linux users—use the `make` command

5. The successful compilation will result in binary files stored in the `bin` and `lib` directories.

Note that Microsoft Visual Studio will generate the .dll binary files in the bin directory, whereas, Linux users will find the same binary files in the lib directory. You can copy all the binary files into one directory where your Lua application resides. This will ensure that the Lua interpreter finds all the necessary binary modules.

There's more...

LuaSDL uses libSDL 1.2, which is more than 5 years old. Despite being no longer maintained, the LuaSDL package is considered as stable.

LuaSDL2 is being developed at the time of writing. You can access the source code from GitHub at `https://github.com/soulik/LuaSDL-2.0.git`.

Designing the main application loop with LuaSDL

LuaSDL offers an event-based application design. LibSDL uses a window to capture input events. Without it, you wouldn't be able to detect key strokes, mouse movement and, of course, you will be without any graphical output.

Getting ready

Before running your Lua script with LuaSDL, make sure you've got the LuaSDL module with all the dependencies in the same directory. However, you can always override the PATH environmental variable so that your application can find the necessary libraries. Note that the path environment variable is managed in the operating system and it's not for the Lua module location!

How to do it...

First, you must load the LuaSDL module file. If this step fails, you are either missing the correct libSDL library or one of the dependencies:

```
require 'LuaSDL'
```

You can define your own assertion check function with the optional SDL error reporting:

```
function SDL_assert(condition, msg)
  local msg = (msg and msg .. ": " .. SDL.SDL_GetError())
  return assert(condition, msg)
end
```

You have to set up the default window parameters as follows:

```
local window_x_pos = 128
local window_y_pos = 128
local window_width = 640
local window_height = 480
local window_bpp = 0
local window_flags = 0
```

LuaSDL must be initialized with `SDL.SDL_Init` before any use:

```
SDL_assert(SDL.SDL_Init(SDL.SDL_INIT_EVERYTHING) >= 0, "Couldn't
initialize SDL")
```

LuaSDL places the window randomly upon creation. You can override this by setting the environmental variable `SDL_VIDEO_WINDOW_POS`:

```
SDL.SDL_putenv(string.format("SDL_VIDEO_WINDOW_POS=%d,%d",window_x
_pos, window_y_pos))
```

To set a window caption, you have to call the `SDL.SDL_WM_SetCaption` function:

```
SDL.SDL_WM_SetCaption("LuaSDL Example", "Example")
```

Now, you can create a window with the `SDL.SDL_SetVideoMode` function, which returns the `SDL_Surface` object as a userdata:

```
local screen = SDL_assert(SDL.SDL_SetVideoMode(window_width,
window_height, window_bpp, window_flags))
```

You can use the event loop invariant or just use a `break` statement on the application exit:

```
local running = true
```

It's more efficient to use the table of event functions than the usual approach with the `if`, `elseif`, and `else` statements. Each table key is an integer constant in this case:

```
local events = {
  [SDL.SDL_MOUSEMOTION] = function(event_struct)
    local event_struct = event_struct.motion
    -- do something when this event occurs
  end,
  [SDL.SDL_MOUSEBUTTONDOWN] = function(event_struct)
    local event = event_struct.button
  end,
  [SDL.SDL_MOUSEBUTTONUP] = function(event_struct)
    local event = event_struct.button
  end,
  [SDL.SDL_KEYDOWN] = function(event_struct)
    local event = event_struct.key
    local key = event_struct.keysym.sym
  end,
  [SDL.SDL_KEYUP] = function(event_struct)
    local event = event_struct.key
    local key = event_struct.keysym.sym
  end,
  [SDL.SDL_VIDEORESIZE] = function(event_struct)
      local event = event_struct.resize
  end,
  [SDL.SDL_QUIT] = function(event_struct)
      running = false
  end,
}
-- prepare local instance of SDL_Event object
local local_event = SDL.SDL_Event_local()

while (running) do
  -- check for events in the poll
  if (SDL.SDL_PollEvent(local_event)~=0) then
    local event_fn = events[local_event.type]
    if type(event_fn)=='function' then
      event_fn(local_event)
    end
  end
end
```

The `SDL.SDL_Quit` function ensures that all the temporary objects are freed upon application exit:

```
SDL.SDL_Quit()
```

How it works...

Using the LuaSDL library must follow a certain pattern to ensure correct management of resources and events. Events are used as a primary source of information about user interaction with your application. The LuaSDL library can detect mouse movement, keyboard input, change of application window size, and a request to close your application.

The whole process of event processing uses event polling where you use the `SDL.SDL_PollEvent` function in each step of the main application loop to obtain information about the event that has occurred. This function may return a value 0 if there are no events to process. In this case, you can use this free time to process game logic. This recipe uses a skeleton table for event processing functions called `events`.

The most important event, `SDL.SDL_QUIT`, is received when the user closes the application window. You should clean up all the resources and LuaSDL state as well. Don't forget to use the `SDL.SDL_Quit` function before exiting your application to ensure all the previously used memory is freed.

2
Events

In this chapter, we will cover the following recipes:

- ▶ Processing input events with LuaSDL
- ▶ Using the keyboard input
- ▶ Using the relative mouse position
- ▶ Using the absolute mouse position
- ▶ Using timers

Introduction

Event-driven design offers a cheap and efficient way to detect user input without the need to check for input device status in each frame. A naïve approach to this is to query all input devices for changes in their state. There are many types of input devices such as keyboard, mouse, joystick, keypad controller, tablet, touch screen, and so on. LuaSDL relies on the library libSDL 1.2, which supports only basic input devices such as keyboard, mouse, and joystick. This version doesn't support the use of multiple devices of the same kind. This limitation has been removed with libSDL 2.x, which is used in LuaSDL 2. LuaSDL 2 is the successor of a former LuaSDL library and it's in the stage of early development at the time of writing. This chapter will cover the use of an older LuaSDL library, as the LuaSDL 2 interface is not so different.

Processing input events with LuaSDL

LuaSDL offers a form of platform-independent abstraction layer to these devices with an inner event pool. You only have to query the event pool for unprocessed events and, if there are any, check for the event type.

Getting ready

Before doing any event processing, your application must initialize internal event pools. This can be achieved with the `SDL.SDL_Init` function, where the only parameter is a bitmask representing which parts of LuaSDL you want to initialize. You can use the bitlib library for the Lua language. Another option would be to use the bit32 internal library if you are using the newer version of the Lua interpreter. The default value here is `SDL.SDL_INIT_EVERYTHING`, which is fine as it starts the event pool automatically. Specifically, you can use the `SDL.SDL_INIT_EVENTTHREAD` or `SDL.SDL_INIT_VIDEO` values to initialize the event pool.

A code sample can be used to initialize the LuaSDL library. It should be used right at the start of the application:

```
require 'LuaSDL'
require 'bit'
-- initialize video device and internal thread for event processing
SDL.SDL_Init(bit.bor(SDL.SDL_INIT_VIDEO,
SDL.SDL_INIT_EVENTTHREAD))
```

How to do it...

You can poll for currently pending events with the `SDL.SDL_PollEvent` function. This function uses the `SDL_Event` object as the only argument and fills this object with event information, if there's any. LuaSDL provides the `SDL.SDL_Event_local` function, which creates the local `SDL_Event` object. Keep in mind that this object is not kept globally. The `SDL_Event` object will be subject to garbage collection after you leave the block where it was defined. The `SDL.SDL_PollEvent` function also returns a value 1 if there is an event that is currently pending or 0 if there aren't any. This approach is quite desirable because you call this function only once for each event loop iteration. If there are no events pending, you can just skip further event processing in that iteration.

First of all, you need to create a local event object. This object will contain event information and can be defined at the start of your application and freed upon application exit.

```
local event = SDL.SDL_Event_local()
```

The application event loop can be defined as a `while` loop:

```
local running = true
while (running) do
  if (SDL.SDL_PollEvent(event) ~= 0) then
    process_event(event)
  end
end
```

Incoming events will be processed in the `process_event` function. This function usually handles more than one type of event, which is defined in the `event.type` variable. Each event type can be processed separately inside the `if-then-else` chain of code blocks or you can rely on the function map stored in a Lua table in the form of an associative array. The Lua language doesn't contain the switch statement known from other programming languages, so you are mostly left with these two options. For other kinds of switch statement alternatives, you can refer to the lua-users wiki page at `http://lua-users.org/wiki/SwitchStatement`.

As long as the amount of event types is small enough, it doesn't really matter which one you use.

Event handling with the if-then-else chain

An example of the `if-else-if` chain is shown in the following code:

```
local function process_event(event)
  if event.type == SDL.SDL_KEYDOWN then
    print("Key pressed:", event.key.keysym.sym)
  elseif event.type == SDL.SDL_KEYUP then
    print("Key released:", event.key.keysym.sym)
  elseif event.type == SDL.SDL_QUIT then
    running = false
  end
end
```

In the first case with event type `SDL.SDL_KEY_DOWN`, the code captures an event of pressing a key on your keyboard. You can get both the key symbol code defined in `event.key.keysym.sym` or a scan code from `event.key.keysym.scancode`. A key symbol code is keyboard-layout dependent, whereas `scancode` is a hardware-dependent value. Usually, you'll want to use a key symbol code if you're developing a game.

The second case with the `SDL.SDL_KEYUP` event type captures an event of key releasing and the last one detects a quit event when the user closes the application window.

Event handling with an associative array

The next example shows how to process events with the associative array represented with the Lua table:

```lua
local events = {
  [SDL.SDL_KEYDOWN] = function(raw_event)
    local event = raw_event.key
    local key = event.keysym.sym
    print("Key pressed:", key)
  end,
  [SDL.SDL_KEYUP] = function(raw_event)
    local event = raw_event.key
    local key = event.keysym.sym
      print("Key released:", key)
  end,
  [SDL.SDL_QUIT] = function(raw_event)
    running = false
  end,
}
local function process_event(event)
  local event_fn = events[event.type]
  if type(event_fn)=='function' then
    event_fn(event)
  end
end
```

In this case, the `process_event` function looks up for a key-value pair in the `events` table. A key part of a pair corresponds to the event type identifier. On the other hand, a value part contains a function that will be invoked. A complete list of valid event type identifiers is shown in a table, which we will look at shortly. In every case, an event function will be called with the current event object placed in the first function argument.

Keep in mind that LuaSDL always uses a generic form of event object. Therefore, to get a certain event attribute, you need to follow this structure:

```lua
event.[structure_name].[structure_attribute]
```

For instance, if you wanted to know what key was pressed, you can use the key symbol identifier from the `key` structure.

```lua
local keySymbol = event.key.keysym.sym
```

The following table shows what event types LuaSDL can handle:

Event types	Description	Structure names	Structure attributes
`SDL_ACTIVEEVENT`	This allows you to gain or lose window focus	Active	gain state
`SDL_KEYDOWN`	This allows you to press down a key on the keyboard	Key	state keysym
`SDL_KEYUP`	This allows you to release a key on the keyboard		
`SDL_MOUSEMOTION`	This enables mouse movement over the application window	Motion	state x,y srel, yrel
`SDL_MOUSEBUTTONDOWN`	This enables pressing a mouse button	Button	which button
`SDL_MOUSEBUTTONUP`	This enables releasing a mouse button		state x, y
`SDL_JOYAXISMOTION`	This enables joystick movement	jaxis	which axis value
`SDL_JOYBUTTONDOWN`	This enables you to press a joystick button	jbutton	which button
`SDL_JOYBUTTONUP`	This enables you to release a joystick button		state
`SDL_JOYHATMOTION`	This enables the joystick to change the hat position	jhat	which hat value
`SDL_JOYBALLMOTION`	This enables the joystick to change the trackball movement	jball	which ball xrel, yrel
`SDL_VIDEORESIZE`	This enables the window to resize	resize	w,h
`SDL_VIDEOEXPOSE`	This enables screen redraw	Not applicable	
`SDL_SYSWMEVENT`	This is a platform-dependent event	syswm	msg
`SDL_USEREVENT`	This is a user-defined event	User	code data1, data2
`SDL_QUIT`	This means that quit was requested	Not applicable	

Each event type has its own attributes. You can use those attributes to obtain information about specific events, for example, the mouse button that was pressed or the key symbol code. The next set of recipes in this chapter will cover the most common use cases of some of the event types.

How it works...

The LuaSDL library is intended to be used with the event polling mechanism, which is used in a loop, as you can see in the following sample code:

```
-- application can be exited be setting running variable to false
local running = true
-- prepare local instance of SDL_Event object
local local_event = SDL.SDL_Event_local()

while (running) do
  -- check for events in the poll
  if (SDL.SDL_PollEvent(local_event)~=0) then
    local event_fn = events[local_event.type]
    if type(event_fn)=='function' then
      event_fn(local_event)
    end
  else
    -- ...do game mechanics
  end
end
```

This application design allows you to react to the input event when needed while idle time can be used to process game mechanics or video rendering. However, special care must be taken to prevent game mechanics from taking too long to finish as this may halt your application or make it less responsive.

See also

- ▸ The *Using the keyboard input* recipe
- ▸ The *Using the relative mouse position* recipe
- ▸ The *Using the absolute mouse position* recipe

Using the keyboard input

LuaSDL offers a simple way of determining what key was pressed or released on your keyboard. Events with event types `SDL.SDL_KEYDOWN` and `SDL.SDL_KEYUP` can react to one keystroke at the time. This is usually fine during a game play. However, if you want to use keyboard shortcuts in a text input field, the previous approach would not be very efficient.

This recipe will show you how to manage keyboard input in a robust way that can be used for both situations—to control a game or to write text into an input field.

Getting ready

Let's say you need your game character to run when a *Shift* key is pressed. There are three key problems. The common PC keyboard has left and right *Shift* keys. These are two different keys with two different key symbol codes. The next thing is that you use these keys with another keyboard key which may or may not be the modifier key. The last problem is putting key states together, so you'll know if the player has pressed the *Shift* + *W* keys at the same time.

There are rare cases where you need to query key status multiple times in one frame. It wouldn't be very efficient to do this every time you need a current state of key modifier. A better solution is to cache key states into a Lua table. A key symbol code will be used as a table key and the value will indicate a key status (0 means released and 1 means pressed). You can assume that the key is released if there is no such entry in the key state table. This assumption doesn't apply to all modifier keys, for example, the *Num Lock* key, so make sure that you initialize modifier key states on application startup. The following code will define tables to store cached information about key states, along with a special table for the conversion of modifier key codes into scan code:

```
local keyStates = {}
local keyModStates = {}
-- a list of key modifiers paired with their scan codes
local modKeysScanCodes = {
  [SDL.KMOD_LSHIFT]=SDL.SDLK_LSHIFT,
  [SDL.KMOD_RSHIFT]=SDL.SDLK_RSHIFT,
  [SDL.KMOD_LCTRL]=SDLK_LCTRL,  [SDL.KMOD_RCTRL]=SDL.SDLK_RCTRLT,
  [SDL.KMOD_LALT]=SDL.SDLK_LALT,  [SDL.KMOD_RALT]=SDL.SDLK_RALT,
  [SDL.KMOD_LMETA]=SDL.SDLK_LMETA,
  [SDL.KMOD_RMETA]=SDL.SDLK_RMETA,
  [SDL.KMOD_NUM]=SDL.SDLK_NUMLOCK,
  [SDL.KMOD_CAPS]=SDL.SDLK_CAPSLOCK,
  [SDL.KMOD_MODE]=SDL.SDLK_MODE,
}
```

This code should be used before event processing takes place.

How to do it...

This recipe will be separated into two parts. This first part will deal with the storing states of normal keys. The second part will manage key modifier states as this is a bit more problematic.

Normal keys

Getting the states of normal keys is pretty straightforward. You just need to detect keyboard input events to store a key state into the `keyState` table. This part of the recipe will use the event functions stored in a table, which is explained in the previous recipe in detail:

```
local events = {
  -- a keyboard key was pressed down
  [SDL.SDL_KEYDOWN] = function(raw_event)
    local event = raw_event.key
    local keySym = event.keysym.sym
    keyStates[keySym] = true
  end,
  -- a keyboard key was released
  [SDL.SDL_KEYUP] = function(raw_event)
    local event = raw_event.key
    local keySym = event.keysym.sym
      keyStates[keySym] = false
  end,
}
```

Modifier keys

Modifier keys need to be processed separately because LuaSDL can't detect certain key combinations within the event processing mechanism. You can try to press both left and right *Ctrl* keys and you'll notice that the second modifier is not detected at all!

The modifier key state can be obtained with the `SDL.SDL_GetModState` function in the form of a bit mask. The following table shows all the modifier key codes:

Modifier key constant names	Key names	Numerical values (in hexadecimal notation)
KMOD_NONE	No modifier key	0x0000
KMOD_LSHIFT	The left *Shift* key	0x0001
KMOD_RSHIFT	The right *Shift* key	0x0002
KMOD_LCTRL	The left *Ctrl* key	0x0040
KMOD_RCTRL	The right *Ctrl* key	0x0080
KMOD_LALT	The left *Alt* key	0x0100

Modifier key constant names	Key names	Numerical values (in hexadecimal notation)
KMOD_RALT	The right *Alt* key	0x0200
KMOD_LMETA	Usually a left Windows (GUI) key	0x0400
KMOD_RMETA	Usually a right Windows (GUI) key	0x0800
KMOD_NUM	The *Num Lock* key status	0x1000
KMOD_CAPS	The *Caps Lock* key status	0x2000
KMOD_MODE	The *Alt Gr* key	0x4000
KMOD_CTRL	Both left and right *Ctrl* keys	0x00C0
KMOD_SHIFT	Both left and right *Shift* keys	0x0003
KMOD_ALT	Both left and right *Alt* keys	0x0300
KMOD_META	Both left and right Windows (GUI) keys	0x0C00

The modifier key state will be processed in a function called processModKeys:

```
local function processModKeys()
  local modState = SDL.SDL_GetModState()
  for keyMod, keySym in pairs(modKeysScanCodes) do
    -- apply binary and operator to obtain modifier key state
    keyModStates[keySym] = (bit.band(modState, keyMod) > 0)
  end
end
```

This function needs to be called in every frame so that you always get the current state of the modifier keys.

How it works...

The second part of this recipe relies on using the binary and the operator to get the modifier key state. As mentioned earlier, the modifier key states are stored in a bit mask. Therefore, to get the actual scan code, it uses the conversion table called modKeysScanCodes. Modifier key states are stored in a local modState variable, which is used in the for loop to do binary tests for all modifier keys. If a modifier key is pressed, the binary AND operator returns nonzero value. The result of this operation is stored in the keyModState table.

Note that the key modifier values such as SDL.KMOD_SHIFT, SDL.KMOD_CTRL, SDL. KMOD_ALT, and SDL.KMOD_META are not included in the modKeysScanCodes table. You can obtain states for these modifier keys by using Boolean operators as follows:

```
local SHIFT_state = (keyModStates[SDL.SDLK_LSHIFT] or
keyModStates[SDL.SDLK_RSHIFT])
```

This will return true if any of the *Shift* keys is pressed.

From this point, if you need to query the keyboard shortcut status for *Shift + W*, you can use the following code:

```
local SHIFT_W_state =
   (keyModStates[SDL.SDLK_LSHIFT] or
   keyModStates[SDL.SDLK_RSHIFT]) and
   keyState[SDL.SDLK_w]
```

See also

> ▶ For a complete list of SDLK_ key symbol constants, you can browse a header file
> SDK_keysym.h from libSDL 1.2, which is also available in the GitHub repository at
> `https://github.com/soulik/LuaSDL/blob/master/src/binding/orig/`
> `SDL_keysym.h`

Using the relative mouse position

The relative mouse position is often used when you need unconstrained mouse movement. A typical example of such a use is a first person shooter game in a 3D environment. The relative mouse position represents how much the mouse pointer position changed in comparison with the previous state in all the axes.

Getting ready

The biggest problem with the relative mouse position is that the mouse pointer is constrained to the application window or the screen. You can solve this by centering the mouse cursor in the center of the application window after computing the relative cursor position or by using direct values from the mouse driver.

The relative mouse position has the big advantage of versatility because you can apply the mouse cursor speed modifier simply by multiplying the relative mouse position with a number. If that number is greater than 1, the mouse cursor will move faster. Multiplying by a number lesser than 1, will slow down the mouse cursor.

How to do it...

The first solution is the most viable in this situation as you don't have to depend on platform-specific features.

The whole solution relies on the following steps:

1. Reset the mouse position to the center of the screen or application window on startup—this is to prevent sudden mouse cursor jumps on startup.

2. Store the current mouse position into temporary variables, `currentX` and `currentY`.

3. Reset the mouse position to the center of the screen or application window.

4. Compute the relative mouse cursor position as the difference between its current position and the screen center position:

    ```
    relativeX = currentX - centerX
    relativeY = currentY - centerY
    ```

5. Repeat from step 2.

Mouse cursor centering can be achieved with the `SDL.SDL_WarpMouse` function, where the parameters are the cursor positions in the *x* and *y* axes. In this case, you can't rely on the `xrel` and `yrel` event attributes because you center the mouse cursor position on every mouse move. As a consequence of this, the `xrel` and `yrel` values will be eliminated with the `-xrel` and `-yrel` values respectively in the next event iteration.

The mouse motion event handler will look like the following code:

```
[SDL.SDL_MOUSEMOTION] = function(_event)
    local event = _event.motion
```

The `centerX` and `centerY` values correspond to the screen center position and will change only on window resize event or on screen resolution change:

```
SDL.SDL_WarpMouse(centerX, centerY)
relativeX, relativeY = event.x - centerX, event.y - center
```

The `totalX` and `totalY` variables will contain unconstrained mouse cursor coordinates:

```
    totalX, totalY = totalX + diffX, totalY + diffY
end
```

By putting the `SDL.SDL_WarpMouse` function inside the mouse movement event handler, you can save some time. There's no need to reset the mouse cursor position at every event loop iteration.

There's more...

You might have noticed that this application doesn't let you move the cursor outside the application. For example, you need to switch to another application, but your mouse cursor is stuck in the middle of the application window. This issue can be solved by handling SDL_ACTIVEEVENT. If your application loses focus, it will stop trying to set the mouse cursor position in the middle of the window. After it gains a window focus, it will reset the mouse position and restore the former mouse event handler.

It's a good idea to move the mouse movement event handler into a separate function. Let's assume that this function is called `mouseMotionHandler`.

This first thing you must do is to do forward declaration of the `events` table.

```
local events
events = {...}
```

This gives you a way to modify the `events` table inside the SDL_ACTIVEEVENT event handler that is defined in this table.

The updated SDL_ACTIVEEVENT handler can look like the following code:

```
[SDL.SDL_ACTIVEEVENT] = function(raw_event)
  local event = raw_event.active
```

First, you need to check whether your application gained or lost focus completely using the following code:

```
    if SDL.And(event.state, SDL.SDL_APPINPUTFOCUS) > 0 then
      if event.gain == 1 then
```

The application gained complete focus and can restore the old mouse motion event handler. Don't forget to put the mouse cursor in the middle of the screen:

```
        SDL.SDL_WarpMouse(centerX, centerY)
        events[SDL.SDL_MOUSEMOTION] = mouseMotionHandler
      else
```

The application lost complete focus; therefore, it can disable the mouse motion handler:

```
        events[SDL.SDL_MOUSEMOTION] = false
      end
    end
end
```

This way your application behaves in a more suitable manner and allows users to use other applications at the same time.

Using the absolute mouse position

The absolute mouse position is used primarily in window applications, where the mouse position constraints are desirable. The mouse position (0,0) corresponds to the upper-left corner of your application window. The maximum mouse position depends always on the size of the window. Take special care when the mouse cursor is outside the application window. The behavior of LuaSDL in this situation is highly dependent on the currently used operating system! In most cases, you won't get any events related to the mouse cursor motion.

The main advantage of this is that you can use the mouse cursor position reported directly by LuaSDL to precisely manipulate GUI elements inside of the application window. This approach is used also with tablet touch input devices, where you always get absolute positions.

How to do it...

The following mouse movement handler function shows a simple way to get the absolute mouse cursor position:

```
[SDL.SDL_MOUSEMOTION] = function(raw_event)
  local event = raw_event.motion
```

The absolute mouse position is stored in x and y attributes:

```
  mouseX = event.x
  mouseY = event.y
end,
```

Using timers

LuaSDL offers support for timer objects. The problematic part is the use of timers. The LibSDL library uses callback functions to call event functions. These callbacks run in another thread and the naïve approach, where you put the Lua function in the position of callback function, would lead to Lua state corruption. There is a better way to accomplish this by using the internal LuaSDL callback function that invokes a special user event.

Timers aren't very precise and they are mostly used in GUI updates. If you need more precision, you'll need to use **High Precision Event Timer** (**HPET**), which is out of the scope of this book.

Getting ready

Each timer object uses a user-defined event that contains unique timer function identifiers represented by integer values. LuaSDL offers a slightly modified version of the `SDL.SDL_AddTimer` function, where it accepts two parameters instead of three. The first parameter is an interval value in milliseconds. The second is the user-defined event object.

How to do it...

The first thing you'll need to do is to define your user-defined event. You can use the `SDL.SDL_Event_local` function to create one:

```
local timerEvent = SDL.SDL_Event_local()
```

The next thing you'll need to do is to set the event code specific for a timer object. You can then create a timer object with the `SDL.SDL_AddTimer` function. This function returns an internal timer ID, which you can use with the `SDL.SDL_RemoveTimer` function to stop the timer.

So far, you've created a user-defined event generator that will generate events at a specified interval. To make this useful, you can define your user event handler with the following code:

```
[SDL.SDL_USEREVENT] = function(_event)
  local event = _event.user
  if event.code > 0 then
    timerCallback(event.code)
  end
end
```

You can use the event code to specify what callback function will be called.

How it works...

After you create the timer object with `SDL.SDL_AddTimer`, LuaSDL calls the real `SDL_AddTimer` function with its own callback function that will periodically push the event you specified in the second function argument into the event queue. Fortunately, event handling in LuaSDL is one of the few things that is thread safe. Timer callback functions don't run strictly in specified intervals. This is because there are platform-specific limitations and, what's more, callback functions only push events into the event queue. Your application can process timer events much later.

There's more...

To make timer handling more efficient, you can define a function that will take two arguments. The first one is the interval and the second is a function or a closure.

This approach uses central table `timers` with all the timer objects and the user event handler will always try to query the timer function from the `timers` table, as shown in the following code:

```lua
local timers = {}
local timerID = 0


-- Each call to createTimer function will create a new timer
   object.
-- Interval argument expects a time in millisecond units
-- Supplied function in the second argument will be called
   repeatedly
local function createTimer(interval, fn)
  assert(type(interval)=='number' and type(fn)=='function')
  local timerObj = {}
  -- Unique timerID number generator with simple incremental
     counting
  timerID = timerID+1
  -- timerEvent will be used to contain timerID user value
  local timerEvent = SDL.SDL_Event_local()
  -- Store a reference for timerEvent object
  -- so it won't be prematurely garbage collected
  timerObj.event = timerEvent
  timerObj.call = fn
  timerEvent.type = SDL.SDL_USEREVENT
      timerEvent.user.code = timerID
  -- Create LuaSDL timer object
  local timer = SDL.SDL_AddTimer(interval, timerEvent)
  timerObj.timer = timer
  -- Destroys current timer object
  timerObj.remove = function()
    SDL.SDL_RemoveTimer(timer)
    timers[timerID] = nil
  end
  timers[timerID] = timerObj
end
```

There remains one small modification in the user event handler, which is as follows:

```
[SDL.SDL_USEREVENT] = function(raw_event)
  local event = raw_event.user
  if event.code > 0 then
    local timer = timers[event.code]
    if timer and type(timer.call)=="function" then
      timer.call()
    end
  end
end
```

The last thing you need to do is to clean up all timers before exiting your application. This is caused by the fact that timer objects from LuaSDL aren't automatically garbage collected. You can achieve this with the following simple iteration:

```
for _, timer in pairs(timers) do
  timer.remove()
end
```

The `remove` function will stop the timer and destroy the timer object. Without this step, you'd be relying on the automatic cleanup functions of the operating system, which is never a good idea. In the worst case, it could cause a memory leak.

3
Graphics – Common Methods

This chapter will cover the following recipes:

- Creating a window in libSDL
- Creating surfaces
- Surfaces manipulation
- Using colors
- Cursor manipulation
- Initializing the graphics mode with OpenGL
- Getting OpenGL information
- Using OpenGL extensions with GLEW and Lua
- Loading images with SDL_image
- Creating textures
- Loading and using bitmap fonts
- Loading and using TrueType fonts
- Displaying the text
- Creating texture atlas with the rover-design pattern
- Using tiles and tilesets in the game

Introduction

This chapter covers the basic principles of using the graphical interface in conjunction of LuaSDL with OpenGL. It covers basic operations on surface objects, using color models, cursor manipulation, image loading, and using textures and fonts. It also contains a few examples of game engine optimizations such as texture atlas and tilesets.

These recipes can be enhanced with the information from subsequent chapters to get better efficiency on resource handling.

Creating a window in libSDL

A window in an application is the most basic part of the drawing process. LibSDL offers a way to create one regardless of the graphical environment or operating system being used. Each window uses the surface object, which contains basic information about the drawing context, such as the inner window size, color depth, pixel format settings and optional flag variables to set up the drawing process. LuaSDL allows you to set up these window parameters in a simple manner.

Moreover, libSDL operates with the screen as the surface object representation. LibSDL 1.2 allows you to use only one window, while the current version of libSDL 2.0 allows multiple windows. This might be the deciding factor when deciding whether to use the older version of LuaSDL or the newer LuaSDL 2.

Getting ready

LibSDL 1.2 offers an old interface to set up a window but it's sufficient for simple games and multimedia applications. Most likely you'll want to use the whole screen for your application, so you'll need to set up a fullscreen mode. You can achieve this with the flag parameter `SDL.SDL_FULLSCREEN` in the `SDL.SDL_SetVideoMode` function. All flag parameters consist of bitmasks, so you need to use the binary OR operator to construct the final flag value.

LibSDL tries to use the accelerated window drawing if it's available on the target platform. Without this feature, all the drawing is processed in software mode, which is substantially slower than hardware-accelerated drawing. You can check for the hardware acceleration feature with the `SDL.SDL_GetVideoInfo` function. It returns a table with the following content:

Field names	Description	Value types
hw_ available	Are hardware surfaces available?	0 means false and 1 means true
wm_ available	Is window manager available?	0 means false and 1 means true

blit_hw	Are hardware-to-hardware blits accelerated?	0 means false and 1 means true
blit_hw_CC	Are hardware-to-hardware color key blits accelerated?	0 means false and 1 means true
blit_hw_A	Are hardware-to-hardware alpha blits accelerated?	0 means false and 1 means true
blit_sw	Are software-to-hardware blits accelerated?	0 means false and 1 means true
blit_sw_CC	Are software-to-hardware colorkey blits accelerated?	0 means false and 1 means true
blit_sw_A	Are software-to-hardware alpha blits accelerated?	0 means false and 1 means true
blit_fill	Are color fills accelerated?	0 means false and 1 means true
video_mem	This is the total amount of video memory in Kilobytes	Returns an Integer value, 0 if not available
vfmt	This is the pixel format of the current video device	SDL_PixelFormat

Be aware that each field except vfmt contains a numerical value.

LibSDL 1.2 doesn't contain full support for DirectX acceleration on Windows platforms, so you may end up with windib video driver. This means you won't be able to use hardware-accelerated surfaces. Software-based blitting is generally a slow process as it accompanies RAM to RAM data copy. In this case, most of you will fall back to OpenGL acceleration, which is fine because OpenGL is known to be platform independent and almost every graphic card supports OpenGL nowadays.

To get the name of the current video driver, you need to call the SDL.SDL_VideoDriverName function. However, there's a catch to call this function properly mainly due to Lua++ binding.

The current workaround looks like this:

```
-- let Lua to allocate a string
local str = string.rep(" ", 256)
str = SDL.SDL_VideoDriverName(str, #str)
```

This will prepare the str variable to be able to contain at most 256 characters, which is sufficient in most cases. The str variable will be filled with a name of the current video driver. Fortunately, the length of the string variable indicates the maximum length of the video driver name. Longer driver names are truncated to the specified length. This issue is resolved in LuaSDL 2.

How to do it...

You can set up your screen with the `SDL.SDL_SetVideoMode` function with formal definition:

```
SDL.SDL_SetVideoMode(width, height, bpp, flags)
```

This function will return the surface object or nil on failure. Screen width and height are in pixels. Each pixel is represented by a color value stored in a binary form. Bits per pixel or the `bpp` parameter specifies how many bits are used to describe one pixel. Each color value uses the RGB (red, green, blue) color representation. Usually, each color channel uses the same amount of bits. However, other surface objects in the libSDL library may use other binary representations for colors. For instance, RGB channels may be in reverse order or there may be a different size for each color channel. The problematics of pixel format description and doing conversion between them is well explained in an article at `https://www.opengl.org/wiki/Image_Format`.

You can also use the `bpp` parameter with zero value in case you want to use the current screen `bpp` setting. This will automatically turn on the `SDL.SDL_ANYFORMAT` flag.

Optional flags define surface capabilities. You can combine them together with the binary OR operator from the bit library. The flag values are described in the following table:

Flag names	Description
`SDL.SDL_SWSURFACE`	The video surface is in the system memory—RAM
`SDL.SDL_HWSURFACE`	The video surface is in the video memory—graphic card memory
`SDL.SDL_ASYNCBLIT`	This involves asynchronous updates of the display surface and a speed increase on systems with multiple processors or cores
`SDL.SDL_ANYFORMAT`	This uses the closest pixel format available
`SDL.SDL_HWPALETTE`	This involves exclusive palette access for SDL. Without this, you may not always get the exact color you request, usually on screens with 8 bpp.
`SDL.SDL_DOUBLEBUF`	This enables the use of hardware double buffering and is valid only with `SDL.SDL_HWSURFACE`.
`SDL.SDL_FULLSCREEN`	SDL will attempt to use a fullscreen mode or tries to set the next higher resolution with the display window centered.
`SDL.SDL_OPENGL`	This prepares the OpenGL rendering context
`SDL.SDL_OPENGLBLIT`	This prepares the OpenGL rendering context with blitting capability.
`SDL.SDL_RESIZABLE`	The window that is created will be resizable.
`SDL.SDL_NOFRAME`	This is the window without the title bar or frames.

How it works...

The first call of the SDL_SetVideoMode function will always try to create a window. It will allocate the necessary memory to store the window content in a surface object. However, this surface object is automatically freed upon the call of the SDL.SDL_Quit function and should not be freed manually.

Note that the SDL_SetVideoMode function will use the pixel format specified by the bpp parameter even if it's not supported by the current hardware. In such cases, the surface object is also called a **shadow** surface and it means that the libSDL library will do automatic pixel format conversion when you display content on the screen. This conversion will slow down screen rendering a bit. You can avoid this by using the SDL.SDL_ANYFORMAT flag in the SDL_SetVideMode function.

Creating surfaces

Surfaces are an object representation of image data buffers. They play the main role in the texture management process. Every image you load needs to be placed onto the surface first. After this, you can use this surface to render your image onto the screen, store it into graphical memory, or do some image manipulation.

Getting ready

Every surface consists of a pixel format description and binary data. The surface object structure is shown in the following table:

Field names	Description
flags	This is the bit mask description of surface properties.
format	This is the surface pixel format.
w	This is the surface width in pixels.
h	This is the surface height in pixels.
pitch	This is the length of the surface scanline in bytes. It specifies how many bytes are used to store a single line surface content and it's used mostly in surface blitting operations. The pitch value is always dividable by 4 to optimize surface processing speed.
pixels	This is the pointer to pixel data in the form of userdata values.
clip_rect	This is the clipping rectangle for the surface. This affects the destination area that can be modified with blitting.
refcount	This is the reference count, which is the internal value and is used primarily when freeing a surface.

All these fields are read-only except for the `pixels` field which can be used to indirectly change the surface content.

The pixel format describes how many bits per pixel your image uses, how many color channels are there, and so on. The following table shows you the structure of the pixel format in detail:

Field names	Description
`palette`	This is the palette structure. It's empty if the value of `BitPerPixel` > 8.
`BitsPerPixel`	This is the number of bits used to represent one pixel. It's usually either 8, 16, 24, or 32.
`BytesPerPixel`	This is the number of bytes used to represent one pixel. It usually uses a number from 1 to 4.
`Rloss`, `Gloss`, `Bloss`, and `Aloss`	This is the precision loss of each color component. It usually presents a size of color channel in bits.
`Rshift`, `Gshift`, `Bshift`, and `Ashift`	This is the binary left shift of each color component.
`Rmask`, `Gmask`, `Bmask`, and `Amask`	This is the binary mask to retrieve each color component.
`colorkey`	This is the transparent color identifier.
`alpha`	This is the overall surface alpha value—transparency.

Usually, there is no need for you to set these values. However, they are important if you load an image with the alpha channel.

How to do it...

You can create a new empty surface with the `SDL.SDL_CreateRGBSurface` function, where its definition is as follows:

```
SDL_CreateRGBSurface(flags, width, height, depth, Rmask, Gmask, Bmask, Amask)
```

The `Flags` parameter is a bitmask that specifies whether the surface is stored in the system or the video memory. You can use these values:

Flag names	Description
`SDL.SDL_SWSURFACE`	Here, the surface will be stored in the system memory. The pixel level access is faster, but blitting operations don't take advantage of hardware acceleration.
`SDL.SDL_HWSURFACE`	Here, the surface will be stored in the video memory. Blitting is hardware accelerated.

Flag names	Description
SDL.SDL_SRCCOLORKEY	Here, the surface will use the colorkey parameter from the pixel format descriptor. This color will represent a transparent color.
SDL.SDL_SRCALPHA	Here, the surface will use the alpha value from the pixel format descriptor to apply transparency on blitting. However, you don't need this flag to load an image with the transparency channel!

It's completely safe to use flags with zero value as they will use SDL.SDL_SWSURFACE by default.

The next parameters are the width and height of the image in pixels.

The last parameters are the color depth and bit masks for each color component. These are fairly important as the incorrect bit masks will result in messed-up colors. Keep in mind that most of the current computers use little endian bit encoding, which is also called **endianness**. This affects the order of the color components in the surface memory. Unfortunately, PNG, JPEG, and many other file formats use big endian encoding. As a result of this, each pixel is stored with color components in the (A)BGR order and you have to convert it to RGB(A). Fortunately, you can deal with this problem easily by setting the correct bit masks for each color component.

The following image shows what happens when the image is loaded with an invalid pixel format:

Let's say you want to create an empty image surface of 16 x 16 pixels with a bit depth of 32-bit and an RGBA pixel format. You would create such a surface with the following code:

```
local surface = SDL.SDL_CreateRGBSurface(0, 16, 16, 32,
0x000000FF, 0x0000FF00, 0x00FF0000, 0xFF000000)
```

If you have used a big endian computer, you would use the code with swapped bit masks:

```
local surface = SDL.SDL_CreateRGBSurface(0, 16, 16, 32,
0xFF000000, 0x00FF0000, 0x0000FF00, 0x000000FF)
```

Surface objects are not freed automatically. Be sure to free up all unused surface objects with the `SDL.SDL_FreeSurface` function:

```
SDL.SDL_FreeSurface(surface)
```

How it works...

The libSDL library always tries to reserve enough memory for the whole image in uncompressed form. So, even if your PNG image file has a few kB in size, it must be decompressed before storing it into memory. You can compute memory consumption in bytes with this simple equation:

```
needed_memory = width * height * color_components_count
```

The situation may change with the use of memory alignment, where each pixel takes 4 bytes (32 bits), even if your image uses a 24-bit color depth. You can check this with the bytes per pixel field in the pixel format of the surface.

You can access the pixel format information with the `format` field:

```
local pixelFormat = surface.format
```

Note that the pixel format information is stored as a userdata with metatable and internally it's just another object.

If you need to change the pixel format of the existing surface, use the `SDL.SDL_ConvertSurface` function, which creates a new surface. The existing pixel data will be correctly converted into the new pixel format. This function has this formal specification:

```
SDL_ConvertSurface(source_surface, new_pixel_format, flags)
```

There's more...

You can always convert the existing surface into the current display pixel format with the `SDL.SDL_DisplayFormat(surface)` function.

There are some occasions where you need to change the pixel format of the surface in a very specific way. A typical example of such a situation is that you have an ARGB surface and you need to transfer this surface into graphic card memory with OpenGL. However, OpenGL supports the RGBA pixel format, which is the closest one. Of course, you can use the SDL. SDL_ConvertSurface function but you need a pixel format object that describes the RGBA format. To do this, you can create a garbage collector-friendly version with the SDL. SDL_PixelFormat_local() function. Be wary that every value in the object must be set because the object itself is not initialized. Otherwise, you can easily cause a memory access violation or segmentation fault. The following example shows how to create a 32-bit RGBA pixel format object:

```
local pf = SDL.SDL_PixelFormat_local()
local bpp = 32
pf.BitsPerPixel = bpp
pf.BytesPerPixel = math.ceil(bpp/8)
pf.Rmask = 0x000000FF
pf.Gmask = 0x0000FF00
pf.Bmask = 0x00FF0000
pf.Amask = 0xFF000000
pf.Rloss = 0
pf.Gloss = 0
pf.Bloss = 0
pf.Aloss = 0
pf.Rshift = 0
pf.Gshift = 0
pf.Bshift = 0
pf.Ashift = 0
pf.colorkey = 0
pf.alpha = 255
pf.palette = nil
```

There's another thing with the current stable version of Lua 5.2. This version allows you to define a custom garbage collection routine for a regular table. This routine can be used to define automatic surface destruction when the surface object is not used anymore.

Take an example of a situation when you create an interface within your application to manage textures for each game level. Textures can take a lot of memory space. When you change the game level, you'll most probably want to use a different set of textures. So, in the end, you'll need to keep a track of all the textures you use. Before loading a new game level, you can free up all the previously used textures and load the new ones. However, there will almost certainly be textures that you use over and over, for example, font textures and decals. You can achieve proper surface tracking with weak tables, where you only keep a note that the surface is being used and it should be freed when it's not needed anymore.

The weak table is a special type of a Lua table, which may contain references to other objects. Additionally, these references aren't considered by the garbage collector, and therefore, it allows the object to be freed even if there's a reference to it in a weak table.

The problem is that you have to implement your own mechanism to manage that and often, it's not done correctly. You'll most likely end up with memory leaks. You can solve this with a Lua table extended with metatable, which will contain the garbage collection routine in the form of a metamethod stored with the __gc key.

The problem is that Lua 5.1 can use the __gc metamethod only on userdata objects with a metatable. The newer versions of the Lua language incorporate the so-called finalizers, which means the __gc metamethod can be called on empty tables when they are garbage collected.

There's a workaround for Lua 5.1 to apply this garbage collection mechanism even on a regular table. The following lines will define the `table.proxy` function that will add the capability to use the __gc metamethod in the Lua 5.1 interpreter:

```
table.proxy = function(t)
   -- newproxy is not available in Lua 5.2+ !!!
   if type(newproxy)=='function' then
     assert(type(t) == 'table', '1st argument should be a table')

     -- create a new proxy object
     local p = newproxy(true)
     local p_mt = getmetatable(p)

     -- set GC meta-method for proxy object
     p_mt.__gc = function()
       local mt = getmetatable(t)
       local gc_fn = mt.__gc
       if type(gc_fn)=='function' then
         gc_fn(t)
       end
     end

     -- store proxy object in a metatable
     local mt = getmetatable(t) or {}; mt.__proxy = p;
     setmetatable(t, mt)
   end
end
```

With the garbage collection routine in tables, you can simply define that, if the object (regular table) is collected, the Lua interpreter will call your custom garbage collection routine, which will correctly free up the memory space used by the object.

The following example shows such a design on the surface object:

```
local surface = function(width, height, bpp, rmask, gmask, bmask,
amask)
  local obj = {}
  local raw = assert(SDL.SDL_CreateRGBSurface(0, width, height,
  bpp, rmask, gmask, bmask, amask))
  local mt = {
    __gc = function()
      SDL.SDL_FreeSurface(raw)
    end,
  }
  obj.blit = function(destination, srcRect, destRect)
    ...
  end
  setmetatable(obj, mt)
  table.proxy(obj)
  return obj
end
```

In this construction, the `surface` function will return a regular table, which is in fact an interface to the surface object with one `blit` method. This function will create a closure upon calling and keeps the raw surface object hidden within the implementation. The `mt` table contains the `__gc` metamethod definition, where the function uses an upvalue `raw` value that contains the surface object. This `raw` value is used to delete the surface object and to free up the unused memory space. The beauty of this is that object deletion is done automatically when the Lua object is no longer used and it's collected.

Surfaces manipulation

The basic surface manipulation usually consists of filling the part or whole surface with color, which can be in fact clearing the surface, and copying the surface content into another surface. As you already know, the surface can also represent the screen content. With these two groups of operations you can do almost anything.

Getting ready

In this recipe, you'll be working with routines that require a definition of a rectangular area over which the operation will occur. The libSDL library uses its own `SDL_Rect` object to define such a rectangular area. You can create this object either with `SDL.SDL_Rect_new` or `SDL.SDL_Rect_local`. The second one is preferred because it contains an automatic garbage collection routine, so you don't have to explicitly call the `SDL.SDL_Rect_delete` function to delete the object. The only downside of this is that you can't set the position nor the size of rectangle in the constructor. This means that you have to set all the parameters after the `SDL_Rect` object is created. The following code shows this in detail:

```
local rectangle = SDL.SDL_Rect_local()
rectangle.x = 16
rectangle.y = 32
rectangle.w = 64
rectangle.h = 64
```

This example contains an `SDL_Rect` object, where the x and y fields represent the position of the upper-left corner of the rectangle; the w and h fields are the width and height of the rectangle.

LibSDL usually allows you to use NULL (nil) value instead of the `SDL_Rect` object if you need to proceed with the operation on the entire surface. You will find such use cases in the `SDL_FillRect` or `SDL_BlitSurface` functions.

How to do it...

Filling a surface with color is done with the `SDL.SDL_FillRect` function. The function specification looks like this:

```
SDL_FillRect(surface, rectangle, color)
```

The `Surface` parameter defines the surface object that you want to fill with color. You can fill the whole surface or just a part of it. The last parameter, `color`, defines what color would be used to fill your surface. You have to be careful to use the `SDL.SDL_MapRGBA` function to get the correct color value because its value is dependent on the surface pixel format. This function has the following specification:

```
SDL_MapRGBA(pixel_format_descriptor, red, green, blue, alpha)
```

You can get the pixel format descriptor of the surface with the following code:

```
surface.format
```

Red, green, blue, and alpha parameters accept integer values in the range, 0-255. This function returns a 32-bit value of the selected color. Of course, you can store these values in a table, so you don't have to recompute them every time. Just keep in mind that these values can mean different colors on the surface with different pixel formats.

The following example shows how to fill the rectangular area of an empty `surface` with a red color. The surface has a size of 64 x 64 pixels and uses the RGBA pixel format with the 32-bit color depth:

```
local color = SDL.SDL_MapRGBA(surface.format, 255, 0, 0, 255)
local rect = SDL.SDL_Rect_local()
rect.x, rect.y, rect.w, rect.h = 16, 16, 32, 32
SDL.SDL_FillRect(surface, rect, color)
```

The result of this can be seen in the following screenshot:

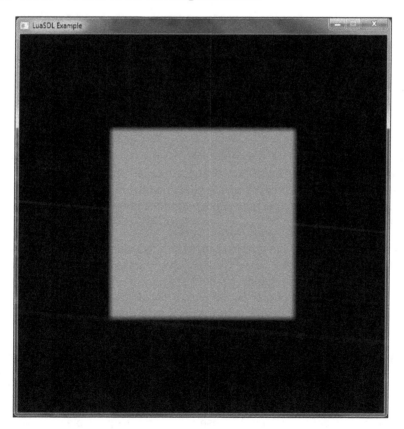

Surface content copying is often called **blitting**. Many graphical APIs use this term to express the operation of putting data into another place. The libSDL library offers a `SDL.SDL_BlitSurface` function to blit surface content into another. This function is quite versatile as it can do automatic conversion of surface data to destination pixel format. Another thing to mention is that you can select what portion of the source surface should be copied into part of the destination surface. The formal specification of this function looks like this:

```
SDL_BlitSurface(source_surface, source_rectangle,
destination_surface, destination_rectangle)
```

Note that the destination surface can be the screen surface object. Such blitting will draw the content of the source surface onto the screen.

In case you only need to convert the surface into another pixel format, you can use the `SDL.SDL_ConvertSurface` function. This function has the following specification:

```
SDL_ConvertSurface(source_surface, target_pixelformat, flags)
```

You can obtain the pixel format object from another valid surface or you can create one yourself with `SDL.SDL_PixelFormat_local()`.

The `flags` parameter accepts the same values as the `SDL_CreateRGBSurface` function.

How it works...

LibSDL uses an internal mechanism to determine whether the conversion is necessary. Blitting between surfaces of the same pixel formats is called internally fastblit. It's much faster because it accompanies only the `memcpy` function to make a copy of the memory region. Optionally, libSDL offers SSE optimization for the blitting function to provide even faster drawing.

Blitting between two regions of the graphical memory is considered to be the fastest method because it's done entirely on the GPU. However, due to the limited availability of hardware acceleration of 2D operations, it's not used very often. Note that this is a different kind of acceleration to the one offered by modern GPUs. Most of the consumer-level graphic cards nowadays are oriented towards the provision of accelerated 3D operations (OpenGL, Direct X, and so on) and hardware video decoding.

Using colors

In games, you might have seen many kinds of graphical effects, such as screen desaturation, HDR image enhancing, or hue shifting. All these effects use the principle of converting between color models to another color representation, which allows you to easily change certain aspects of drawing things on screen. This recipe will try to explain how to convert between color models and how to use them in further image processing.

Usually, colors are defined by three color components—red, green, and blue. This color representation is also known as RGB. There are more methods to define a color. These methods are also called color models. They describe that each one is used in different situations. For example, the RGB color model uses additive color mixing. This is because computer displays use these three colored lights to mix the final color you can see on the screen. Printers use the CMYK color model, which uses subtractive color mixing. This is based on mixing colors like when you are painting on paper. Color mixing on paper behaves differently to mixing colored lights. However, there are many more color models. HSL or HSV color models can be used to a color in terms of hue, saturation, and lightness, or a value. These color models allow you to easily change the color saturation or any other color parameter.

Note that graphic cards use internally RGB color models and it's commonly extended with alpha channels to define the transparency. However, in the end, the result in the GPU framebuffer always uses RGB triplets for colors.

Another point to mention is that color conversion is exact between the RGB and HSL color models, whereas conversion between RGB and CMYK is not so precise. This is because HSL is just another color representation developed for computer graphics applications to make color handling simpler. In contrast to that, the CMYK color model is bound to color mixing processes in printers. While colors on computer display produce the light, colors on a sheet of paper adjust the reflected light to the perceiver. The color representation on a paper is dependent on the paper material, surrounding light and a halftone rasterizing method. These facts can help you with the choice of color model for your situation.

Getting ready

This recipe will show you how to convert between the three most commonly used color models. The methods that are described here can be used inside your application, for example, for color picking and as a part of your fragment shader code, where you can adjust color rendering on screen—color desaturation.

How to do it...

The most common color models used in games are RGB, HSL, and CMYK. The first part of this recipe will deal with conversions between the RGB and HSL color models. The second part will cover conversions between RGB and CMYK color models. RGB color models play a central role as they are used internally in graphic cards:

1. Converting a color from HSL to RGB;

```
function hsl2rgb(h, s, l)
  local r, g, b
  if s == 0 then
    r,g,b = l,l,l -- achromatic
```

```
      else
        local p, q
        local function hue2rgb(t)
          t = math.fmod(t, 1)
          if t < 1/6 then
            return p + (q - p) * 6 * t
          elseif t < 1/2 then
            return q
          elseif t < 2/3 then
            return p + (q - p) * (2/3 - t) * 6
          else
            return p
          end
        end
        if l < 0.5 then
          q = l * (1 + s)
        else
          q = l + s - l * s
        end
        p = 2 * l - q
        r = hue2rgb(h + 1/3)
        g = hue2rgb(h)
        b = hue2rgb(h - 1/3)
      end
      return r, g, b
    end
```

2. Converting a color from RGB to HSL:

```
    function rgb2hsl(r, g, b)
      local max = math.max(r, g, b)
      local min = math.min(r, g, b)
      local h,s, l = (max + min) / 2 -- luminance
      s, l = h, h
      if max == min then
        h,s = 0,0 -- achromatic
      else
        local d = max - min;
        if l > 0.5 then
          s = d / (2 - max - min)
        else
          s = d / (max + min)
        end
        if max == r then
```

```lua
    if g < b then
      h = (g - b) / d + 6
    else
      h = (g - b) / d + 0
    end
  elseif max == g then
    h = (b - r) / d + 2
  elseif max == b then
    h = (r - g) / d + 4
  end
  h = h / 6
end
return h, s, l
end
```

3. Converting a color from CMYK to RGB:

```lua
function cmyk2rgb(c, m, y, k)
  local r, g, b
  r = 1.0 - (c * (1.0 - k) + k)
  g = 1.0 - (m * (1.0 - k) + k)
  b = 1.0 - (y * (1.0 - k) + k)
  return r, g, b
end
```

4. Converting a color from RGB to CMYK:

```lua
function rgb2cmyk(r, g, b)
  local c, m, y, k
  if (r == 0) and (g == 0) and (b == 0) then
    c, m, y, k = 0, 0, 0, 1
  elseif (r == 1) and (g == 1) and (b == 1) then
    c, m, y, k = 0, 0, 0, 0
  else
    c = 1.0 - r
    m = 1.0 - g
    y = 1.0 - b
    local minK = math.min(r, g, b)
    c = (c - minK) / (1.0 - minK)
    m = (m - minK) / (1.0 - minK)
    y = (y - minK) / (1.0 - minK)
    k = minK
  end
  return c, y, m, k
end
```

In the case of converting the HSL color model into RGB, the algorithm first tries to determine whether the color is achromatic. This means saturation is 0 and so there's no point in computing hue. Such computation is quickly over because the resulting RGB color is computed only with lightness. If the saturation is greater than zero, the `hue2rgb` function is used to determine a linear combination of the R, G, and B color channels. The following figure shows how the color channels are combined:

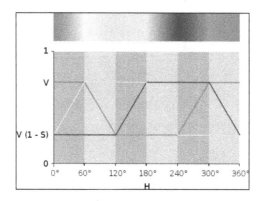

The P and Q quotients are dependent on lightness and saturation and they form the final values of the R, G and B channels.

Conversion from RGB to the HSL color models starts with finding what color channel has the greatest (maximum) and lowest (minimum) value. The next thing is the lightness value, which you can derive by getting the mean value or the minimum and maximum values. If the minimum and maximum values are equal, it means that the color is achromatic—zero color saturation. Otherwise, there is a saturation which you can get by using the following formula:

```
if lightness <= 0.5 then saturation := (max-min)/(max+min)
if lightness > 0.5 then saturation := (max-min)/(2-max-min)
```

Now you're left with computing the hue. You can refer to the previous figure to see the relation between the color channel with the maximum value and the position on the hue palette. The color spectrum can be divided into six parts, where the maximum channels are paired next to each other, except the red channel. If the red color is the maximum, you'll be looking either on the left or on the right side of the spectrum. You can get a finer position by getting the parameter of the linear combination of the other channels. The generalized formula will look like this:

```
h = N + (B - A)/(max - min)
```

Here, N would be the part of sextant, B would be the rising channel on the right, and A would be the falling channel on the left. The value of the finer position is in the range of (-1,1). The final value of the hue can be obtained by dividing the hue by 6, which will map the value into the range of (0,1).

CMYK to RGB color model conversion uses a set of formulas, which are as follows:

- R = (1-C)*(1-K)
- G = (1-M)*(1-K)
- B = (1-Y)*(1-K)

Note that CMYK uses subtractive color mixing. Therefore, the red color is mixed from the negative color of cyan, the green color is mixed from the negative color of magenta, and the blue color is mixed from the negative color of yellow.

The RGB to CMYK formula is a bit more complicated and is listed as follows:

- K = 1 - Max(R, G, B)
- C = (1 - R - K)/(1 - K)
- M = (1 - G - K)/(1 - K)
- Y = (1 - B - K)/(1 - K)

All color models mentioned in this recipe work with the channel range of (0,1).

Cursor manipulation

This recipe incorporates the basic principles of mouse cursor manipulation such as showing and hiding the mouse cursor.

Be aware that libSDL offers fairly limited support for mouse cursor images. These are constrained by using 2 bits for each pixel on an image (1 bit for data and 1 bit for mask) and by image width, which must be a multiple of 8 bits.

There's a much better way to display a mouse cursor. You can use mouse movement events to get the current mouse cursor position and draw an image on the resulting position. This gives you much more flexibility because you can use the cursor image with more than 1 bit for pixels, set up mouse movement smoothing, acceleration, and so on.

This recipe will show you how to implement a custom mouse cursor. This might be especially useful in a case where you need to emphasize an item location under the cursor.

Getting ready

LibSDL provides its own cursor drawing routine, which is turned on by default. If you want to use your own cursor image, you need to turn the default cursor off first.

This recipe will need you to include the GL module, which contains the most important OpenGL functions. This module is defined by the `gl` namespace.

This recipe assumes that you didn't change viewing frustum scaling. This means that screen coordinates use a range (-1,1) in each direction and the point at (0,0) position is the center of the screen. It's also assumed that you have enabled `GL_TEXTURE_2D` texturing target. The cursor texture should be bound to the current texturing target:

```
gl.Enable(GL_TEXTURE_2D)
gl.BindTexture(GL_TEXTURE_2D, cursor_texture_identifier)
```

How to do it...

First, you need to turn off the default cursor with the `SDL.SDL_ShowCursor` function:

```
SDL.SDL_ShowCursor(0)
```

Alternatively, you can turn the default cursor on with the following code:

```
SDL.SDL_ShowCursor(1)
```

Now, you need to get a source of the mouse cursor position. It's preferred to use events for obtaining the mouse cursor position, but you can also use an `SDL.SDL_GetMouseState` function as follows; it returns the state of mouse buttons and a cursor position:

```
local buttons, x, y = SDL.SDL_GetMouseState()
```

This position is relative to the position of the application window and you can safely use it to position the surface on the screen.

Now, you can draw the cursor image on the screen with each screen update. Let's assume that `window_width` contains the width of the current application's window and `window_height` contains the height of the window. The `Mouse` variable is a Lua table with both mouse cursor coordinates `x` and `y`. The mouse cursor size is defined by two variables, `c_w` and `c_h`.

Be aware that OpenGL uses a different Cartesian coordinate system by default than you are used to. The following figure shows how the coordinates are oriented:

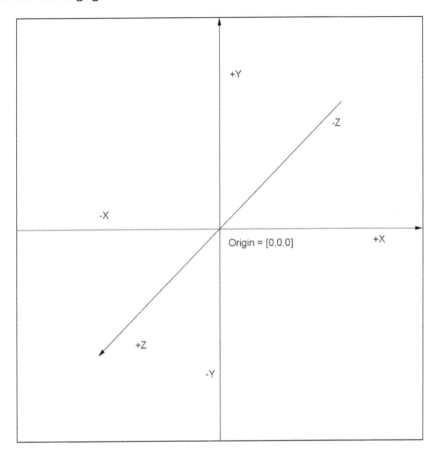

All the coordinates are limited to the range (-1,1), where 0 corresponds to the center. That's why you'll need to divide all the input coordinates with window width and height respectively.

First, you need to define the cursor picture size:

```
local c_width, c_height = 32/window_width, 32/window_height
```

Next, you'll need to transform mouse cursor coordinates into a range of (-1, 1) in both directions:

```
local x = (mouse.x/window_width)*2-1
local y = -((mouse.y/window_height)*2-1)-c_height
```

Notice, that the y coordinate is multiplied by -1. That's because (-1,-1) in OpenGL corresponds to the lower-left corner of the window.

Now, you can draw a simple textured rectangle on the screen with OpenGL functions as follows:

```
gl.Begin(gl_enum.GL_QUADS)
  gl.Color4f(1,1,1,1)
  gl.TexCoord2f(0, 0)
  gl.Vertex2f(x, y)
  gl.TexCoord2f(1, 0)
  gl.Vertex2f(x+c_width, y)
  gl.TexCoord2f(1, 1)
  gl.Vertex2f(x+c_width, y+c_height)
  gl.TexCoord2f(0, 1)
  gl.Vertex2f(x, y+c_height)
gl.End()
```

How it works...

Are you still able to detect the mouse movement and position even if you hide the mouse cursor. The burden of cursor rendering becomes your responsibility.

Cursor rendering should be processed on every time frame so that the user can attain the best interactivity with your application. Cursor is usually drawn as the closest polygon to the viewer along with GUI elements. However, you're not limited to this traditional cursor rendering. For example, you can make the cursor polygon a part of your game. This means you can apply physics, collisions, feedback, and so on.

See also

 ▸ The *Loading images with SDL_image* recipe
 ▸ The *Creating textures* recipe

Initializing the graphics mode with OpenGL

The OpenGL library allows you to draw any 2D or 3D graphical scene on the computer screen. Its advantage is that many current graphic cards offer acceleration features. It's much faster than drawing to surfaces that are stored in the system memory.

This recipe introduces the LuaGL module, which allows you to call OpenGL functions from Lua. However, not every function is available on all systems. Therefore, the LuaGL module uses the features of the GLEW library, which does all the dynamic function binding and you can detect whether certain OpenGL features are available.

Getting ready

Lua itself doesn't offer direct access to the OpenGL functions. To use any of the OpenGL functions, you'll need the OpenGL wrapper library that provides an interface to those functions. Fortunately, there's one available on GitHub repository for free. You can download it with the `git` command:

```
git clone --recursive https://github.com/soulik/luagl.git
```

You'll need the recent version of the CMake 3.1 tool as well to prepare the project files. These can be prepared with the following commands executed in the `luagl` directory:

mkdir luagl/build
cd luagl/build
cmake ..

After that, you'll need to compile it to binary form with the C++ compiler. The resulting binary library will be present in the `build/bin` directory and it will be called `luagl.dll` or `luagl.so` (on Unix-based systems).

How to do it...

First of all, you'll need to set up the OpenGL attributes before creating a window to set the internal pixel format, which will be used in your graphic card. You can use the `SDL_GL_SetAttribute` function provided by libSDL. The minimal setup will look like the following code:

```
SDL.SDL_GL_SetAttribute(SDL.SDL_GL_RED_SIZE, 8)
SDL.SDL_GL_SetAttribute(SDL.SDL_GL_GREEN_SIZE, 8)
SDL.SDL_GL_SetAttribute(SDL.SDL_GL_BLUE_SIZE, 8)
SDL.SDL_GL_SetAttribute(SDL.SDL_GL_ALPHA_SIZE, 8)
SDL.SDL_GL_SetAttribute(SDL.SDL_GL_DEPTH_SIZE, 16)
SDL.SDL_GL_SetAttribute(SDL.SDL_GL_DOUBLEBUFFER, 1)
```

This will force OpenGL to use 8 bits for each color component, 16 bits for the depth buffer and turns on double buffering.

There are also more attributes you can use:

Attribute names	Default values	Description
SDL_GL_RED_SIZE	3	This is the minimum number of bits for the red channel of the color buffer
SDL_GL_GREEN_SIZE	3	This is the minimum number of bits for the green channel of the color buffer
SDL_GL_BLUE_SIZE	2	This is the minimum number of bits for the blue channel of the color buffer

Attribute names	Default values	Description
SDL_GL_ALPHA_SIZE	0	This is the minimum number of bits for the alpha channel of the color buffer
SDL_GL_BUFFER_SIZE	0	This is the minimum number of bits for the frame buffer
SDL_GL_DOUBLEBUFFER	1	This enables double buffering
SDL_GL_DEPTH_SIZE	16	This is the minimum number of bits for the depth buffer element
SDL_GL_STENCIL_SIZE	0	This is the minimum number of bits for the stencil buffer element
SDL_GL_ACCUM_RED_SIZE	0	This is the minimum number of bits for the red channel of the accumulation buffer
SDL_GL_ACCUM_GREEN_SIZE	0	This is the minimum number of bits for the green channel of the accumulation buffer
SDL_GL_ACCUM_BLUE_SIZE	0	This is the minimum number of bits for the blue channel of the accumulation buffer
SDL_GL_ACCUM_ALPHA_SIZE	0	This is the minimum number of bits for the alpha channel of the accumulation buffer
SDL_GL_STEREO	0	This enables stereo 3D output and requires libSDL 2+
SDL_GL_MULTISAMPLEBUFFERS	0	This is the number of buffers for multisample antialiasing and requires libSDL 2+
SDL_GL_MULTISAMPLESAMPLES	0	This is the number of samples used for antialiasing and requires libSDL 2+
SDL_GL_ACCELERATED_VISUAL	1	This forces hardware acceleration for OpenGL. 0 means software rendering; it requires libSDL 2+
SDL_GL_CONTEXT_PROFILE_MASK	0	The types of profile for OpenGL context are the Core profile, Compatibility profile, and ES profile; these require libSDL 2+

You can regard these attributes as hints for libSDL to set up OpenGL.

With double buffering enabled, you have to swap buffers on each screen update. Otherwise, you won't see the results on screen as they'll remain in the frame buffer only. To swap the buffer, you'll need to use the SDL.SDL_GL_SwapBuffers function.

If you're developing a game for mobile devices, you might want to use libSDL 2, where you can also set the required OpenGL profile to the `SDL.SDL_GL_CONTEXT_PROFILE_ES` value.

```
SDL.SDL_GL_SetAttribute(SDL.SDL_GL_CONTEXT_PROFILE_MASK,
SDL.SDL_GL_CONTEXT_PROFILE_ES)
```

For specific information regarding the OpenGL ES profile, you can refer to the Kronos reference pages at `http://www.khronos.org/opengles/sdk/docs/man/`.

After this initialization phase, you can set up the video mode. The following example creates a window with a size of 800 x 600 pixels with a 32-bit color depth and OpenGL support:

```
SDL.SDL_SetVideoMode(800, 600, 32, SDL.SDL_OPENGL)
```

To use fullscreen mode, you'll need to use the binary OR operator to add the `SDL.SDL_FULLSCREEN` flag into the last parameter. Fortunately, LuaSDL provides binary operators which are not a part of the Lua language until version 5.2:

```
SDL.SDL_SetVideoMode(800, 600, 32, SDl.Or(SDL.SDL_OPENGL,
SDL.SDL_FULLSCREEN))
```

Note that switching between the fullscreen and windowed modes requires a new GL context. This means you have to reload all data (this includes textures) into GPU memory again! That's why many older games require such a long time to recover when toggling the fullscreen mode. Modern games and libSDL 2 don't have this problem.

How it works...

Upon calling `SDL.SDL_SetVideoMode` with the OpenGL flag, libSDL automatically creates a new OpenGL context and sets it as the current one. LibSDL does this because OpenGL context creation and context selection is always platform dependent.

The OpenGL context represents an individual working environment and stores all the states associated with the current instance of OpenGL. An application can use multiple OpenGL contexts, for example, multithreaded application or multiple OpenGL windows with different states in each one. Contexts can share certain information such as textures, buffer objects, and GLSL objects. Frame buffers and vertex objects are not shareable.

Having a new OpenGL context also means that every state variable is reset to the default values. This includes model-view, projection, texture, and color matrices. It is recommended to set these matrices into appropriate values for your situation.

Getting OpenGL information

As you may already know, there are multiple versions of OpenGL. Each version offers a standard set of functions while other functions may be marked as deprecated. What's more, graphic card manufacturers try to extend these standard OpenGL functions with so-called extensions. Some extensions are specific to graphic cards and have a prefix in their names. Other ones have become standardized over time. For instance, an extension for vertex shader programs is called `ARB_vertex_program` and it's provided by the OpenGL Architecture Review Board. There is also a vendor-specific version of this extension called `NV_vertex_program` provided by the NVidia company in their GPUs. Many extensions start with the vendor-specific version, then they are reworked by the OpenGL ARB. In the final stage, they may be incorporated into the core specification of OpenGL. There are other extensions with names starting with GLX or WGL prefixes, which indicates that these extensions are specific to certain operating systems. GLX is used in Unix-based systems and WGL is oriented towards the Microsoft Windows operating system. To get the current list of known extensions, you can visit `https://www.opengl.org/registry/`.

Getting ready

Before using the extensions, you'll need to check whether they are present in the current system. You can query for their existence with the `gl.Get` function. This function is quite versatile and can also be used to check the current OpenGL version, as well as the shading language version. Its specification is as follows:

```
gl.Get(format, name)
```

The `format` parameter specifies the returning value type. The valid `format` specifiers are shown in the following table:

Format specifiers	Description
s(1)	This returns a string
i(n)	This returns an array of integer elements with the size of n items
f(n)	This returns an array of float number elements with the size of n items
d(n)	This returns an array of double number elements with the size of n items
b(n)	This returns an array of Boolean elements with the size of n items

The list for available `name` values is quite comprehensive and differs with each OpenGL version. You can always get the full list from the OpenGL reference manual page for the `glGet` function, which you can find on the web page `http://www.opengl.org/sdk/docs/man/xhtml/glGet.xml`.

However, this recipe will mention a few of the most used `name` parameters to get a basic picture of the current system.

How to do it...

This recipe will show you how to obtain four of the most queried information from OpenGL.

Getting the OpenGL version

To get the OpenGL version, you'll need to call:

```
local version = gl.Get("s(1)", GL_VERSION)
```

This will return a string in one of these three forms:

- A.B
- A.B.C
- OpenGL ES-DD A.B

Letter A represents a number of the major version. Letter B is the minor version number and letter C stands for a release number.

The last form can be seen on OpenGL ES hardware (mobile devices), where the DD letters represent the name of the profile. There are two profiles, which are as follows:

- CM—Common profile
- CL—Common Lite profile

Getting the graphic card vendor

You can get a graphic card vendor name with a call:

```
local vendor = gl.Get("s(1)", GL_VENDOR)
```

This will tell you if the graphic card is made by NVidia Corporation, AMD, Intel, or some other company and tells you which vendor-specific extensions you are able to use on the current system.

Getting the graphic card name

The name of current graphic card can be obtained with a call:

```
local renderer = gl.Get("s(1)", GL_RENDERER)
```

The `renderer` string contains the name of the graphic card but it often contains other vendor-specific information. Its format is not standardized and is intended to be human readable.

Getting the extensions list

To get a list of all the supported extensions, you'll need to call:

```
local extensions = gl.Get("s(1)", GL_EXTENSIONS)
```

This will return the space delimited list of extension names, which you can process further into the Lua table:

```
local extensions_list = {}
for extension in extensions:gmatch("([%w_]+)") do
  extensions_list[extension] = true
end
```

Now, you can easily determine whether the specific extension is present on the current system. This is useful, for example, in determining whether there is support for shading language or not.

However, there is the GLEW library to contain the extensions management in order.

How it works...

The `Gl.Get` function offers a powerful querying capability. It unifies the `glGetBoolean`, `glGetInteger`, `glGetFloat`, `glGetDouble`, and `glGetString` functions into one. The catch is that you'll need to know what data type is relevant to the parameter name. Improper use can have unpredictable results, for example, an application crash. However, most of the parameters use the numeric format.

Using OpenGL extensions with GLEW and Lua

The GLEW library handles the correct mapping of the OpenGL function's entry points. This way you won't have issues with calling nonexistent extension functions if that extension is not available on the current system.

Getting ready

Support for the GLEW library is included in the OpenGL wrapper module called GL. First, you need to include this library in the Lua environment with the following code:

```
local gl = require 'luagl'
```

The GLEW library is initialized with the call of the `gl.InitGLEW` function.

How to do it...

With the GLEW library initialized, you are able to query for the presence of the specified extension or the OpenGL version. To do this, you'll need to call the `gl.IsSupported` function. The only parameter of this function is an extension name or the `GL_VERSION_{version}` string. This function also accepts more than one string parameter delimited with space. It will return true if such a combination is supported on the current system, otherwise it will return false.

Let's take a look at how to determine whether your system supports point sprites:

```
local point_sprites_supported = gl.IsSupported("GL_VERSION_1_4
GL_ARB_point_sprite")
```

This is how you would determine whether there's support for the vertex program:

```
local vertex_shader_supported =
gl.IsSupported("GL_ARB_vertex_shader")
```

Now, you can safely call functions that handle vertex shader programs.

How it works...

The GLEW library scans all the available extensions on initialization and makes appropriate dynamic bindings to OpenGL extension-specific functions. Without GLEW, this was usually done with the `xxxGetProcAddress` function that returns the function address. The three-letter prefix `xxx` is replaced with either `wgl` or `glx`, depending on the platform.

Loading images with SDL_image

This recipe will show you how to load images from various file formats. SDL_image supports the file formats BMP, CUR, GIF, ICO, JPG, LBM, PCX, PNG, PNM, TGA, TIF, XCF, XPM, and XV. SDL_image is a part of the LuaSDL module.

All images are loaded into the new surface object. File formats with support for transparent pixels (it's not the same as the alpha channel) would have set the color key attribute on the surface.

Getting ready

The SDL_image library depends on third-party libraries to load JPEG and PNG files. Make sure that you have the libjpeg, libpng, and zlib libraries installed. SDL_image doesn't require any additional initialization. LuaSDL handles this internally.

How to do it...

There are two ways of loading images:

- **Loading an image file directly to surface**: This method uses the `SDL.SDL_IMG_Load` function, where the only parameter is the image filename. If there is such a file and it is accessible to the application, `SDL.SDL_IMG_Load` will try to guess a file format by its extension. Finally, if everything goes well, it'll return a surface object with the image. Otherwise, it'll return a nil value.

  However, there's a downside because you can't detect whether the file doesn't exist or is unreadable. Another thing is that if the extension doesn't correspond with the file format, this function will fail.

  The following code shows you how to use this function to load an image file:

  ```
  local surface = assert(SDL.SDL_IMG_Load("image.png"))
  ```

- **Loading an image file with the use of RWop**: RWop is a form of file I/O abstraction offered by libSDL. This means libSDL offers you a way to load files regardless of the platform. Another thing to mention is that you can easily load file content from the text string or system memory.

  The SDL_image library supports loading image files with the RWop file object and also encourages users to use this way because it's much safer and you can also detect specific problems when something fails during image loading.

  To load an image file, you need to create the RWop file object with the `SDL.SDL_RWFromFile` function. The following example shows you how to do this:

  ```
  local image_file = assert(SDL.SDL_RWFromFile("image.png",
  "rb"))
  ```

The first parameter is the file path and the second is a string representing the mode to be used for opening the file. The mode is usually `rb`, which means that you are using the file for reading binary data. After this step, you can load an image from the RWop object provided with the `SDL.IMG_Load_RW` or `SDL.IMG_LoadTyped_RW` function. While the first function will always try to detect the image format, the second one accepts an image format specification. Both these functions use the second parameter to determine whether the submitted RWop object can be closed automatically. This is especially useful if you don't plan to read that file again. These functions will return the surface object with the image upon success. The image type can specified by one of these strings in uppercase BMP, CUR, GIF, ICO, JPG, LBM, PCX, PNG, PNM, TGA, TIF, XCF, XPM, and XV.

The following example shows how to use these functions to load the image from the RWop object:

```
local image_auto = assert(SDL.IMG_Load_RW(image_file, 1))
local image_png = assert(SDL.IMG_LoadTyped_RW(image_file, 1,
"PNG"))
```

How it works...

Even if you choose to load the image file with the `SDL.SDL_IMG_Load` function, it uses the `RWop` object internally. If an error occurs, you can rely only on the `SDL.SDL_GetError` function to get a better view on what went wrong.

The resulting image will be stored into a new surface object with the corresponding pixel format. Always check for the pixel format of the resulting surface to avoid confusion later. A typical example can be a PNG file, which supports 1, 2, 4, 8, 16, 24, and 32-bit color depth with or without palette, grayscale with the alpha channel or even 64-bit color depth.

Creating textures

OpenGL offers the use of 1D, 2D, and 3D textures. 2D textures are the most commonly used, even in 3D games. Support for 3D textures was introduced with OpenGL 1.2. A 3D texture can be thought as a layered 2D texture. 1D textures can be used in situations where the texture doesn't change along one dimension, for example, a rainbow.

Getting ready

OpenGL, by default, doesn't use any textures. All polygons are rendered with solid color, defined by colors on the vertices. This method of rendering is called Flat shading. Optionally, these vertex colors can be interpolated with so-called Smooth shading or Gouraud shading. The difference between these two modes becomes apparent with vertex lighting as you can see in the following figure:

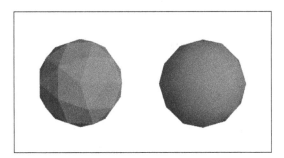

To use textures, you'll need to toggle the texturing state with the `gl.Enable` function. There are altogether three states for texturing—GL_TEXTURE_1D, GL_TEXTURE_2D, and GL_TEXTURE_3D. Each one allows you to use a certain type of texture. You can also disable texturing with the `gl.Disable` function. This might be desirable when drawing a wireframe around an object.

How to do it...

Texture creation consists of four steps:

1. Generating the texture object.
2. Binding the texture to a texture target.
3. Setting up texture parameters (optional, but recommended).
4. Uploading the desired content to a texture object.

First of all, you'll need to get a valid texture object. You can get it with the `gl.GenTextures` function, which will return a Lua table with texture identifiers. This function has only one parameter that specifies how many texture objects you want to create:

```
local textures = gl.GenTextures(1)
local texture_id = textures[1]
```

The preceding code extracts the texture object identifier in the second line. This identifier will be used in later steps.

The next step is to decide what kind of texture you'll be using. There are three kinds of textures to choose from—GL_TEXTURE_1D, GL_TEXTURE_2D, and GL_TEXTURE_3D. This choice will affect the texturing target name in subsequent instructions.

With the texturing target name, you can bind the texture object to the current texturing unit with the `gl.BindTexture` function. The first parameter of this function is the texture target name and the second is the texture object identifier. The Lua code for this step might look like this:

```
gl.BindTexture(GL_TEXTURE_2D, texture_id)
```

With the texture object bound, you can set up the texture parameter. This step isn't necessary, but the default texture parameters can lead to unpredictable behavior and bad texture quality. Therefore, you should use the `gl.TexParameter` function. Actually, there are two versions of this function. The first one is called `gl.TexParameteri`, which only accepts integer values. Then, there is the second `gl.TextParameter` function that accepts the float number. With this texture parameter setting, you can set up texture wrapping/tiling and texture filtering. The example of texture parameters' setting is shown as follows:

```
gl.TexParameteri(GL_TEXTURE_2D, GL_TEXTURE_WRAP_S,
GL_CLAMP_TO_EDGE)
gl.TexParameteri(GL_TEXTURE_2D, GL_TEXTURE_WRAP_T,
GL_CLAMP_TO_EDGE)
gl.TexParameteri(GL_TEXTURE_2D, GL_TEXTURE_MIN_FILTER, GL_LINEAR)
gl.TexParameteri(GL_TEXTURE_2D, GL_TEXTURE_MAG_FILTER, GL_LINEAR)
```

This will set the texture to wrap on both dimensions, which are specified by the s and t coordinates. The s coordinate is usually the horizontal and the t coordinate is regarded as vertical. There is also an r coordinate which is used on 3D textures as the depth coordinate. The other two parameters, `GL_TEXTURE_MIN_FILTER` and `GL_TEXTURE_MAG_FILTER`, correspond to the texture filtering method used on texture minifying and texture magnifying. The minifying filter is used when the surface area is greater than the texture and the magnifying filter is used on smaller surface areas. This is most notable on 3D scenes, where the textured object might move towards or away from the viewing camera.

The following table contains the available values for these parameters:

Parameter names	Parameter values	Description
`GL_TEXTURE_WRAP_x`	`GL_CLAMP`	The coordinates are clamped to range (0,1).
	`GL_CLAMP_TO_BORDER`	The coordinates are clamped to range $<\dfrac{-1}{2N}, 1+\dfrac{1}{2N}>$, where N is the texture size in the specified direction. The texture border is taken into account.
	`GL_CLAMP_TO_EDGE`	The coordinates are clamped to range $<\dfrac{1}{2N}, 1-\dfrac{1}{2N}>$, where N is the texture size in the specified direction. The texture border is taken into account.
	`GL_REPEAT`	The texture is tiled by omitting the integer part of the texture coordinate.
	`GL_MIRRORED_REPEAT`	The texture is tiled with mirroring used on every second repetition.

Parameter names	Parameter values	Description
GL_TEXTURE_MIN_FILTER	GL_NEAREST	This returns the nearest texture element—texel.
	GL_LINEAR	This is the linear interpolation that is used between texels.
	GL_NEAREST_MIPMAP_NEAREST	This uses the nearest texel in combination with mipmapping, where the mipmap is selected by the nearest selection criteria.
	GL_LINEAR_MIPMAP_NEAREST	This uses linear interpolation on texels with mipmapping. Mipmap is selected by the nearest selection criteria.
	GL_NEAREST_MIPMAP_LINEAR	This uses the nearest texel with mipmapping. The resulting mipmap is a linear combination of the two closest mipmaps.
	GL_LINEAR_MIPMAP_LINEAR	This uses linear interpolation on texel with mipmapping. The resulting mipmap is a linear combination of the two closest mipmaps.
GL_TEXTURE_MAG_FILTER	GL_NEAREST	This returns the nearest texel.
	GL_LINEAR	This is the linear interpolation that is used between texels.

The difference between the nearest and linear texture filtering can be seen in the following two screenshots:

An example of the nearest texture filtering is as follows:

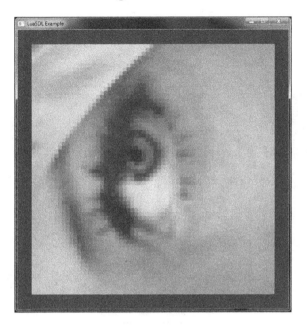

An example of the linear texture filtering is as follows:

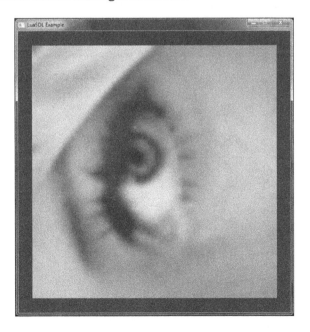

These two methods suffer from the moiré pattern effect when used on the 3D scene when the surface goes into distance. To resolve this issue, mipmapping can be used. Mipmapping represents a method of down sampling the texture into smaller versions. The original texture version is used when the surface is close enough. As the surface is farther, the smaller versions of the texture are used. This can be regarded as a simple form of level of detail automation. Fortunately, graphic cards can generate mipmaps automatically if you choose mipmap filtering. The following figure shows the scene without mipmapping on the left and with mipmapping on the right-hand side:

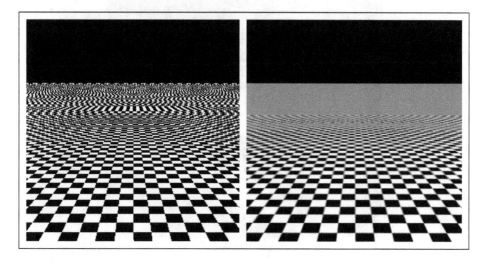

Finally, you can set the size, pixel format, and content of the texture. To do this, you need to call either the `gl.TexImage1D`, `gl.TexImage2D` or `gl.TexImage3D` function. These functions will submit the texture into the graphic card and reserve the corresponding space in memory for the texture. This example shows the usage of the 2D version, which is the most commonly used:

```
local texture_target = GL_TEXTURE_2D
local mipmap_level = 0
local internal_format = GL_RGBA
local width = surface.w
local height = surface.h
local border = 0
local format = GL_RGBA
local data = surface.pixels
gl.TexImage2D(texture_target, mipmap_levels, internal_format,
width, height, border, format, data)
```

A texture target should correspond to the gl.TexImage version; although, a different texture target can be used to convert, for example, from 1D image to 2D image. The mipmap-level parameter will set the original level of detail for mipmapping. The internal format specifies how the image will be stored in the graphical memory. The Border parameter creates a border around the texture. The border color can be changed with the GL_TEXTURE_BORDER_COLOR texture parameter. The Format parameter specifies the input image format. This is usually GL_RGB or GL_RGBA if you're using an image with the alpha channel. The last parameter contains the texture data. This parameter can also be 0, which means that nothing will be stored in this texture. This is useful if you're going to generate the texture on-the-fly.

Note that the gl.TexImage function will reserve memory space with each call and it's not suitable to update texture content!

The last thing to do is to free the texturing target with the following line of code:

```
gl.BindTexture(texture_target, 0)
```

This means that you won't be doing anything with the texture. The zero value is reserved for the default texture in OpenGL. This technique is often called texture unbinding.

How it works...

OpenGL always uses numeric identification of the texture object. As a result of this, manipulation with OpenGL objects is much simpler and portable.

Internally, OpenGL doesn't care if a certain portion of the memory is used by a 2D texture or vertex buffer. This gives the programmer much flexibility and it's also very dangerous at the same time. Therefore, always try to be consistent with the use of OpenGL objects.

The internal format parameter of gl.TexImage can be supplied with a number of channels or with one of the many internal formats OpenGL supports. The most notable formats are GL_RGB, GL_RGBA, GL_LUMINANCE, or GL_INTENSITY. The last two formats are often used with grayscale images.

The data parameter refers to the pointer value which LuaGL interconnects with light user data type. You can use this fact to easily supply an array of pixels or any other data.

There's more...

If you need to update the existing texture or just a portion of it, you can use the gl.TexSubImage function. There are three versions of this function for each texture target, which are gl.TexSubImage1D, gl.TexSubImage2D, and gl.TexSubImage3D. These functions have the following specifications:

```
gl.TexSubImage1D(texture_target, mipmap_level, xoffset, width,
format, data)
```

```
gl.TexSubImage2D(texture_target, mipmap_level, xoffset, yoffset,
width, height, format, data)
gl.TexSubImage3D(texture_target, mipmap_level, xoffset, yoffset,
zoffset, width, height, depth, format, data)
```

With these functions, you can also set the offsets for each dimension. Notice that these functions don't do any texture resizing. Image resizing must be done on a surface level with the `SDL.GFX_zoomSurface` function. The function specification looks like this:

```
SDL.GFX_zoomSurface(surface, x_zoom_factor, y_zoom_factor,
antialiasing)
```

This function will return a new surface object. Zoom factors smaller than 1 will cause the resulting image to be smaller in that direction and factors greater than 1 will stretch the image. You can also turn on antialiasing, which makes the resulting image nicer. Antialiasing is a method of reducing visible artefacts that usually occur during image resizing.

Functions such as `gl.TexImage` and `gl.TexSubImage` support a zero value in their data parameter. This is a special case when OpenGL allows you to copy the texture into another.

The following screenshot shows the modification of the existing surface with `gl.TexSubImage2D`:

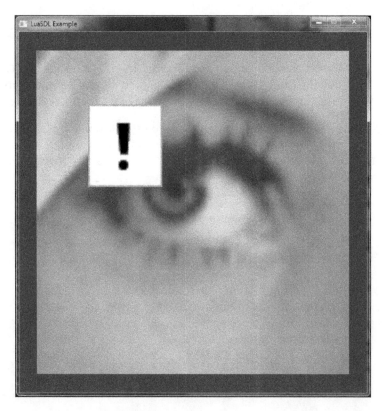

Loading and using bitmap fonts

Bitmap fonts are used mainly with monospaced fonts. Mainly, that's because you can evenly divide bitmap into rectangular areas. Each of these areas contains one font character. Usually, such font characters are sorted by ASCII coding or use a part of this coding. Once you have loaded the image file with the bitmap font, you can easily access each font character finding its rectangular coordinates. These coordinates can be stored in a Lua table which makes character lookup fast. This kind of font is quite popular mainly because each font character has equal spacing between characters, so you don't have to handle problems with font kerning.

The following example shows a bitmap font stored in an image:

This recipe will deal with single glyph rendering.

Getting ready

First you need to load the bitmap font into graphical memory. Let's assume that the `font_texture_id` variable contains a valid texture object, which contains the font image. The `Font_texture_width` and `font_texture_height` variables will contain the texture size. The `Glyph_width` and `glyph_height` variables will contain the glyph size. Now, the only information you'll need is the glyphs count in the single line in font texture. This will be addressed in the `glyphs_per_line` variable.

The next thing you'll need is texturing support. You can turn it on with the following code:

```
gl.Enable(GL_TEXTURE_2D)
```

Finally, you can bind the font texture into the texture target:

```
gl.BindTexture(GL_TEXTURE_2D, font_texture_id)
```

How to do it...

Glyph rendering will be done in the GL_QUADS mode. This means each glyph will consist of four vertices connected into one polygon. Each vertex will be described by its position and texture coordinates. Texture coordinates play the most important role in this case. Texture coordinates in OpenGL use the range (0,1), so you'll need to convert the position from your font texture into this range. You can achieve this with the following equations:

```
local font_texture_x = glyph_width*(glyph_index%glyphs_per_line)
local font_texture_y =
glyph_height*math.floor(glyph_index/glyphs_per_line)
local texcoord_x0 = font_texture_x/font_texture_width
local texcoord_y0 = font_texture_y/font_texture_height
local texcoord_x1 = texcoord_x0 + glyph_width/font_texture_width
local texcoord_y1 = texcoord_y0 + glyph_height/font_texture_height
```

The Glyph_index variable is the glyph index with range (0,N), where N is the total number of glyphs in the font image. Coordinates are used to describe corresponding corners as you can see in the following figure:

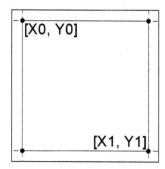

You can store these coordinates into the Lua table to improve the game performance.

Now you can finally use this information to render font glyph on screen. Glyph will be drawn in a rectangular polygon. The glyph position on the screen will be defined by two coordinates, x and y. The size of the rectangular polygon will use two variables, w and h. The code to draw this rectangle will look like this:

```
gl.Begin(GL_QUADS)
    gl.Color4f(1,1,1,1)
    gl.TexCoord2f(texcoord_x0, texcoord_y0)
    gl.Vertex2f(x, y)
```

```
    gl.TexCoord2f(texcoord_x0, texcoord_y1)
    gl.Vertex2f(x, y+h)
    gl.TexCoord2f(texcoord_x1, texcoord_y1)
    gl.Vertex2f(x+w, y+h)
    gl.TexCoord2f(texcoord_x1, texcoord_y0)
    gl.Vertex2f(x+w, y)
  gl.End()
```

Notice that there's only one definition of the polygon color. OpenGL accepts this by using the same color on all vertices. Another thing to mention is that this font glyph renderer will overwrite the whole rectangular area. This is because OpenGL doesn't know which parts should be transparent yet. This issue can be resolved by using the OpenGL blending function.

How it works...

Bitmap fonts rely on regular positions of characters. This allows the designer to easily divide the bitmap font with the grid and draw font bitmaps pixel by pixel. The main disadvantage is that each letter must be of the same size. The larger letter often consists of 2, 4 or more parts. In the old days of DOS, this technique was often used to generate graphics in text mode, where the font in the system memory was regularly updated.

Font bitmaps often use white color because you can easily change that color with vertex coloring with the `gl.Color4f` function.

Each font glyph is defined by four vertices. The vertex definition must follow the instructed order—`color`, `texcoord`, and `vertex` or `texcoord`, `color`, and `vertex`.

There's more...

Glyph coordinate equations can be used with texture tiles too. In fact, the bitmap font is a tileset!

See also

- ▶ The *Displaying the text* recipe
- ▶ The *Using tiles and tilesets in the game* recipe

Loading and using TrueType fonts

TrueType fonts present a higher quality font rendering with the use of font outlines. Each font character is called a glyph. TTF files contain not only outlines but also the glyph's information. Glyph rendering from outlines is much slower than drawing bitmap font characters on screen. This is mainly because these glyphs are being drawn on-the-run and font rendering may be enhanced with antialiasing, which is costly. Because of this, applications using TrueType fonts often cache font glyphs into textures.

The SDL_ttf library manages the loading of the TrueType font files. Everything you need to use these files is included in the LuaSDL library.

This recipe will deal with loading font glyph in surface object, which you can store into the texture or as a smaller part of the bigger texture—texture atlas.

Getting ready

First, you'll need a TTF file with font data. Let's assume that you already have one called font.ttf. The next thing you'll need to know is what font size will be used. This is important because the SDL_ttf library uses this size to set the proper glyph metrics on scalable fonts and to choose the glyph set on nonscalable fonts.

The SDL_ttf library needs initialization before the first use. You can initialize it with the function call:

```
SDL.TTF_Init()
```

The same goes for freeing the resources when you're about to quit the application. You should always call SDL.TTF_Quit() at the end.

How to do it...

There are four versions of the function you can use to load the SDL.TTF_OpenFont, SDL.TTF_OpenFontIndex, SDL.TTF_OpenFontRW, and SDL_TTF_OpenFontIndexRW font. The first two use filename to load the font file. The other two use the RWop object. The functions with the index keyword accept one additional parameter with the font face index. Their specifications are as follows:

```
SDL.TTF_OpenFont(font_filename, font_size)
SDL.TTF_OpenFontIndex(font_filename, font_size, font_face_index)
SDL.TTF_OpenFont(rwop, free_src, font_size)
SDL.TTF_OpenFontIndex(rwop, free_src, font_size, font_face_index)
```

The `free_src` parameter set to 1 will free the `RWop` object after successful load. In this case, the recipe will be using the last version of the function.

First, you need to open the font file:

```
local rwop = assert(SDL.SDL_RWFromFile("font.ttf","rb"))
```

Now, you can read the content from the font file:

```
local font_size = 12
local face_index = 0
local font = assert(SDl.TTF_OpenFontIndexRW(rwop, 1, font_size,
face_index))
```

Now that you have successfully loaded the font file, you can read the font information and glyphs. You'll need the font ascent and descent values to be able to set correct glyph positions.

The next step is to render a glyph. Each glyph contains information about glyph positioning. Without it, the characters wouldn't sit on the baseline because each glyph usually has a different size. To get the glyph positioning information, you need to call `SDL.TTF_GlyphMetrics`. Each glyph has different metrics, so you need to obtain this information for each glyph. Fortunately, you can store glyph metrics in the Lua table. You can use the method shown in the following sample:

```
local glyph_metrics = {}
local text = "Hello world ABCDEF"
for i=1,#text do
  local code = string.byte(text, i)
  if not glyph_metrics[code] then
    local _, minx, maxx, miny, maxy, advance =
    SDL.TTF_GlyphMetrics(font, code)
    glyph_metrics[code] = {
      minx = minx,
      maxx = maxx,
      miny = miny,
      maxy = maxy,
      advance = advance,
    }
  end
end
```

Glyph metrics are useful if you are rendering texts that change often. If this is not the case, you can safely use the internal `SDL_ttf` text renderer to produce surface objects that contain whole text with characters at the right places.

The final part of this recipe is text rendering. There are altogether 12 functions that provide text rendering. Their description is shown in the following table:

Function names	Description
`SDL.TTF_RenderText_Solid`	This renders text in Latin1 encoding in solid mode
`SDL.TTF_RenderUTF8_Solid`	This renders text in UTF8 encoding in solid mode
`SDL.TTF_RenderUNICODE_Solid`	This renders text in UNICODE encoding in solid mode
`SDL.TTF_RenderGlyph_Solid`	This renders a UNICODE glyph in solid mode
`SDL.TTF_RenderText_Shaded`	This renders text in Latin1 encoding in shaded mode
`SDL.TTF_RenderUTF8_Shaded`	This renders text in UTF8 encoding in shaded mode
`SDL.TTF_RenderUNICODE_Shaded`	This renders text in UNICODE encoding in shaded mode
`SDL.TTF_RenderGlyph_Shaded`	This renders a UNICODE glyph in shaded mode
`SDL.TTF_RenderText_Blended`	This renders text in Latin1 encoding in blended mode
`SDL.TTF_RenderUTF8_Blended`	This renders text in UTF8 encoding in blended mode
`SDL.TTF_RenderUNICODE_Blended`	This renders text in UNICODE encoding in blended mode
`SDL.TTF_RenderGlyph_Blended`	This renders a UNICODE glyph in blended mode

You must have noticed that there are three rendering modes:

- **Solid**: While solid mode is the fastest, it uses an 8-bit surface with palette. Color index 0 is used as a color key—transparent color. Color index 1 is used for text foreground color. The text is not very smooth.

- **Shaded**: This mode is slower but nicer. It uses an 8-bit surface. Color index 0 is used as a background. Other colors are used as varying degrees of foreground color. This text is not transparent and it's surrounded with a solid box filled with background color.

- **Blended**: This mode is the slowest. It uses a 32-bit surface with the alpha channel. What's more, the text is antialiased.

You should always use the blended mode with OpenGL. Not only does the text look better, but the process of uploading the texture into the graphic card memory is much easier.

You can draw a single character with any of the `SDL.TTF_RenderGlyph_xxx` functions. The following example will be using the blended mode:

```
local color = SDL.SDL_Color_local()
color.r,color.g,color.b = 255,255,255
```

```
local glyph_surface =
assert(SDL.TTF_RenderGlyph_Blended(font, string.byte("A",1),
color))
```

You can blit `glyph_surface` directly to the screen surface object or transfer it into the OpenGL texture. However, be sure to check the pixel format of the `glyph_surface` object! The color channel mask can be quite different from what the OpenGL function `gl.TexImage` expects. The order of the color channels in `glyph_surface` must match the internal texture format! Otherwise, you can expect incomplete texture, invalid texture colors or even segmentation faults (crashes).

Don't forget to call `SDL.TTF_CloseFont` to free the font object:

```
SDL.TTF_CloseFont(font)
```

How it works...

Font glyph uses metrics information to maintain the correct glyph placement. A summary of these metrics can be found in the following figure:

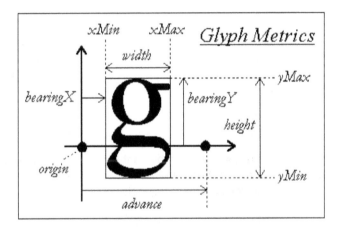

The font ascent and descent values can help you with the vertical positioning of characters. Ascent is the distance from the top of the font to the baseline. Descent is the distance from the baseline to the bottom of the font. You can get these two parameters with the `SDL.TTF_FontAscent(font)` and `SDL.TTF_FontDescent(font)` functions.

See also

▸ The *Displaying the text* recipe
▸ The *Creating texture atlas with the rover design pattern* recipe

Displaying the text

Text rendering if often the base part of any graphical engine. The text rendering engine can be divided into two groups:

- ▸ The bitmap font rendering engine
- ▸ The TrueType font rendering engine

The main difference is that bitmap fonts are usually proportional and glyph placement is quite easy as each glyph uses the same spacing and all glyphs use the texture of the same size. On the other hand, TrueType font rendering is more complex as it uses glyphs of different sizes. Each glyph has its own characteristics and you can't easily determine how much space will be taken by text.

This recipe will cover the second case with TrueType font rendering. Bitmap font rendering can be easily derived from this recipe with a few changes.

Getting ready

Before you start, make sure you have a valid `font` object with font information. You'll also need to apply a blending function so that the transparent parts of the glyph won't be visible. Otherwise, you will see only solid rectangles instead of characters. This can be set somewhere after you have created the OpenGL window:

```
gl.Enable(GL_BLEND)
gl.BlendFunc(GL_SRC_ALPHA, GL_ONE_MINUS_SRC_ALPHA)
```

Let's assume that `glyph_textures` is a Lua table that always contains valid font glyph textures. You can generate textures on-the-fly and store them into this table from which you can reuse them repeatedly, so it won't cause a major slowdown.

Also, don't forget to turn on texture rendering by using the following code:

```
gl.Enable(GL_TEXTURE_2D)
```

How to do it...

This recipe will contain the whole text drawing function, which you can reuse and modify to suit your needs.

First, you need to obtain the basic font information by using the following code:

```
local font_descent = SDL.TTF_FontDescent(font)
local font_lineskip = SDL.TTF_FontLineSkip(font)
local glyph_metrics = {}
```

These two font parameters are sufficient for text rendering. The text drawing function will be called `ttf_print`:

```lua
function ttf_print(x, y, color, size_factor, text)
  local size_factor = size_factor or 1
  -- pos_x and pos_y store current glyph position on screen
  local pos_x, pos_y = x, y
  -- loop through all string characters
  for I=1, #text do
    -- character code
    local code = string.byte(text,i)
    -- obtain cached glyph metrics
    local metrics = glyph_metrics[code]
    -- store glyph metrics into cache if the glyph
    -- is used for the first time
    if not metrics then
      local _, minx, maxx, miny, maxy, advance =
      SDL.TTF_GlyphMetrics(font, code)
      metrics = {
        minx = minx,
        maxx = maxx,
        miny = miny,
        maxy = maxy,
        advance = advance,
      }
      glyph_metrics[code] = metrics
    end
    -- obtain glyph image
    local glyph_texture = glyph_textures[code]
    if glyph_texture then
      gl.BindTexture(GL_TEXTURE_2D, glyph_texture)
```

Variables `tc_x0`, `tc_y0`, `tc_x1`, and `tc_y1` contain texture coordinates for glyphs. In this case, all the glyphs use the same texture coordinates, but this can vary depending on your implementation of texture storage. These coordinates will be unique for each glyph if you use texture atlas:

```lua
      local tc_x0, tc_y0, tc_x1, tc_y1 = 0, 0, 1, 1
      local glyph_x = pos_x + metrics.minx * size_factor
      local glyph_y = pos_y + (font_descent - metrics.maxy) *
      size_factor
      local glyph_width = (metrics.maxx - metrics.minx) *
      size_factor
      local glyph_height = (metrics.maxy - metrics.miny) *
      size_factor
```

Glyphs will use rectangular polygons. Note that the order of vertices is important. The reverse order will cause disappearing of the polygons because their orientation will be inside the screen and not outside to the viewer:

```
-- draws a rectangle filled with glyph image
gl.Begin(GL_QUADS)
    gl.Color4f(color.r, color.g, color.b, 1)
    gl.TexCoord2f(tc_x0, tc_y0)
    gl.Vertex2f(glyph_x, glyph_y)

    gl.TexCoord2f(tc_x1, tc_y0)
    gl.Vertex2f(glyph_x + glyph_width, glyph_y)

    gl.TexCoord2f(tc_x1, tc_y1)
    gl.Vertex2f(glyph_x + glyph_width, glyph_y + glyph_height)

    gl.TexCoord2f(tc_x0, tc_y1)
    gl.Vertex2f(glyph_x, glyph_y + glyph_height)
gl.End()
```

Each glyph should be moved a bit horizontally. Otherwise, the glyphs will overlap each other.

```
pos_x = pos_x + metrics.advance * size_factor
```

Optionally, you can emulate newlines by incrementing the `pos_y` variable with the `font_lineskip` parameter and resetting the `pos_x` variable to x:

```
        end
      end
    end
```

You can manage the rendered font size by changing the `size_factor` parameter. Factor 1 means the original size.

How it works...

SDL_ttf works internally with UNICODE encoding to determine the index of glyph. Glyph textures should use points with a considerably larger size as downsizing the texture is usually handled pretty well by GPU. Resizing low resolution glyph textures doesn't provide good results. Higher resolution glyphs take more memory space, of course. It's always good to find a balance between quality and memory consumption.

You can see this resolution problem in the series of the two following figures. The first one shows the result of downsizing high resolution glyphs on GPU:

The second one shows scaling up the low resolution glyphs:

See also

▶ The *Loading and using bitmap fonts* recipe
▶ The *Loading and using TrueType fonts* recipe

Creating texture atlas with the rover-design pattern

Texture management becomes important with increasing the number of textures. An intuitive approach of using different OpenGL texture objects for each game texture presents the major bottleneck with rapid texture switching. That's because every time you change active texture unit, the graphic card needs to change its internal state. This problem can be eliminated using fewer larger textures that contain smaller images. This can be compared to a texture atlas where images are placed next to each other. These images can be accessed using different texture coordinates for every image.

Texture atlas can use evenly-spaced images with the same size or use some placement algorithm to place images of unequal sizes efficiently.

The first method was used in older games and is often used in games in which the images have the same size. Such texture atlas is often pregenerated to save the game loading time. Every time the game needs to use a different set of images, a new texture atlas is loaded into memory. The disadvantage is that these texture atlases may contain the same images from other atlases and you can't add a new image to them. These texture atlases are often called tiles.

The second method uses dynamic generated texture atlases. These are generated on-the-fly and each new image takes a specific place. Image placement can be controlled by a certain algorithm, which can make the placement more compact so that the space is used more efficiently. One of the algorithms is called the rover design pattern. This algorithm can be found, for example, in games from the id software company.

Getting ready

The texture atlas technique uses storing smaller images into one big texture. The basic prerequisite is at least one free texture that can be used as storage. This texture should at least be as big as the largest image you'll be using. In a memory-constrained environment, you can do proportional resizing of the image so that it fits into the texture atlas. LuaSDL offers this kind of function called `SDL.GFX_zoomSurface` and it's specified using the following function definition:

```
local surface = SDL.GFX_ZoomSurface(surface, scale_x, scale_y,
smooth)
```

This function will accept the source surface object in the first argument. Scale values present scaling factors and the last argument is a numeric flag value to enable antialiasing for zooming. The next sample code will scale the image down to half of its original size with smoothing enabled:

```
local scale_x = 0.5
local scale_y = 0.5
local dst_surface = SDL.GFX_ZoomSurface(src_surface, scale_x,
scale_y, 1)
```

The total size of the atlas texture can be set dynamically to achieve a certain level of texture detail. This is commonly found in modern games where you have an option in the settings to set the texture quality.

How to do it...

This example of texture atlas algorithm will use a texture atlas with the size of 512 x 512 pixels. You can use it every time you need to place a new image into the texture atlas. It will return coordinates in the texture atlas for the specified size of the image. If there is not enough space for the image, it will return false:

```
local atlas = {
   width = 512,
   height = 512,
   fill = {},
   full = false,
}
```

```lua
local function allocBlock(width, height)
  local allocated = atlas.fill
  local i,j,best1,best2,x,y = 0,0,atlas.height,0,0,0
  for i=0, atlas.width-width do
    best2 = 0
    for k=0,width-1 do
      local column = allocated[i+k]
      j = k
      if not column then
        column = 0
        allocated[i+k] = column
      end
      if (column >= best1) then
        break
      end
      if (column > best2) then
        best2 = column
      end
    end
    if j == width-1 then
      -- valid area
      x = i
      y, best1 = best2, best2
    end
  end
  if (best1 + height) > atlas.height then
    return false
  end
  for i=0, width-1 do
    allocated[x+i] = best1 + height
  end
  return x,y
end
```

How it works...

The texture atlas function uses the `atlas` table to store the information about free space in the texture atlas. Free space lookup works just like the famous *Tetris* game with the board flipped upside-down. This algorithm works in two nested loops. The first one (the outer loop) tries to place the block of specified size from the left side to the right side. The second one (the inner loop) checks whether there are any obstacles in the current block placement. If there aren't any, the placement is regarded as valid and the function returns this position.

Note that the order of placement is important in this case. Smaller objects should be placed first, although there might be better methods with additional heuristics.

The texture atlas can look like the following figure:

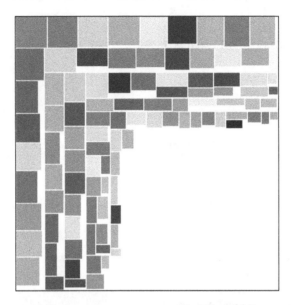

Using tiles and tilesets in the game

Tiles are usually referred to as small subimages that are part of a bigger image. Tiles usually have the same size, so they are easily compacted into one rectangular area. You can see tiles mostly in 2D games, especially in platform games, RPGs and even 3D action games. The rectangular property makes tiles very efficient in the question of accessing specific subimages from a large tileset. You can store the whole tileset into the graphical memory, and with the knowledge of the subimage positions, you can easily select the tiles you need.

You can observe that many small game animations consist of a connected set of tiles—called **tileset**. Tilesets can define an animation as an ordered list of tile indices. Tile indices are often accompanied with destination coordinates so you can make an animated movement with the same tile.

The main advantage of the Lua language is that it has excellent support for structural data description. Therefore, you can use Lua tables to describe tiles and tilesets.

This recipe will show you an example of the tileset engine.

Getting ready

First, let's assume that you've already loaded the tileset image into a texture single object with a size of 512 x 512 pixels. This texture object will be identified by the `texture` variable, which will be obtained from the Lua table `textures`. It may look like the following screenshot:

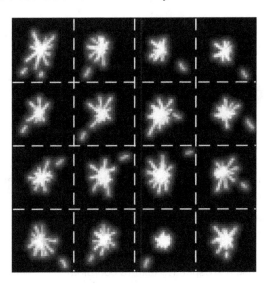

From this, you can see that this image is an animation divided into 4 x 4 sections. These sections are the tiles you'll be using.

To select one specific tile, you can either rely on regular tile placement or use the tileset descriptor defined by the Lua table:

```lua
local tilesets = {
  ['sparkle'] = {
    filename = "sparkle.png",
    w = 512, h = 512,
    tiles = {
      ['sparkle_01'] = {
        x=0, y=0, w=128, h=128,
      },
      ['sparkle_02'] = {
        x=128, y=0, w=128, h=128,
      },
      ['sparkle_03'] = {
        x=256, y=0, w=128, h=128,
      },
      ['sparkle_04'] = {
        x=384, y=0, w=128, h=128,
      },
```

```
        ['sparkle_05'] = {
          x=0, y=128, w=128, h=128,
        },
        ...
      }
    }
  }
```

Now that you have described all the tiles from the sparkle tileset, you can proceed to the function that will retrieve tile information from this table.

How to do it...

The process of drawing a tile consist of three phases:

- The first phase will obtain tile coordinates that correspond to the tileset name and to the name of the tile. The result will be four coordinates that will need to be transformed according to the texture matrix configuration and the texture object identifier that contains the tileset image.

- The second phase will map the obtained coordinates to a valid range of texture coordinates, which is usually (0,1).

- The last phase will draw a textured rectangular polygon at the specified place. Each vertex will use its respective texture coordinate.

These phases can be enhanced with other parameters such as tile coloring, rotation, offset from tile origin point, and so on.

The function for the first phase will consist of two input parameters, the name of the tileset and the name of the tile. It will return the texture object identifier, texture size, and four coordinates that describe the rectangular region of the tileset image:

```
function getTile(tileset_name, tile_name)
  local tileset = tiles[tileset_name]
  if tileset then
    local texture = textures[tileset.filename]
    if texture then
      local tile = tileset.tiles[tile_name]
      if tile then
        return texture, tileset.w, tileset.h, tile.x, tile.y,
        tile.w, tile.h
      end
    end
  end
  return false
end
```

In the second phase, you'll need to convert tile coordinates to texture space so that they can be used directly with the OpenGL gl.TexCoord2f function. The whole conversion is based on mapping from pixel coordinates into the numeric range (0,1). It's important to do this because OpenGL uses this range by default. Otherwise, you will get barely visible downscaled tile images.

Coordinate conversion will be done in the transformCoordinates function and will accept texture atlas dimensions and four tile coordinates. The result will consist of four pairs of coordinates that can be used directly with the OpenGL gl.TexCoord function:

```
function transformCoordinates(tileset_width, tileset_height, x, y,
w, h)
  local out_x = x/tileset_width
  local out_y = y/tileset_height
  local out_w = w/tileset_width
  local out_h = h/tileset_height
  return {
    {x = out_x, y = out_y },
    {x = out_x + out_w, y = out_y },
    {x = out_x + out_w, y = out_y + out_h},
    {x = out_x, y = out_y + out_h},
  }
end
```

Now you can step into the last phase of tile rendering. This function will use the previous functions to construct an array of texture coordinates and use them to draw a textured rectangle on screen:

```
function drawTile(tileset_name, tile_name, x, y, scale_factor)
  local texture, ts_w, ts_h, t_x, t_y, t_w, t_h =
  getTile(tileset_name, tile_name)
  if texture then
    local scale_factor = scale_factor or 1
    local tex_coord = transformCoordinates(ts_w, ts_h, t_x, t_y,
    t_w, t_h)
    gl.BindTexture(GL_TEXTURE_2D, texture)
    gl.Begin(GL_QUADS)
      gl.Color4f(1, 1, 1, 1)
      gl.TexCoord2f(tex_coord[1].x, tex_coord[1].y)
      gl.Vertex2f(x, y)

      gl.TexCoord2f(tex_coord[2].x, tex_coord[2].y)
      gl.Vertex2f((x + t_x) * scale_factor, y)

      gl.TexCoord2f(tex_coord[3].x, tex_coord[3].y)
```

```
        gl.Vertex2f((x + t_x) * scale_factor, (y + t_y) *
        scale_factor)

        gl.TexCoord2f(tex_coord[4].x, tex_coord[4].y)
        gl.Vertex2f(x, (y + t_y) * scale_factor)
     gl.End()
   end
 end
```

With this function, you can place tiles anywhere on screen. The polygon position is defined by the x and y parameters. Optionally, you can also scale the tile with the `scale_factor` parameter. With the default scale, the tile size will be the same as it is in the tileset.

How it works...

This recipe uses the power of the Lua language to describe any data structure with the Lua tables in a very brief way. Because of this, tileset data doesn't have to be stored in a special file. It can be read directly by the Lua interpreter into the variable.

The transformation of texture coordinates is necessary to map coordinates into valid texture space. Textures usually use coordinates in the range of (0,1), although you are not explicitly limited to it. The behavior of the coordinates across the specified range is defined by the texture object parameters, `GL_TEXTURE_WRAP_S` and `GL_TEXTURE_WRAP_T`. If the texture uses the `GL_REPEAT` mode, you can safely use coordinates that don't fall into the range (0,1). Otherwise, you will get a clamped result as shown in the following figure:

With correct texture coordinates, the `drawTile` function will bind the corresponding texture object into the 2D texture target. From this point, this texture will be used in subsequent operations. This function uses intermediate mode to draw a rectangular polygon. This means this group of vertices enclosed by the `gl.Begin` and `gl.End` functions will be drawn immediately.

This whole polygon will use white color for all vertices, which results in tile rendering with the same colors as the tileset image. The vertex color can be used to modify polygon colorization. If you have used `gl.Color4f(0, 0, 0, 1)`, the vertices would be black and so would be the whole polygon. The vertex color is usually multiplied with the texture color. However, this behavior can be changed with vertex program, vertex shader, or fragment shader.

Notice that these vertices are in a certain order. This order assures that the polygon will be drawn facing the viewer—you. This order can be changed with the `gl.FrontFace` function. This function accepts one of these parameters, `GL_CW` and `GL_CCW`. The first one renders polygons in a clockwise fashion and the second one renders polygons counterclockwise, which is the default value.

See also

- The *Loading images with SDL_image* recipe
- The *Creating textures* recipe
- The *Loading and using bitmap fonts* recipe

4
Graphics – Legacy Method with OpenGL 1.x–2.1

This chapter will deal with the following recipes:

- ▶ Drawing primitives in immediate mode
- ▶ Setting up blending
- ▶ Moving, rotating, and scaling objects
- ▶ Setting up the orthogonal and perspective cameras
- ▶ Setting up materials
- ▶ Setting up lighting
- ▶ Using display lists
- ▶ Setting up the vertex buffer

Introduction

There are two ways of using OpenGL. The first one was used over many years from the introduction of the first version of OpenGL. This method uses the so-called immediate mode. This means that every command is processed immediately and the graphic card uses a fixed pipeline. It's mostly used in Hello World samples because it's very easy to use.

The second one uses a dynamic programmable pipeline, which is a bit more difficult to use and it allows you to achieve optimal application performance.

This chapter will cover this first method, so you can learn the basics of OpenGL. The Lua scripting language will help you with your first prototype of the OpenGL application. You'll learn how to draw graphical primitives, change their parameters, position, rotation and scale. The next thing you'll learn will be object matrix transformations, accompanied by other types of matrix transformations. The last part will deal with the basics of using display lists and vertex buffers.

Display lists and vertex buffers played an important role in the last few years before the introduction of the programmable pipeline on graphic cards. It was the only way of uploading and using a bigger amount of vertex data.

Drawing primitives in immediate mode

The OpenGL drawing process consists of drawing graphic primitives. These are basic shapes such as points, lines, triangles, quadrilaterals and polygons. There are also special cases when you can use the OpenGL utility functions (GLUT) to draw more complex objects such as curves, spheres, NURBS curves, and so on. However, this chapter is oriented toward basic OpenGL operations. More information about this library can be found at `https://www.opengl.org/resources/libraries/glut/`.

Immediate mode drawing commands consist of the `gl.Begin` and `gl.End` blocks. Each of these blocks contain the element drawing specification. For instance, there's only one specification for drawing points, but there are three modes of drawing a set of lines. You can draw each line separately or you can connect them in a way that each line segment will connect to the previous segment.

This recipe will show you how to use each individual type of primitive in certain situations with visual samples.

Getting ready

To get access to the OpenGL functions from the Lua language, you'll need to use the LuaGL binding library. You can use LuaGL available at the GitHub repository `https://github.com/soulik/luagl`.

Refer to the *Initialize graphics mode with OpenGL* recipe in *Chapter 3, Graphics – Common Methods*, to get the usable binary module for LuaGL.

First, you'll need to get the LuaGL module loaded in the Lua source code. You can do this with the following code:

```
local gl = require 'luagl'
```

The next thing you'll need is a list of the OpenGL constants. This list of constants is a part of LuaGL project and can be found at `https://github.com/soulik/luagl/blob/master/src/gldefs.lua`.

This list is constantly updated with each new OpenGL revision or with the introduction of a new graphic card. This way you can manually update this list and add a new constant without recompilation. Upon including this file, a new global table, gl_enum, is defined. You can query a value of the constant like this:

```
gl_enum.GL_POINTS
```

This will return the same value as the C macro definition GL_POINTS. This list is imported from the GLEW library header file, which should contain the most up-to-date list of OpenGL constants.

Each vertex consists of these basic parameters—position, color, and texture coordinates. The vertex position can be defined by these two functions—gl.Vertex2f(x, y) and gl.Vertex3f(x, y, z). The function parameters x, y, and z are coordinates for each dimension of 3D space. Note that the final vertex position on screen can be modified by transformation matrix operations such as rotation, translation, and scaling. The next functions set the color of the next vertex gl.Color3f(r, g, b) and gl.Color4f(r, g, a). Color components use a numerical range (0,1). The last vertex parameters are texture coordinates for the next vertex. These can be set with the functions: gl.TexCoord2f(u, v) and gl.TexCoord3f(u, v, w). U, V, and W are texture coordinates in the 2D or 3D space of a texture. These are usually in a range (0,1), but you are allowed to use any range you need. Coordinates from this range are used in conjunction with the wrapping mode set to GL_REPEAT so that the texture repeats itself.

How to do it...

Each primitive definition block begins with the gl.Begin command. This command accepts one argument with a primitive type specification. As of OpenGL version 2.1, there were 10 possible primitive types. This list was later extended with special cases of primitive drawing modes. Primitives are defined by a set of vertices. Each vertex need at least one position specification. You can also set the vertex color and vertex specific texture coordinates. Do note that if you don't set vertex color, OpenGL will use the default color—red. The same goes for default texture coordinates with zeroes in all dimensions. Vertex parameters must be set before setting the vertex position.

Drawing points

The simplest primitive is a point. Each point consists of exactly one vertex. Point primitives are mostly used with particle effects. In conjunction with the point sprites technique and GLSL shaders, you can create various effects such as a flame or water flow. The point sprites technique uses textures instead of simple points. In this case, textures are always oriented toward the viewer. More about GLSL shaders can be found in *Chapter 5, Graphics – Modern Method with OpenGL 3.0+*.

The point drawing code can look like the following:

```
gl.Begin(gl_enum.GL_POINTS)
  -- A
  gl.Color4f(1, 0, 0, 1)
  gl.Vertex3f(-0.5, -0.5, 0)
  -- B
  gl.Color4f(0, 1, 0, 1)
  gl.Vertex3f(0.5, -0.5, 0)
  -- C
  gl.Color4f(0, 0, 1, 1)
  gl.Vertex3f(0.5, 0.5, 0)
  -- D
  gl.Color4f(1, 1, 0, 1)
  gl.Vertex3f(-0.5, 0.5, 0)
gl.End()
```

This will draw four colored points with the size of one pixel. Points of this size are hardly seen. You can the change point size in pixels with the `gl.PointSize` function. This function will accept a positive floating point number that specifies the point diameter. However, OpenGL uses the square shape for points by default. You can change this behavior to use the circular shape with:

```
gl.Enable(gl_enum.GL_POINT_SMOOTH)
```

Note that you need to set these point parameters before drawing. Otherwise, the changes will apply to the next drawing block.

An example of the previous sample output will look like the following screenshot:

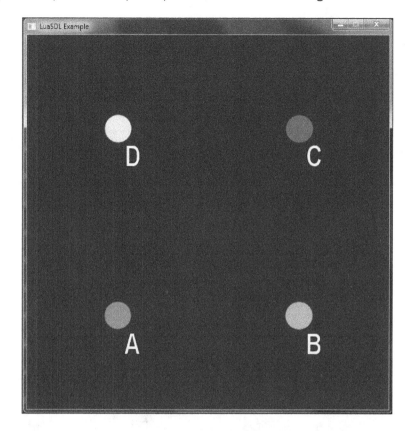

Drawing lines

The next primitive type is lines. Lines consist of two vertices. One primitive can be made up of more than one line. In this case, you can tell OpenGL if you'd like to specify each line with a pair of two vertices or with just the final vertex, where the first one is determined by the previous vertex position. Vertex color and texture coordinates must be defined before the `gl.Vertex` function.

The drawing code block is mostly the same as in the point drawing code:

```
gl.Begin(gl_enum.GL_LINES)
   -- A
   gl.Color4f(1, 0, 0, 1)
   gl.Vertex3f(-0.5, -0.5, 0)
   -- B
   gl.Color4f(0, 1, 0, 1)
   gl.Vertex3f(0.5, -0.5, 0)
```

```
    -- C
    gl.Color4f(0, 0, 1, 1)
    gl.Vertex3f(0.5, 0.5, 0)
    -- D
    gl.Color4f(1, 1, 0, 1)
    gl.Vertex3f(-0.5, 0.5, 0)
gl.End()
```

This code would draw straight horizontal lines with 1 pixel width. You can adjust the line width with the `gl.LineWidth` function. OpenGL guarantees that you can use lines with 1 pixel width. However, the upper limit is specific to your system. You can check the available range with `gl.Get('f(2)',gl_enum.GL_LINE_WIDTH_RANGE)`. This will return a Lua table with minimum and maximum values of line width. There is also an option to enable line smoothing, so that they don't look so jagged. You can enable this with:

```
gl.Enable(gl_enum.GL_LINT_SMOOTH)
```

The resulting output will look like this:

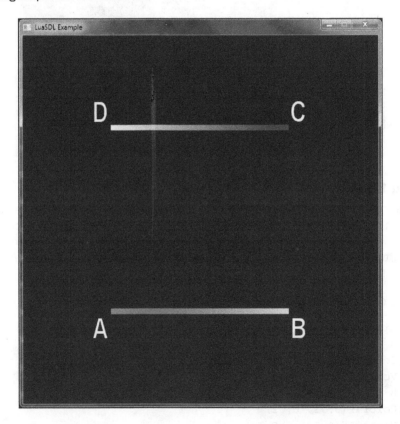

Drawing line strips

Line strips are used to draw a sequence of connected lines. A typical example of usage can be linear graphs or curved trails. You can reuse the previous code where you change the primitive type only:

```
gl.Begin(gl_enum.GL_LINE_STRIP)
  ...
gl.End()
```

The resulting image would look like this:

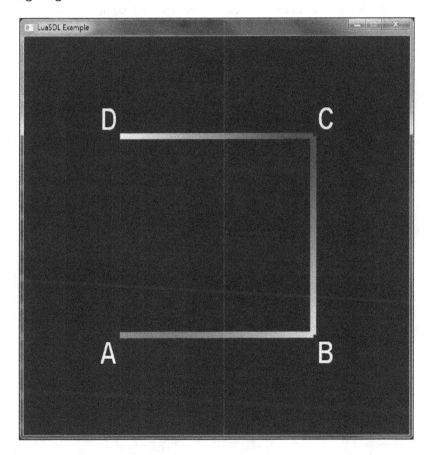

Drawing line loops

You must have noticed that standard OpenGL doesn't provide functions for drawing circles or any other closed outline shapes—hollow polygons. You have to do this by yourself with line loops. Line loops behave just like the line strips, except the last vertex is connected to the first one with a line. This is fairly useful when drawing object outlines:

```
gl.Begin(gl_enum.GL_LINE_LOOP)
    ...
gl.End()
```

This code uses the same vertices as the previous example with point primitives and results in a colorful rectangle, as shown in the following screenshot:

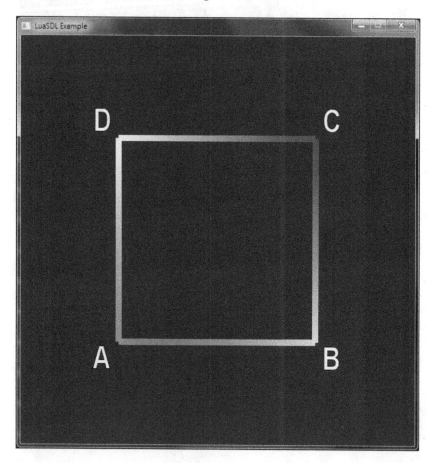

Drawing triangles

So far, you've been shown how to draw points, lines, and hollow polygons. The following parts will deal with filled primitives, such as triangles, quadrilaterals and polygons. Triangles often represent the basic part of more complex 2D or 3D objects as any polygon can be decomposed into triangles. Every triangle consists of exactly three vertices. The following code will draw a single-colored triangle where each vertex will have its own color; OpenGL can do automatic color interpolation in the area between vertices:

```
gl.Begin(gl_enum.GL_TRIANGLES)
  -- A
  gl.Color4f(1, 0, 0, 1)
  gl.Vertex3f(-0.5, -0.5, 0)
  -- B
  gl.Color4f(0, 1, 0, 1)
  gl.Vertex3f(0.5, -0.5, 0)
  -- C
  gl.Color4f(0, 0, 1, 1)
  gl.Vertex3f(0.5, 0.5, 0)
gl.End()
```

The result will look like this:

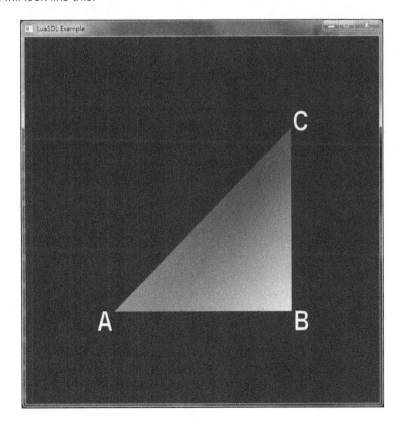

Note that, in this case, every triangle needs to be specified separately. For instance, to draw two triangles, you'd need to use the `gl.Vertex3f` function six times. The `gl.Begin` and `gl.End` blocks might contain vertex specifications for more than one graphical primitive of the same type.

Drawing triangle strips

Triangle strips are most often used when drawing various beams and trails. Let's assume that the first triangle is defined by a sequence of vertices marked with the letters **A**, **B**, and **C**. The next triangle can be constructed by adding one vertex **D**, where this triangle would contain vertices **B**, **C**, and **D**. This method is more efficient than defining every triangle separately. You can see the construction process in the following screenshot:

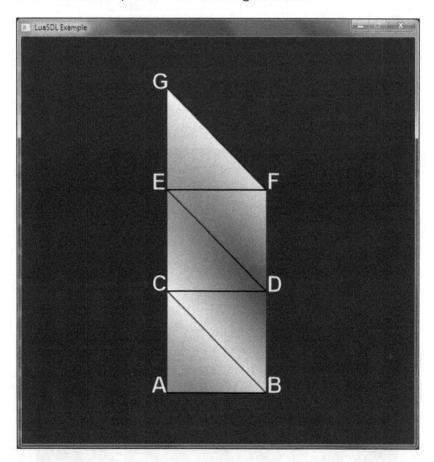

This picture consists of five triangles defined by seven vertices. If you wanted to draw this in the `GL_TRIANGLES` mode, you would need to pass 15 vertices to OpenGL. Keep in mind that passing data between CPU and GPU directly affects video game performance. Both sides are limited by the currently available RAM bandwidth.

The following code sample will draw five connected triangles from the preceding screenshot:

```
gl.Begin(gl_enum.GL_TRIANGLE_STRIP)
    -- A
    gl.Color4f(1, 0, 0, 1)
    gl.Vertex3f(-0.25, -0.75, 0)
    -- B
    gl.Color4f(0, 1, 0, 1)
    gl.Vertex3f(0.25, -0.75, 0)
    -- C
    gl.Color4f(1, 1, 0, 1)
    gl.Vertex3f(-0.25, -0.25, 0)
    -- D
    gl.Color4f(0, 0, 1, 1)
    gl.Vertex3f(0.25, -0.25, 0)
    -- E
    gl.Color4f(1, 0, 1, 1)
    gl.Vertex3f(-0.25, 0.25, 0)
    -- F
    gl.Color4f(0, 1, 1, 1)
    gl.Vertex3f(0.25, 0.25, 0)
    -- G
    gl.Color4f(1, 1, 1, 1)
    gl.Vertex3f(-0.25, 0.75, 0)
gl.End()
```

Drawing triangle fans

Triangle fans are similar to triangle strips. They are more efficient than drawing every triangle separately. Triangle fans are mostly used for drawing filled arcs, circles, convex polygons or even simpler concave polygons such as a star shape. It works in a way that the first vertex in the list is used as a central vertex, the second one corresponds to the last vertex used in the previous triangle, and finally, you define the last one. A sample code is as follows:

```
gl.Begin(gl_enum.GL_TRIANGLE_FAN)
    -- A
    gl.Color4f(1, 0, 0, 1)
    gl.Vertex3f(0.0, 0.0, 0)
    -- B
    gl.Color4f(0, 1, 0, 1)
    gl.Vertex3f(0.0, -0.75, 0)
    -- C
    gl.Color4f(1, 1, 0, 1)
    gl.Vertex3f(0.5, -0.5, 0)
    -- D
```

```
    gl.Color4f(0, 0, 1, 1)
    gl.Vertex3f(0.75, 0.0, 0)
    -- E
    gl.Color4f(1, 0, 1, 1)
    gl.Vertex3f(0.5, 0.5, 0)
    -- F
    gl.Color4f(0, 1, 1, 1)
    gl.Vertex3f(0.0, 0.75, 0)
    -- G
    gl.Color4f(1, 1, 1, 1)
    gl.Vertex3f(-0.5, 0.5, 0)
gl.End()
```

This code will draw five triangles from the list of seven vertices. You can see the result with the description in the following screenshot:

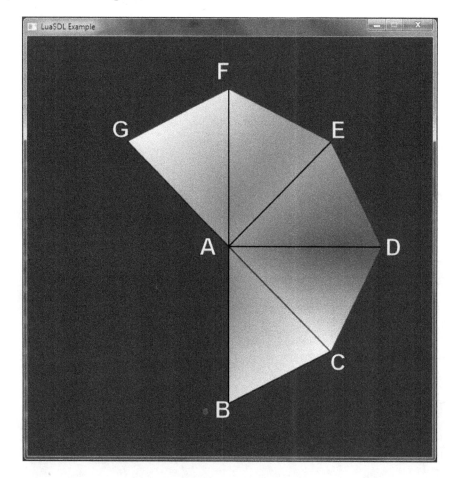

Drawing quads

Quads are primitives that consist of exactly four vertices. It's expected that these four vertices are in 1 plane. Otherwise, the result is unpredictable. This primitive type is mostly used with rectangular surfaces such as you can find in games with tiles and sprites. Quads are also used with font rendering because each glyph is made out of a separate rectangle. A quad definition will look like the following code:

```
gl.Begin(gl_enum.GL_QUADS)
  -- A
  gl.Color4f(1, 0, 0, 1)
  gl.Vertex3f(-0.5, -0.5, 0)
  -- B
  gl.Color4f(0, 1, 0, 1)
  gl.Vertex3f(0.5, -0.5, 0)
  -- C
  gl.Color4f(1, 1, 0, 1)
  gl.Vertex3f(0.5, 0.5, 0)
  -- D
  gl.Color4f(0, 0, 1, 1)
  gl.Vertex3f(-0.5, 0.5, 0)
gl.End()
```

This will render a single colored rectangular polygon, as shown in the following screenshot:

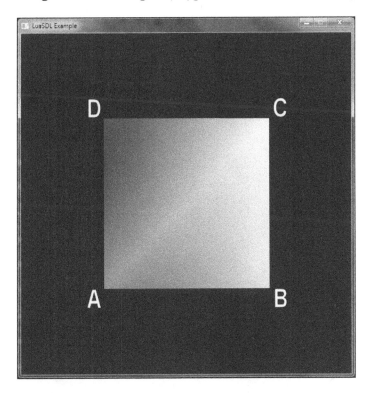

Drawing quad strips

Quad strips are connected quads that share exactly one edge. The last two vertices from the previous quad are used as the first two vertices in the new quad. This can be used to draw beams or trails just like triangle strips. The main difference between quad and triangle strips is that the neighboring quads share two vertices along with vertex attributes, whereas triangle strips share only one vertex with its attributes. This is mostly noticeable when you apply texture coordinates on vertices. The following code will draw two colored quads:

```
gl.Begin(gl_enum.GL_QUAD_STRIP)
   -- A
   gl.Color4f(1, 0, 0, 1)
   gl.Vertex3f(-0.25, -0.5, 0)
   -- B
   gl.Color4f(0, 1, 0, 1)
   gl.Vertex3f(0.25, -0.5, 0)
   -- C
   gl.Color4f(1, 1, 0, 1)
   gl.Vertex3f(-0.5, 0.0, 0)
   -- D
   gl.Color4f(0, 0, 1, 1)
   gl.Vertex3f(0.5, 0.0, 0)
   -- E
   gl.Color4f(1, 0, 1, 1)
   gl.Vertex3f(-0.25, 0.5, 0)
   -- F
   gl.Color4f(0, 1, 1, 1)
   gl.Vertex3f(0.25, 0.5, 0)
gl.End()
```

This will lead to drawing a hexagonal shape that consists of two quads, as you can see in the following screenshot:

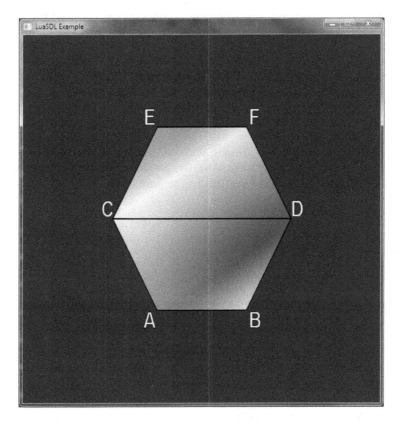

Note that the order of vertices differs from the usual quads. In this case, vertices follow the zigzag movement.

Drawing polygons

Polygonal primitives can be used to draw convex objects only and they are quite limited in terms of performance. The same object can be drawn much faster with triangles than with the polygon. Therefore, programmers are mostly discouraged from using this type of primitive.

How it works...

Drawing blocks `gl.Begin` and `gl.End` may consist of functions that specify vertex attributes only. Any other command in these blocks is considered as an error.

Examples contained in this recipe use the default camera settings. Therefore, the x coordinates represent the horizontal position from left to right in a range (-1,1). The y coordinates are the vertical position from bottom to top in a range (-1,1) and the z coordinates represent the depth in a range (-1,1). The positive values are nearer to the viewer and the negative values are farther from the viewer.

Note that drawing objects with the `gl.Begin` and `gl.End` blocks is slow because each call transfers data from the CPU to the graphic card. The graphic card waits until the data transfer is complete and this also has a negative effect on the performance.

See also

  ▶ The *Using display lists* recipe
  ▶ The *Setting up the vertex buffer* recipe

Setting up blending

OpenGL allows you to change the way textures are drawn. This process is called blending and it's often used when combining multiple textures. However, blending can also be applied to texture rendering on screen. OpenGL uses a so-called "blending function" to define the mathematical function that calculates the final color value. For example, the `GL_FUNC_ADD` blending function defines additive blending, which is used when mixing colored lights in a scene.

This function uses two values:

  ▶ The source value is usually a color or alpha channel value of the texture you are currently using. The source value is also called a fragment.
  ▶ The destination value is a color or alpha channel value that's on the destination surface or the screen.

You can't directly put values into the blending function. What you are allowed to do is to use one of the predefined functions to be used for the source value or the destination value.

Note that the blending function is also used with the modern rendering techniques introduced by dynamic programmable pipelines—GLSL shaders, which will be covered in *Chapter 5, Graphics – Modern Method with OpenGL 3.0+*.

Getting ready

By default, OpenGL doesn't use blending in the process of rendering the scene. You can enable it with the `gl.Enable(gl_enum.GL_BLEND)` function call. With blending turned on, you can apply transparency control with the blending function.

How to do it...

As you can see, there are many possible combinations for the final form of the blending equation. However, there are only a few combinations found that are used in games. These are additive blending, subtractive blending, and alpha blending.

Additive blending

This type of blending is commonly used for particles that affect the light. For instance, you can use it for water particles, blood splats, laser beams, fire, and so on. You can set up additive blending with the following code:

```
gl.Enable(gl_enum.GL_BLEND)
gl.BlendFunc(gl_enum.GL_SRC_ALPHA, gl_enum.GL_ONE)
gl.BlendEquation(gl_enum.GL_FUNC_ADD)
```

This assumes that the particle texture has an alpha channel. If this is not the case, you'll need to set the source blending function to the `GL_ONE` constant. An example of additive blending can be seen in the following screenshot:

Subtractive blending

Subtractive blending is mostly used with smoke particles, decals, or paintings that cover a surface. In this situation, you can use the following code:

```
gl.Enable(gl_enum.GL_BLEND)
gl.BlendFunc(gl_enum.GL_ONE_MINUS_SRC_COLOR, gl_enum.GL_SRC_COLOR)
gl.BlendEquation(gl_enum.GL_FUNC_ADD)
```

This type of blending is often used with a grayscale picture where the white color is fully transparent and the black color is opaque. The result is shown in the following screenshot:

Alpha blending

Alpha blending is similar to subtractive blending with the exception that the alpha channel is used to control transparency instead of the color lightness. This gives you an advantage over subtractive blending because you can draw colored decals over surfaces. For instance, you can draw nails on wood, signs on walls and so on. The code for alpha blending is as follows:

```
gl.Enable(gl_enum.GL_BLEND)
gl.BlendFunc(gl_enum.GL_SRC_ALPHA, gl_enum.GL_ONE_MINUS_SRC_ALPHA)
gl.BlendEquation(gl_enum.GL_FUNC_ADD)
```

Remember that this code works only with pictures that have an alpha channel. Otherwise, the picture will overdraw previous content.

The correct use of alpha blending is shown in the following screenshot:

How it works...

The general form of the blending equation looks like this:

```
final value = blending_equation(fragment_color * source_factor,
pixel_color * destination_factor)
```

The blending function in the equation uses two parameters: the source value and the destination value. The exact form of the blending function depends on the choice of the blending equation, which you can change with the `gl.BlendEquation` function. You can choose one of the equations given in the following table:

Equations	Mathematical operators
GL_FUNC_ADD	output = src + dest
GL_FUNC_SUBSTRACT	output = src - dest
GL_FUNC_REVERSE_SUBSTRACT	output = dest - src
GL_MIN	output = min(src, dest)
GL_MAX	output = max(src, dest)

OpenGL uses `GL_FUNC_ADD` by default, which is great for antialiasing and transparency.

The source and destination factors are determined by the choice of the blending function. The list of blending functions is shown in the following table:

Blending functions	Description
GL_ZERO	$(0,0,0,0)$
GL_ONE	$(1,1,1,1)$
GL_SRC_COLOR	(R_s, G_s, B_s, A_s)
GL_ONE_MINUS_SRC_COLOR	$(1,1,1,1) - (R_s, G_s, B_s, A_s)$
GL_DST_COLOR	(R_d, G_d, B_d, A_d)
GL_ONE_MINUS_DST_COLOR	$(1,1,1,1,) - (R_d, G_d, B_d, A_d)$
GL_SRC_ALPHA	(A_s, A_s, A_s, A_s)
GL_ONE_MINUS_SRC_ALPHA	$(1,1,1,1) - (A_s, A_s, A_s, A_s)$
GL_DST_ALPHA	(A_d, A_d, A_d, A_d)
GL_ONE_MINUS_DST_ALPHA	$(1,1,1,1) - (A_d, A_d, A_d, A_d)$
GL_CONSTANT_COLOR	(R_c, G_c, B_c, A_c)
GL_ONE_MINUS_CONSTANT_COLOR	$(1,1,1,1) - (R_c, G_c, B_c, A_c)$
GL_CONSTANT_ALPHA	(A_c, A_c, A_c, A_c)
GL_ONE_MINUS_CONSTANT_COLOR	$(1,1,1,1) - (A_c, A_c, A_c, A_c)$
GL_SRC_ALPHA_SATURATE	$(R_d * G_d * B_d * i, 1)$ $i = min(A_s, 1 - A_d)$

The color component values are specified by R—red, G—green, B—blue, and A—alpha. The subscript s specifies the source color channel, *d* is for the destination color channel, and the c subscript refers to the constant color channel that you can set with the `gl.BlendColor` function. The `gl.BlendColor` function uses the same parameters as `gl.Vertex4f`. To get a better idea of how blending works, you can refer to the following screenshot, where the source image uses a transparent picture of the Lua logo and the destination is the famous picture of Lena. The samples use all the possible combinations of the blending functions—for the source it is the horizontal direction and for the destination it is the vertical direction:

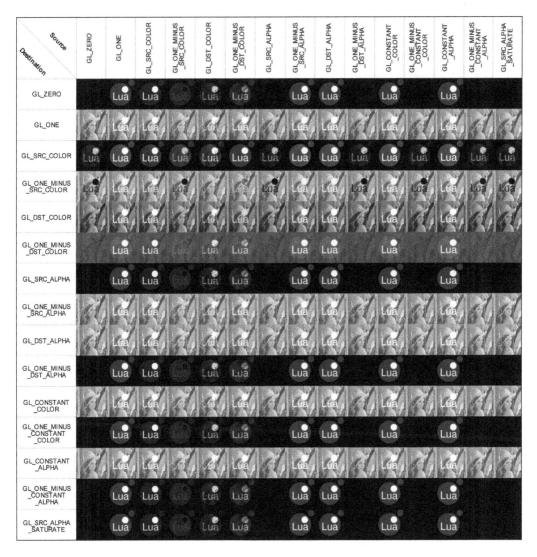

Moving, rotating, and scaling objects

OpenGL offers you stack-based matrix transformations. These transformations include translating—moving, rotating, and scaling. Stacking means that previous transformations can affect succeeding transformations and they create the hierarchical structure. A typical example may be a human-like arm simulation. The arm consists of several parts connected with joints. Each part's position and orientation is dependent on the position and orientation of the previous part. Similar rules of dependency apply to all parts of the solar system. Planets orbit around stars and moons orbit their planets at the same time.

This recipe will show you how to create a simple scene with your own animated miniature of the solar system.

Getting ready

The core to success with scene animation is to understand how matrix transformations affect parts of your scene. There are four main rules to remember:

> ▶ Each transformation changes the state of the local coordinate system, so the order of transformations is important.

> ▶ Matrix transformation doesn't affect the previous transformations—it doesn't propagate backwards.

> ▶ The matrix state can be reset, stored, and restored from stack, which is, of course, limited by its maximum depth in specific matrix mode. Matrix modes will be explained later in the *How it works...* section of this recipe.

> ▶ There are four types of matrices—the model view matrix, projection matrix, texture transformation matrix, and color transformation matrix.

The best way to design the transformation system is to draw a simple scheme of transformations. It's always good to think of matrix transformations as a movement of your arm and fingers. When you rotate your arm, you'll also move your fingers into another position. When you move your fingers, it doesn't affect the position of your arm. This recipe will refer to the following scheme diagram:

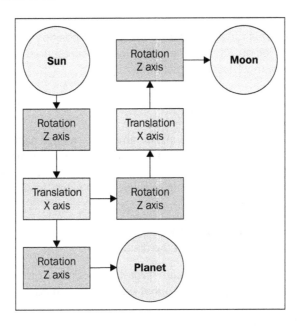

This recipe will use the default matrix settings, where the world will start at the origin position (0,0,0) and you'll only be using the model view matrix.

The entire solar system will be stored in a structure made up of the Lua tables. Each solar system will have its own planets and each planet will have its own moon. Every space object will contain its size, color, and distance from the center of the rotation, outer and inner angular speed, and its objects. The configuration of the solar system can look like this:

```lua
local stars = {
  {size = 0.3, color = {1,1,0,1}, planets = {
    {distance = 0.2, outerSpeed = 1, innerSpeed = -1,
      size = 0.05, color = {1,0,0,1},},
    {distance = 0.4, outerSpeed = 0.5, innerSpeed = 0.3,
      size = 0.09, color = {0.8,1,0,1}, moons = {
        {distance = 0.15, outerSpeed = 2, innerSpeed = 1,
          size = 0.04, color = {0.8,0.7,0.7,1},},
    }},
    {distance = 0.9, outerSpeed = 0.4, innerSpeed = -0.5,
      size = 0.2, color = {0.2,0.7,1,1}, moons = {
        {distance = 0.2, outerSpeed = -2, innerSpeed = -1,
          size = 0.04, color = {0.9,0.9,0.9,1}, },
        {distance = 0.3, outerSpeed = -1.5, innerSpeed = -1,
          size = 0.03, color = {0.7,0.7,0.9,1},},
    }},
  }}
}
```

Space objects will be drawn with the `drawObject` function, which will accept one parameter—object color. This function will draw an object at position (0,0,0) with the specified color. You can decide whether the object will be represented by a rectangle, sphere, or anything you want. That's all you'll need for now.

How to do it...

First, you'll want to start with a star—the sun. For simplicity, you can assume that the sun will be the center of your small world. You can assume that the sun is static. The next step is to set the position of the planets. Each planet orbits around the sun, so you'll need to apply rotation. Don't worry, the sun already has its position and it won't be affected by the following transformations.

Each planet has its own distance, especially if you don't want the planets to collide. So, the next transformation will be the translation to set the distance.

The next thing you'll probably want is the planet rotation around its own axis. Now, the problem is, how to place moons around the planet so that each moon can have its own rotation, which isn't affected by the rotation of the planet. You can do this by saving the matrix state before you do the planet rotation around its own axis. You can do the same with planets, so each one will have its own rotation speed and distance. After you have placed the planet, you can restore the matrix state and rotate the moon around the planet.

After this, you only need to set the moon distance from the planet by translation, and finally, you can rotate the moon around its own axis.

The following code will process all the stars, planets, and the moon step by step:

```
gl.MatrixMode(gl_enum.GL_MODELVIEW)
for _, star in ipairs(stars) do
  gl.LoadIdentity()
  gl.PushMatrix()
  gl.Scalef(star.size, star.size, 1)
  drawObject(star.color) - draw the star
  gl.PopMatrix()

  for _, planet in ipairs(star.planets) do
    gl.PushMatrix()
    planet.outerAngle = math.fmod((planet.outerAngle or 0) +
    planet.outerSpeed, 360)
    planet.innerAngle = math.fmod((planet.innerAngle or 0) +
    planet.innerSpeed, 360)

    gl.Rotatef(planet.outerAngle, 0, 0, 1)
    gl.Translatef(planet.distance, 0, 0)
```

```
gl.PushMatrix()
gl.Rotatef(planet.innerAngle, 0, 0, 1)
gl.Scalef(planet.size, planet.size, 1)
drawObject(planet.color) - draw the planet
gl.PopMatrix()

if planet.moons then
  for _, moon in ipairs(planet.moons) do
    gl.PushMatrix()
    moon.outerAngle = math.fmod((moon.outerAngle or 0) +
    moon.outerSpeed, 360)
    moon.innerAngle = math.fmod((moon.innerAngle or 0) +
    moon.innerSpeed, 360)

    gl.Rotatef(moon.outerAngle, 0, 0, 1)
    gl.Translatef(moon.distance, 0, 0)
    gl.PushMatrix()
    gl.Rotatef(moon.innerAngle, 0, 0, 1)
    gl.Scalef(moon.size, moon.size, 1)
    drawObject(moon.color) - draw the moon
    gl.PopMatrix()
    gl.PopMatrix()
  end
  end
  gl.PopMatrix()
end
end
```

This will result in an animated scene of the solar system model. The following screenshot shows the resulting solar system model with textured space objects:

How it works...

This first thing this recipe does is to set the active matrix mode with the `gl.MatrixMode` function. This function accepts four matrix modes:

Matrix mode names	Guaranteed minimum stack depth	Description
GL_MODELVIEW	32	This mode applies transformations to the current set of objects in the scene.
GL_PROJECTION	2	The projection matrix affects the current camera view. It's usually used for setting up the zooming factor, aspect ratio of the screen, and perspective correction.
GL_TEXTURE	2	This mode is used to adjust the texture placement as it operates on the texture coordinates.
GL_COLOR	2	The color matrix applies transformations to colors. However, due to poor support, it's rarely used.

After this, the code loops through all the stars, where each star starts with a model view matrix resets into identity matrix. The next operation is to scale with the `gl.Scalef` function, but because this operation will also scale the entire solar system, you'll need to store the current matrix into stack memory with the `gl.PushMatrix` function. After scaling, you can draw the star, which is based on some generic space object with the unit size. Scaling will multiply the size of this star. After you have drawn your star, you can restore the model view matrix before scale transformation.

The next step is planets. Each planet starts with storing the current matrix state, which is restored after you have finished drawing the planet. After storing, you need to place the planet. You will need to think of the placement, such as playing 2D tanks artillery game or the famous *Worms* game. First, you set the direction and then you set the distance. You'll need to rotate the coordinate system about the *z* axis, which is directed toward you, perpendicular to the screen. This angle will change over time because matrix transformations aren't considered *stable*. The mathematical stability issue with floating point numbers is well known in the field of computer science. Each matrix operation will introduce a certain level of inaccuracy, which is the direct result of how floating point numbers work. The following example shows a simplified case of floating point numbers' inaccuracy with adding numbers to the sum:

```
local sum_of_numbers = 0
local iterations = 3
for i=1,iterations do
  sum_of_numbers = sum_of_numbers + 1/iterations
  print(("%f"):format(sum_of_numbers))
end
```

```
    -- is the result equal to 1?
    print("Sum equals to 1?", sum_of_numbers == 1)
```

After running this code, you'll get these four lines on the output screen:

```
0.333333
0.666667
1.000000
Sum equals to 1? true
```

As you'd expect, a value of one third is represented by an infinite sequence of digits. The second line contains rounded values of two thirds. The last line contains `true` if the sum is equal to 1. Computers can only store a limited amount of information; therefore, you'll always get an approximate value. Floating point number rounding can be handy in a limited set of cases. On the other hand, it introduces the so-called **rounding error** if you're working with smaller numbers, which is not unusual in matrix math. Try to change a number of iterations up to 6, and you'll see that, with six iterations, the resulting sum value is not equal to 1 anymore!

You can read more about floating-point numbers in Wikipedia article at `https://en.wikipedia.org/wiki/Floating_point`.

Unless you're doing science stuff, you can mitigate inaccuracy problems by storing the exact state of the matrix for later use.

Rotation is done with the `gl.Rotatef(degrees, x, y, z)` function, where the angle should be in the range (0,360) and the x, y, and z parameters are normalized direction vectors. A normalized vector has a length of 1 unit. Rotation around the X axis uses the direction vector (1,0,0), rotation around the Y axis uses the vector (0,1,0), and rotation around the Z axis uses the vector (0,0,1).

Now, you can set the planet's distance from the sun with translation over the X axis with the `gl.Translatef(x,y,z)` function. After this, you can scale and rotate the planet around its own axis of rotation if the planet has no moons. Scaling and rotation will affect the moons, so you'll need to use the `gl.PushMatrix` function before applying scaling and rotation. After drawing your planet, you can restore the matrix with the `gl.PopMatrix` function. The following process with moons is practically the same as with drawing planets.

The transformation matrix is defined by a 4 x 4 numerical matrix, which means there are four rows by four columns. The first three columns represent the position of the axes. The last column presents the origin point:

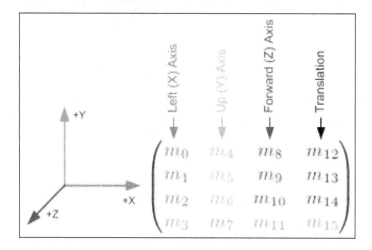

This recipe example uses six types of matrix operations, which are as follows:

▸ Load matrix identity

▸ Push matrix into stack

▸ Pop matrix from stack

▸ The translation matrix

▸ The rotation matrix

▸ The scale matrix

Every matrix operation, except push and pop, is defined by a special form of transformation matrix. For instance, the identity matrix contains one on the diagonal from the top left to the bottom right edge of the matrix. Any other field contains a zero value. Transformation matrices are applied to vertices by matrix multiplication. The following diagram shows the application of a 4 x 4 translation matrix on the 4 x 1 vector of vertex coordinates:

$$\begin{pmatrix} 1 & 0 & 0 & 1 \\ 0 & 1 & 0 & 2 \\ 0 & 0 & 1 & 3 \\ 0 & 0 & 0 & 1 \end{pmatrix} \cdot \begin{pmatrix} 0 \\ 1 \\ 2 \\ 1 \end{pmatrix} = \begin{pmatrix} 1 \\ 3 \\ 5 \\ 1 \end{pmatrix}$$

This sample uses the vertex at location (0,1,2). The last element of the vertex location vector is the *w* coordinate, which is also known as the homogeneous coordinate. This *w* coordinate can help the with representation of affine transformations such as translation or perspective correction. For instance, directional vectors use a *w* value equal to 0, while positional vectors use *w = 1*. You can find out more about affine transformations in the article at `https://en.wikipedia.org/wiki/Transformation_matrix#Affine_transformations`.

On the left-hand side, there is a translation matrix that moves the vertex in all axes by (1,2,3). The right-hand side of multiplication contains positional vectors with *w* equal to 1 and it's placed at the point with (0,1,2) coordinates in the Euclidean space. This vector transformation will result in homogeneous coordinates (1,3,5,1). However, you'll most probably need a Euclidean space coordinate, which can be easily obtained by dividing the first three coordinates by the *w* coordinate. The final result will consist of a point in the Euclidean space with coordinates (1,3,5), which can be directly used to set a new vertex position.

Also, do note that the multiplication between matrix and vector in this example results in a vector with a size of 4 x 1 (four rows and one column). This is a result of the matrix multiplication rule. A vector can be regarded as a matrix with one column or one row respectively. Let's assume that you want to multiply two matrices with sizes A x B and B x C. This will always result in a matrix with a size of A x C.

The identity matrix

The identity matrix has a special property that multiplies any 4 x 4 matrix with a 4 x 4 identity matrix, and the resulting matrix will remain the same as the original matrix. The identity matrix also presents the neutral operation as it doesn't change anything. The identity matrix has the following form:

$$\begin{pmatrix} 1 & 0 & 0 & 0 \\ 0 & 1 & 0 & 0 \\ 0 & 0 & 1 & 0 \\ 0 & 0 & 0 & 1 \end{pmatrix}$$

The translation matrix

The translation matrix is similar to the identity matrix with the exception that the last column contains **X**, **Y**, and **Z** coordinates that shift the origin of the coordinate system:

$$\begin{pmatrix} 1 & 0 & 0 & X \\ 0 & 1 & 0 & Y \\ 0 & 0 & 1 & Z \\ 0 & 0 & 0 & 1 \end{pmatrix}$$

The scale matrix

The scale matrix is based on the identity matrix, where the scale is defined as a scaling factor in each dimension. These scaling factors are positioned in the diagonal of the matrix. You can see this in the following diagram:

$$
\begin{pmatrix}
X & 0 & 0 & 0 \\
0 & Y & 0 & 0 \\
0 & 0 & Z & 0 \\
0 & 0 & 0 & 1
\end{pmatrix}
$$

The rotation matrix

The rotation matrix is a bit more complicated. Its columns contain positions of the axes for the rotated coordinate system. This matrix can be decomposed into simpler matrices that contain rotation in one direction. For instance, complex rotation in all axes in 3D space can be decomposed into three matrices. The first one rotates the coordinate system in the x dimension, the second one rotates in the y dimension, and the last one rotates in the z dimension. Note that the order of rotation matrices is important. Because of this, rotation around the z and the x axes is different from the rotation around the x and the z axes. Rotation matrices have two forms. One for the right-handed coordinate system and one for the left-handed system. OpenGL uses the standard right-handed coordinate system. Also, that's why positive y coordinates are directed towards the top of the screen.

The form of the rotation matrix around the x axis is as follows:

$$
R_x(\theta) = \begin{pmatrix}
1 & 0 & 0 & 0 \\
0 & \cos(\theta) & \sin(\theta) & 0 \\
0 & -\sin(\theta) & \cos(\theta) & 0 \\
0 & 0 & 0 & 1
\end{pmatrix}
$$

The rotation matrix about the y axis has the following form:

$$
R_y(\theta) = \begin{pmatrix}
\cos(\theta) & 0 & -\sin(\theta) & 0 \\
0 & 1 & 0 & 0 \\
\sin(\theta) & 0 & \cos(\theta) & 0 \\
0 & 0 & 0 & 1
\end{pmatrix}
$$

The matrix for rotation about the z axis has the following form:

$$
R_z(\theta) = \begin{pmatrix}
\cos(\theta) & \sin(\theta) & 0 & 0 \\
-\sin(\theta) & \cos(\theta) & 0 & 0 \\
0 & 0 & 1 & 0 \\
0 & 0 & 0 & 1
\end{pmatrix}
$$

There's more...

You can use textured rectangles for each type of space object, so you might be able to recognize whether the space object is a star, a planet, or a moon.

You can load your own transformation matrices into OpenGL with the `gl.LoadMatrix` and `gl.LoadTransposeMatrix` functions. These functions accept one Lua table with 16 elements of the 4 x 4 matrix. You are also allowed to apply your own matrix multiplication with the `gl.MultMatrix` and `gl.MultTransposeMatrix` functions. Be aware that this matrix multiplication is slower because you are sending a bunch of data from CPU to GPU with each function call.

See also

▸ The *Setting up the orthogonal and perspective cameras* recipe

Setting up the orthogonal and perspective cameras

The camera view is affected by the projection matrix. The projection matrix allows you to set up the camera position, rotation and the size of visible space.

Games mostly use two modes of camera projection. The first one is the orthogonal mode, which can be used to draw 2D scenes on the screen. This mode doesn't use the perspective camera, so the object's distance doesn't affect its size. On the other hand, the perspective mode causes farther objects to be visibly smaller than the nearer objects.

Getting ready

This recipe will assume that the current screen dimensions are stored in the variables `screen_width` and `screen_height`. These variables might change their values when you resize the application window or change the screen resolution. You might want to update these variables on resize event.

How to do it...

Camera space operations are divided into two parts. The first one shows how to use orthogonal projection for 2D screen elements and the second one will refer to perspective projection, which is used primarily for 3D scenes.

The orthogonal mode

The orthogonal mode is used commonly with UI elements, which are on the 2D surface of the screen. It causes parallel projection. This mode can be applied with the `gl.Ortho` function, which will set up the projection matrix. The following code shows you how to use this function properly:

```
local left, right = 0, screen_width
local top, bottom = 0, screen_height
local near, far = -1, 1
gl.MatrixMode(gl_enum.GL_PROJECTION)
gl.LoadIdentity()
gl.Ortho(left, right, bottom, top, near, far)
```

This will cause a change to the coordinate system. The vertex coordinate (0,0) will be positioned on the top-left corner of the screen. The bottom-right corner will correspond to the coordinate (`screen_width`,`screen_height`). Remember that you don't have to change the size of the orthogonal view with every change of the window size. The size of the orthogonal projection can be viewed as a grid where you divide the screen into even parts. If you need to divide the screen space into 10 x 10 even parts, you'll be using the following code:

```
gl.Ortho(0,10, 10, 0, -1, 1)
```

The perspective mode

This perspective mode is commonly used in 3D graphics, where you need to do perspective correction, move or rotate the camera, and change the field of view (FOV). To keep things simple, you can use the OpenGL utility library function `gl.Perspective`, which has the following specification:

```
gl.Perspective(fov, screen_aspect_ratio, zNear, zFar)
```

The first parameter `fov` defines the field of view in the Y direction in degrees. The screen aspect ratio is a ratio of the screen width to the screen height. The last two parameters `zNear` and `zFar` specify the position of the near and far clipping plane. Both the values must be positive numbers. Precision of the depth buffer is affected by the `zNear` and `zFar` ratio, which is defined as the `zFar` value divided by `zNear`. The greater the ratio, the greater will be the bits of depth buffer that are lost.

You can apply matrix transformation on the camera as well. With this, you can achieve camera movement, rotation, and scaling.

How it works...

The whole process of transformation from 3D space to 2D space is based on matrix multiplications. Transformation matrices are presented as a state in OpenGL. This means once you set up a certain transformation matrix, it will be used until you change it. This recipe won't cover matrix transformations in detail as this is a subject for the whole book. A visual representation of the whole transformation process can be seen in the following diagram:

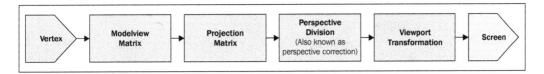

There's more...

The OpenGL function, gl.Frustum, presents a simple way to compute the transformation matrix for perspective corrections, which is important in realistic 3D scenes. It defines the viewing volume for the current scene and has the following specification:

```
gl.Frustum(left, right, bottom, top, near, far)
```

The first four parameters define a size of the viewable portion on the screen. The last two parameters are used to define the viewing distance.

As you can see, this function is very similar to the gl.Ortho function in terms of parameters. However, instead of using screen edges, this function uses clipping planes. For a better understanding, see the following diagram:

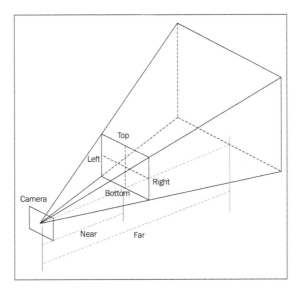

The following code shows how the `gl.Perspective` function works in relation to the `gl.Frustum` function. As you can see, the `gl.Perspective` function is actually a shortcut that computes positions of clipping planes and submits them directly to the `gl.Frustum` function:

```
function computeFrustum(fov, screen_aspect_ratio, zNear, zFar)
    -- tangent value refers to the half of the size of
    -- viewable screen portion
    local tangent = math.tan(math.rad(fov/2))
    local bottom = tangent*zNear
    local top = -bottom
    local right = bottom*screen_aspect_ratio
    local left = -right
    return left, right, bottom, top, zNear, zFar
end
```

The result of this function can be used directly on the `gl.Frustum` function.

You can use the `gl.Viewport` function to select the screen area that will be used for rendering. You can use this function to do split screen rendering.

See also

> ▸ The *Moving, rotating, and scaling objects* recipe

Setting up materials

Lighting can add certain dynamics into your 3D scene or game, which can make it more immersive. Everything you see is a light that reflects from surfaces. Some part of the visible light is absorbed by the material on a surface. The rest of the visible light spectrum defines the material color. You can say that the surface material reacts with the light in a certain way. Therefore, OpenGL attributes light processing into parts—material and lighting.

OpenGL tries to approximate light distribution and reflection by five material attributes, which are as follows:

> ▸ `GL_DIFFUSE`: This specifies the color of the surface and is mostly the attribute you will want to use
> ▸ `GL_AMBIENT`: This affects all vertices equally and often simulates ambient light
> ▸ `GL_SPECULAR`: This is the color of the highlight
> ▸ `GL_EMISSION`: This is the emitted light color, which can be used for surfaces that emit light, such as lamps or LEDs
> ▸ `GL_SHININESS`: This specifies the size of the highlighted area; smaller values are often used for metal surface simulation

Getting ready

Material settings are applied only when lighting is enabled. You can enable lighting with this line:

```
gl.Enable(gl_enum.GL_LIGHTING)
```

Otherwise, scene objects will use the vertex color defined by the `gl.Color` function. The recipe will assume that your scene contains white omnidirectional light. This light can simulate the light bulb.

How to do it...

Materials are applied to polygons in a similar fashion as vertex colors. They can be used on the front side or the back side of the polygons. You can set the material properties with the `gl.Materialf` and `gl.Materialfv` functions. The following code will set up the material for the front side of the polygons:

```
local m_diffuse  =  {0.8, 0.0, 0.0, 1.0}
local m_ambient  =  {0.0, 0.0, 0.5, 1.0}
local m_specular = {1.0, 1.0, 1.0, 1.0}
local m_emission = {0.0, 0.0, 0.0, 1.0}
local m_shininess = 50
local m_side = gl_enum.GL_FRONT

gl.Materialfv(m_side, gl_enum.GL_DIFFUSE, m_diffuse)
gl.Materialfv(m_side, gl_enum.GL_AMBIENT, m_ambient)
gl.Materialfv(m_side, gl_enum.GL_SPECULAR, m_specular)
gl.Materialfv(m_side, gl_enum.GL_EMISSION, m_emission)

gl.Materialf(m_side, gl_enum.GL_SHININESS, m_shininess)
```

This example will set a bright red material for all polygons that are rendered after this code. You can see the result in the following screenshot:

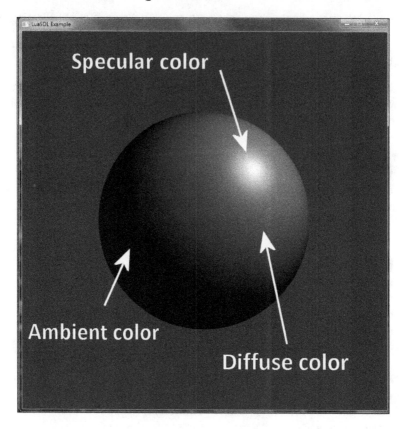

Notice that the `gl.Materialfv` function accepts the Lua table, whereas `gl.Materialf` accepts a number.

How it works...

OpenGL uses material values and light parameters to determine the final vertex color. The vertex color is a composition of the global ambient color, local ambient color, diffuse color, specular color, and emission color. Each component is basically a result of the multiplication of a light component, a material component, and a normal vector.

There's more...

Setting material attributes every time is fairly expensive. What's more, the `gl.Color` function doesn't work with the material and you can't include the material color in a vertex buffer. Fortunately, you can use the `gl.ColorMaterial` function that binds `gl.Color` to the material color attribute. The following example will bind the `gl.Color` function to the `GL_DIFFUSE` attribute:

```
local r,g,b,a = 1.0, 1.0, 1.0, 1.0
gl.ColorMaterial(gl_enum.GL_FRONT, gl_enum.GL_DIFFUSE)
gl.Enable(gl_enum.GL_COLOR_MATERIAL)
gl.Color4f(r, g, b, a)
```

Note that the material's diffuse color also has the alpha channel, which can be used to apply object transparency. Other material attributes don't use the alpha channel!

See also

> ▸ The *Setting up lighting* recipe

Setting up lighting

The fixed pipeline of OpenGL allows you to set up simple lighting. This lighting system is mostly used for static scenes with a few light sources. This is mostly because it has a few limitations:

> ▸ OpenGL guarantees that there are at least eight light sources available.
>
> ▸ It only supports Gouraud shading—vertex color interpolation
>
> ▸ There are predefined equations for normal mapping and attenuation. You can only change a few parameters.

If you're okay with these limitations, you can use this lighting system without the need of CPU-computed lighting or GPU shaders. Games such as *Quake* and *Quake 2* use vertex colors and light map textures to compute lighting on CPU, which is expensive, but these games use certain tricks to keep the performance at an acceptable level. For instance, *Quake 2* uses compressed normal vectors that can be compressed into 1 byte.

Getting ready

This recipe will operate not only with vertex position coordinates but also with normal vectors. Normal vectors are important as they specify the facing direction of polygons. These normal vectors are applied on triangles usually, but they can be used on vertices.

How to do it...

First, you'll need to obtain normal vectors. If you don't already have them, you can compute them for each triangle. Let's say that the triangle contains three vertices v1, v2, and v3. Each vertex has three coordinates: x, y, and z. A normal vector can be defined as a cross product of two vectors that define edges of the triangle. You can use triangle vertices v1, v2, and v3 to obtain these two vectors U and V. Finally, the U and V vectors can be used to compute the normal vector. The whole procedure is explained in the following lines, for which, first you need to obtain the U and V vectors:

```
U.x = v2.x - v1.x
U.y = v2.y - v1.y
U.z = v2.z - v1.z

V.x = v3.x - v1.x
V.y = v3.y - v1.y
V.z = v3.z - v1.z
```

Now you can use these vectors to compute the normal vector N:

```
N.x = U.y*V.z - U.z*V.y
N.y = U.z*V.x - U.x*V.z
N.z = U.x*V.y - U.y*V.x
```

The last thing you'll need to do is normal vector normalization. It means that the vector will always have a length of 1 unit. You can perform normalization by first obtaining the current length of the normal vector:

```
length = math.sqrt(N.x*N.x + N.y*N.y + N.z*N.z)
```

Now, you'll need to divide each normal vector coordinate with this length:

```
N.x = N.x/length
N.y = N.y/length
N.z = N.z/length
```

Finally, with normal vector N, you can draw a triangle:

```
gl.Begin(gl_enum.GL_TRIANGLES)
  gl.Normal3f(N.x, N.y, N.z)
  gl.Vertex3f(v1.x, v1.y, v1.z)
  gl.Vertex3f(v2.x, v2.y, v2.z)
  gl.Vertex3f(v3.x, v3.y, v3.z)
gl.End()
```

From now, this triangle will be able to reflect light because OpenGL knows in which direction the triangle is facing. In some cases, you'll need to change the direction of the normal vector to the opposite direction in relation to a different order of vertices, which is defined by winding. This may be important if you change the definition of the front-facing and back-facing polygons with the gl.FrontFace function. By default, OpenGL uses gl.FrontFace(gl_enum.GL_CCW), which means that the front face of the triangle is the one facing the normal vector that is computed from the vertices submitted in the counterclockwise direction.

A light source can be defined with three basic properties—diffuse color, specular color, and ambient color. These properties can be set with the following code:

```
local light_source = gl_enum.GL_LIGHT0
local light_diffuse =  {1, 1, 1, 1}
local light_specular = {1, 1, 1, 1}
local light_ambient =  {0, 0, 0, 1}

gl.Lightfv(light_source, gl_enum.GL_DIFFUSE, light_diffuse)
gl.Lightfv(light_source, gl_enum.GL_SPECULAR, light_specular)
gl.Lightfv(light_source, gl_enum.GL_AMBIENT, light_ambient)
```

This will produce a white light source. Each light source has its own identifier gl_enum.GL_LIGHTx, where x is a number from 0 to 7. You can turn the light source on or off with the following command:

```
gl.Enable(light_source)  -- to turn on
gl.Disable(light_source)  -- to turn off
```

You can also set other light source parameters such as light source position or direction, light spot size and direction, and light attenuation. These parameters can be set by using the following code:

```
local light_position = {0.2, 0.2, 0.4, 1.0}
local light_spot_direction = {0, 0, 0}
local light_attenuation_constant = 1
local light_attenuation_linear = 0.04
local light_attenuation_quadratic = 0.08
local light_spot_cutoff = 120

gl.Lightfv(light_source, gl_enum.GL_POSITION, light_position)
gl.Lightfv(light_source, gl_enum.GL_SPOT_DIRECTION,
light_spot_direction)
gl.Lightf(light_source, gl_enum.GL_CONSTANT_ATTENUATION,
light_attenuation_constant)
gl.Lightf(light_source, gl_enum.GL_LINEAR_ATTENUATION,
light_attenuation_linear)
gl.Lightf(light_source, gl_enum.GL_QUADRATIC_ATTENUATION,
light_attenuation_quadratic)
gl.Lightf(light_source, gl_enum.GL_SPOT_CUTOFF, light_spot_cutoff)
```

Special care should be taken to light position the vector. As you can see, it uses four coordinates *x*, *y*, *z*, and *w*. The last coordinate *w* can be set to 0 or 1. A zero value means that the light source is directional. This can be used for light panels, big screens, and so on. If the *w* coordinate equals to 1, the light source is positional. This is often viable for light bulbs, car lights, or spot lights.

How it works...

The final vertex color is defined by this equation:

```
C = global_ambient * material_ambient + material_emission

for each light L
  C = C + light_attenuation * spotlight_factor * (
    light_ambient * material_ambient +
    light_diffuse * material_diffuse * normal . vectorLC +
    light_specular * material_specular *
    (normal . vectorRV) ^ shininess
  )
```

Every light on the scene contributes to the final vertex color. This equation uses the dot product with the vertex normal vector to determine the surface light intensity. In the first case, it's used with `vectorLC`, which contains direction of the light source to the vertex position. As you can see, camera orientation does not play any role in diffuse lighting.

In the second case, the dot product is used together with `vectorRV`, which contains the camera orientation vector. This is used to produce a shiny surface effect and it can be controlled with the shininess value. A lower shininess value will result in brighter light reflection.

The light attenuation value is based on the following equation:

```
light_attenuation = 1 / (a + b*r + c*r^2)
```

The distance between vertex and the light source is represented by the `r` variable. Other variables: a, b, and c are attenuation factors:

- Constant attenuation—a
- Linear attenuation—b
- Quadratic attenuation—c

Attenuation determines how much will the light intensity decrease with increasing distance between the light source and object.

There's more...

If your object looks too "blocky" with lighting, you might need to apply some kind of interpolation for normal vectors. This recipe applies them for whole polygons. You can use linear interpolation to obtain normal vectors for each vertex. The normal vector for the vertex can be computed in the following fashion. Let's assume that you want to compute the vertex normal vector for the V1 vertex, which is a part of the triangle with the normal vector N1. This vertex V1 is also a part of an other two triangles with normal vectors N2 and N3. A new normal vector N1V1 for vertex V1 will be computed as follows:

```
N1V1.x = (N1.x + N2.x + N3.x)/3
N1V1.y = (N1.y + N2.y + N3.y)/3
N1V1.z = (N1.z + N2.z + N3.z)/3
```

Now, when you compute normal vectors for each vertex, you can submit them for each vertex and you'll get smooth surface with lighting.

See also

▸ The *Setting up materials* recipe

Using display lists

Display lists present a way to duplicate scene objects. They use a block structure such as the gl.Begin and gl.End function pairs. Almost every OpenGL call is stored into display list except those that manipulate with buffers and memory content. Display lists were intensively used and misused in the past to make scene rendering faster. However, they are now deprecated in relation to vertex buffers, which offer superior performance.

Getting ready

Before using the display list, you need to generate the display list object with the gl.GenLists(range) function. This function accepts one argument that represents the number of continuous display lists to be generated. It returns an identifier of the first display list.

The included sample code will assume that the dl_id variable contains a valid display list identifier.

How to do it...

The display list can be filled with instructions in a block that is enclosed by the `gl.NewList` and `gl.EndList` commands. The `gl.NewList` function has this specification:

```
gl.NewList(display_list_identifier, mode)
```

There are two modes that the display list builder will work with:

Display list modes	Description
GL_COMPILE	Here, the display list is only compiled but is not executed. It is useful if you're preparing a display list for later use.
GL_COMPILE_AND_EXECUTE	Here, the display list is compiled and executed. It behaves like an ordinal command block but the display list can reproduce the entire command block many times over.

The sample code with the usage of display lists is as follows:

```
gl.NewList(dl_id, gl_enum.GL_COMPILE)
  gl.Begin(gl_enum.GL_TRIANGLES)
  -- A
  gl.Color4f(1, 0, 0, 1)
  gl.Vertex3f(-0.5, -0.5, 0)
  -- B
  gl.Color4f(0, 1, 0, 1)
  gl.Vertex3f(0.5, -0.5, 0)
  -- C
  gl.Color4f(0, 0, 1, 1)
  gl.Vertex3f(0.5, 0.5, 0)
  gl.End()
gl.EndList()
```

After this, you can execute the display list with the `gl.CallList` or `gl.CallLists` commands. These commands present a convenient way to call repetitive tasks with one command. The following example shows the usage of both functions:

```
gl.CallList(dl_id)
gl.CallLists({dl_id, ...})
```

After you no longer need the display list, you have to delete the display list with the `gl.DeleteLists(display_list_identifier, range)` function.

How it works...

Display lists compile the entire command block for efficient execution. Games often use display list compilations during the loading screen, where it prepares all the important data for the gameplay.

Note that the display lists contain only command calls. You are allowed to do the nesting of display lists with the `gl.CallList(another_display_list)` function call inside the display list, but the content of another display list is not transferred. Therefore, you can easily replace the content of the child display list.

Another thing is that, once the display list is compiled, you might only replace the whole display list content.

See also

 ▸   The *Setting up the vertex buffer* recipe

Setting up the vertex buffer

The vertex buffer offers another technique of improving performance. Instead of using the `gl.Vertex` function for each vertex, you can load vertices into the memory in a batch. This is considerably faster because you only use one function call instead of hundreds or thousands of calls.

Getting ready

Vertex buffers are represented by **vertex buffer objects** or **VBO** in short. VBO was introduced as an extension of OpenGL and you can check its presence in the extension list with the extension name `GL_ARB_vertex_buffer_object`. Fortunately, LuaGL contains support for the GLEW library, which manages extension initialization.

The vertex buffer object must be initialized with the `gl.GenBuffers` function. This function will only reserve the buffer object identifiers and returns a Lua table with the buffer object identifiers. Further buffer object specification must be done with the `gl.BufferData` function.

This recipe assumes that you already have a valid buffer object generated with the following code:

```
local vbo_ids = gl.GenBuffers(2)
local vbo_vertices = vbo_ids[1]
local vbo_colors = vbo_ids[2]
```

There are two vertex buffer objects generated, where vbo_vertices will contain vertex positions and vbo_colors, which will contain the color information for the vertices.

How to do it...

The usage of the vertex buffer objects is, in many ways, similar to texture object management. There are also the gl.BindBuffer and gl.BufferSubData functions. That's why the gl.BufferData function is used mostly for buffer initialization and gl.BufferSubData is used to update buffer contents.

First, you must fill the vertex buffer object with data. You can do this by selecting the current buffer object with the gl.BindBuffer function:

```
gl.BindBuffer(gl_enum.GL_ARRAY_BUFFER, vbo_vertices)
```

After this, you can fill the buffer with data:

```
local data = {
   -0.5, -0.5, 0,
   0.5, -0.5, 0,
   0.5, 0.5, 0,
}
local usage = gl_enum.GL_STATIC_DRAW
gl.BufferData(gl_enum.GL_ARRAY_BUFFER, data, usage)
```

By using the GL_STATIC_DRAW constant for usage parameter, you give OpenGL a hint that you don't intend to change the buffer content very often. This may help to improve performance. You can do the same for vertex color data:

```
gl.BindBuffer(gl_enum.GL_ARRAY_BUFFER, vbo_colors)
local data = {
   1, 0, 0, 1,
   0, 1, 0, 1,
   0, 0, 1, 1,
}
local usage = gl_enum.GL_STATIC_DRAW
gl.BufferData(gl_enum.GL_ARRAY_BUFFER, data, usage)
```

The final step is setting the OpenGL client state, which will tell OpenGL what kind of data will be used:

```
gl.EnableClientState(gl_enum.GL_VERTEX_ARRAY)
gl.EnableClientState(gl_enum.GL_COLOR_ARRAY)
```

Now, you're ready to use those vertex buffers in your scene. OpenGL uses a special way of using buffer data. It consists of using `gl.BindBuffer` to select the buffer object and then calling the pointer version of the `gl.Vertex`, `gl.Color`, or `gl.TexCoord` functions. The following code shows how this process looks:

```
gl.BindBuffer(gl_enum.GL_ARRAY_BUFFER, vbo_vertices)
gl.VertexPointer(3)
gl.BindBuffer(gl_enum.GL_ARRAY_BUFFER, vbo_colors)
gl.ColorPointer(4)
gl.DrawArrays(gl_enum.GL_TRIANGLES, 0, 3)
```

This will draw a colored triangle on the screen.

How it works...

Vertex buffers are defined by the `gl.BufferData` function. This function accepts three arguments: the buffer type, data, and data usage hint. The vertex buffer objects use the `GL_ARRAY_BUFFER` type. Buffer data is defined by the Lua table, which is converted into an array of float data type internally. The last parameter might help you with performance optimization. You can use one of the values listed in the following table:

Usage type	Description
GL_STREAM_DRAW	Here, the data will be modified by the application once and used a few times for drawing. This usage is desirable for streaming movies or animations into the OpenGL texture.
GL_STREAM_READ	Here, the data will be modified by OpenGL once and used a few times in the application query command.
GL_STREAM_COPY	Here, the data will be modified by OpenGL once and used a few times for drawing. You can use this for postprocessing effect buffers.
GL_STATIC_DRAW	Here, the data will be modified by the application once and used many times for drawing. This is often used for world rendering.
GL_STATIC_READ	Here, the data will be modified by OpenGL once and used many times in the application query command.
GL_STATIC_COPY	Here, the data will be modified by OpenGL once and used many times for drawing.
GL_DYNAMIC_DRAW	Here, the data will be modified by the application repeatedly and used many times for drawing.
GL_DYNAMIC_READ	Here, the data will be modified by OpenGL repeatedly and used many times in the application query command.
GL_DYNAMIC_COPY	Here, the data will be modified by OpenGL repeatedly and used many times for drawing.

When using vertex buffers, you need to choose which vertex parameters will be used. That's why there is a need for the `gl.EnableClientState` functions. For the purpose of vertex buffer object management, there are eight client states, which are listed in the following table:

Client state names	Corresponding pointer functions
GL_COLOR_ARRAY	gl.ColorPointer
GL_EDGE_FLAG_ARRAY	gl.EdgeFlagPointer
GL_FOG_COORD_ARRAY	gl.FogCoordPointer
GL_INDEX_ARRAY	gl.IndexPointer
GL_NORMAL_ARRAY	gl.NormalPointer
GL_SECONDARY_COLOR_ARRAY	gl.ColorPointer
GL_TEXTURE_COORD_ARRAY	gl.TexCoordPointer
GL_VERTEX_ARRAY	gl.VertexPointer

The functions `gl.VertexPointer` and `gl.ColorPointer` use only one parameter that specifies how many elements are there in the buffer for one vertex. In this case, each vertex uses X, Y, and Z coordinates. Therefore, `gl.VertexPointer` uses three elements. The colors are defined by four color channels: R, G, B, and A, which is why the `gl.ColorPointer` function uses four elements.

There's more...

Vertex buffers are also a standard feature of the new OpenGL 4.0+ standard. The immediate mode is deprecated from this version, so vertex buffers are the only way of transferring vertex data into the graphic card memory. This is also valid for the mobile profile of OpenGL ES 2.0.

5
Graphics – Modern Method with OpenGL 3.0+

This chapter will cover the following recipes:

- ▶ Loading and using GLSL shaders
- ▶ Using uniform variables with shaders
- ▶ Writing a vertex shader
- ▶ Writing a fragment (pixel) shader
- ▶ Drawing primitives by using vertex buffers
- ▶ Rendering to texture
- ▶ Applying highlights and shadows to the scene
- ▶ Bumpmapping

Introduction

This chapter will deal with programming and using dynamic rendering pipeline in OpenGL. While shaders have been available since OpenGL 2.0, their first versions are now considered deprecated. A wide variety of graphic cards now support at least OpenGL 3.3, which implements the currently valid specification of GLSL shaders. This chapter will focus on GLSL version 3.3, which is relevant for OpenGL 3.3.

Shaders are small programs that define the behavior of the graphic card for scene rendering. They are usually written in C-like language and compiled into binary form by the graphical driver. Shader programs are compiled at runtime. Just out of curiosity, a newer version of OpenGL 4.1 allows you to compile shader programs into binary form, which can be saved into a file and used later without re-compilation.

Shaders provide substantially better flexibility than a fixed pipeline and present a door to parallel graphical processing on GPU.

The immediate mode for the fixed rendering pipeline used rendering commands enclosed in the `gl.Begin` and `gl.End` pairs. Dynamic rendering pipeline no longer uses these commands. Instead, it relies on massive usage of vertex buffers for data storage. Usually, you fill the vertex buffer with vertex data such as color, position, texture coordinates, and normal vectors. This data is used by shader programs to render vertices. This approach is much faster because you're encouraged to transfer vertex data in batches. Frequent calls from the application to the GPU cause stalling of rendering processes, and therefore, decrease the overall performance.

This chapter will also show a few tricks with rendering to texture, which can be used for postprocessing effects. The final set of recipes will deal with the Phong shading effect and the bumpmapping effect.

Loading and using GLSL shaders

Shader programs must be compiled before use. Fortunately, OpenGL offers an interface to load shader programs in text form. The shader source code uses a syntax similar to the C code with several limitations. For instance, you can't perform recursive function calls. After compilation, you can check whether there were any errors in the process.

Shaders can use input values from your application. These input values are called **uniforms**. You can use these values in any part of the rendering pipeline, which consists of several shader program stages:

- **Vertex shader**: This performs operations on vertex attributes: vertex color, position, normal vector and many others
- **Tessellation control shader**: This controls tessellation amount on polygons
- **Tessellation evaluation shader**: This computes the interpolated vertex positions after tessellation
- **Geometry shader**: This performs per vertex operations on polygons
- **Fragment shader**: This operates on fragments after the rasterization process; the results are stored into the frame buffer, the depth buffer, or the stencil buffer

Only vertex and fragment shaders are mandatory for basic rendering of operations. The following diagram shows the complete rendering pipeline:

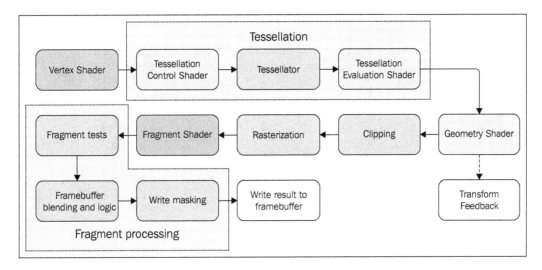

The red parts are mandatory shaders; the optional shaders are in orange. Blue and white parts present steps that aren't fully controllable by the user.

Getting ready

Before using GLSL shaders, you should always check whether the current graphic card supports them. For this, you can use the `gl.IsSupported` function. It accepts one string parameter that consists of the OpenGL extension names and version names. For example, the following code tests whether there is support for OpenGL 3.0, vertex and fragment shaders in the current system:

```
assert(gl.IsSupported("GL_VERSION_3_0 GL_ARB_vertex_shader
GL_ARB_fragment_shader"))
```

Each string part is delimited with one space and always starts with the `GL_` prefix. After this check, you can be confident using GLSL shaders or any other extension. Otherwise, you might end up producing memory access violation or segmentation fault, as the required functions aren't available.

A list of valid extension names can be found at http://glew.sourceforge.net/glew.html.

You'll need the valid shader source code. You can use the following example of the vertex shader source code:

```
local shader_source = [[
#version 330 //use GLSL specification version 3.3
layout (location = 0) in vec3 VertexPosition;
layout (location = 1) in vec4 VertexColor;
layout (location = 2) in vec2 VertexTexCoord;

out vec4 Color;
out vec2 TexCoord;

void main(){
  gl_Position = vec4(VertexPosition.xyz, 1.0);
  Color = vec4(VertexColor.rgba);
  TexCoord = vec2(VertexTexCoord.xy);
}
]]
```

This vertex shader uses GLSL version 3.3 and does basic preparation of vertex attributes for the next stage.

How to do it...

GLSL shaders and programs use special OpenGL objects. These must be created before using. You can create the shader object with the `gl.CreateShader` function. It accepts the shader stage identifier and results in a numerical object identifier. Let's assume that this shader object identifier is stored in the `shader_object` variable with the following code:

```
local shader_stage = gl_enum.GL_VERTEX_SHADER
local shader_object = gl.CreateShader(shader_stage)
```

Now you can use this shader object to load your shader's source code:

```
gl.ShaderSource(shader_object, shader_source)
```

After this step, you can compile the shader with the `gl.CompileShader` function. You can check the shader compilation status with this code:

```
local compilation_status = ""
local status = gl.GetShaderiv(shader_object,
gl_enum.GL_COMPILE_STATUS)
if status == gl_enum.GL_FALSE then
  compilation_status = gl.GetShaderInfoLog(shader_object)
end
```

The `status` variable contains a numerical value, which is set to `GL_TRUE` if the compilation is successful. Otherwise, it's set to `GL_FALSE` and you can obtain the textual error message with the `gl.GetShaderInfoLog` function.

After successful compilation, you can link shader objects into shader programs, but first you must create one with the `gl.CreateProgram` function. It returns a numerical identifier for the shader program. Let's store this value into the `shader_program` value as shown in the following code:

```
local shader_program = gl.CreateProgram()
```

Now you can attach the shader objects into the shader program with the following command:

```
gl.AttachShader(shader_program, shader_object)
```

With this step done, you can finally link shaders into the program with the command:

```
gl.LinkProgram(shader_program)
```

You should always check for the last linking operation status with the following code:

```
local link_status = ""
local status = gl.GetProgramiv(shader_program,
gl_enum.GL_LINK_STATUS)
if status == gl_enum.GL_FALSE then
   link_status = gl.GetProgramInfoLog(shader_program)
end
```

After the shader program is linked, the shader objects are not needed anymore and you can safely delete them with:

```
gl.DeleteShader(shader_object)
```

The shader program can be used with the following code:

```
gl.UseProgram(shader_program)
```

If there's no need for the shader program, you can delete it with the following code:

```
gl.DeleteProgram(shader_program)
```

How it works...

The GLSL shader loading process consists of two steps. The first step is the shader stage compilation into the shader object. It works in a similar fashion as in a C compiler, where the source code is compiled into binary object files. The compilation is followed by the linking process. Shader objects are linked into one shader program. This presents the final result of the GLSL shader preparation process. Of course, your application might contain more than one shader program and you can switch between them. On some rare occasions, it's better to merge more shaders into one and separate them with conditional blocks. This approach introduces additional overhead to the shader code especially in fragment shader, but this might be better than switching shaders. There's no general rule for this, so you'll need to experiment.

When you're writing your own shaders, you should always take into account the amount of shader runs for each element. For instance, the vertex shader is used on every vertex, whereas the fragment shader is almost always used many more times as it operates on fragment elements. You can think of fragments as pixels on the frame buffer. So, whenever you're writing a program for the fragment shader, try to think about implementing it in the vertex shader first. This way you can further optimize your shaders, especially if you intend to use them in an application on mobile devices.

See also

- ▶ The *Using uniform variables with shaders* recipe
- ▶ The *Writing a vertex shader* recipe
- ▶ The *Writing a fragment (pixel) shader* recipe

Using uniform variables with shaders

Uniform variables present a way to pass variables from the application into GLSL shaders. However, you are limited to pass numerical values, vectors, and matrices only.

The dynamic rendering pipeline doesn't use immediate mode functions to set up vertices or matrices. This means functions such as `gl.Vertex`, `gl.Rotate`, `gl.Translate`, and `gl.Scale` are of no use anymore. For this situation, vertices are stored in vertex buffers. Other variables such as model view and projection matrix have to be supplied by uniform variables. These variables are also used often to set up or change the behavior of the shader program during runtime. For example, you can adjust the glowing effect amount in your shader program.

Getting ready

Each uniform variable has its own numerical location identifier. This identifier is used to access almost any uniform variable. The location identifier is limited to primitive values such as integer, float, and vectors. Matrices present a special case where you can upload the whole matrix in one step, but you can retrieve only one element from the shader program at one time. You can obtain a uniform variable location with the `gl.GetUniformLocation` function. There are three ways to use this function:

- ▶ The location of a single primitive value:

    ```
    local location = gl.GetUniformLocation(shader_program,
    "variable_name")
    ```

- ▶ The location of an array element:

    ```
    local location = gl.GetUniformLocation(shader_program,
    "array_variable[1]")
    ```

- ▶ The location of a structure element:

    ```
    local location = gl.GetUniformLocation(shader_program,
    "structure_variable.element")
    ```

Let's assume that `shader_program` is the valid identifier for the shader program. This function returns the location identifier of the specified uniform variable. If such a variable doesn't exist in the shader program or is discarded in the process of compilation, the returned value is -1. The uniform variable is discarded if it isn't actively used in the shader program.

How to do it...

Now that you've got the location of the uniform variable, you can either set the content of the uniform variable or obtain its value.

Writing into uniform variables

You can set the uniform variable by one of these three functions: `gl.Uniformi`, `gl.Uniformf`, and `gl.UniformMatrix`. The first one is used in integer values, the second is for float number, and the last one is for matrices.

Both `gl.Uniformi` and `gl.Uniformf` accept two to five parameters. The first one is always the location of the uniform variable. The second one can be a primitive numeric value or Lua table. Lua tables are usually used for vectors. The following examples show how to set a primitive float number and a vector of floats:

```
local primitive_value = 1.5
local vector = {1.0, 2.0, 3.0}
gl.Uniformf(location, primitive_value)
```

```
gl.Uniformf(location, vector[1], vector[2], vector[3])
gl.Uniformf(location, vector)
```

Setting up matrices is a bit more difficult. Matrix values have to be stored in a flat Lua table. Matrix sizes can vary from 2 x 2 to 4 x 4 elements. You can also let the `gl.UniformMatrix` function to transpose your matrix. It means that matrix rows will be swapped with matrix columns. This is useful if you're supplying matrices that consist of multiple vectors. The following example shows how to upload the whole matrix of size 4 x 4:

```
local x,y,z = 1,2,3
local translation = {
    1, 0, 0, x,
    0, 1, 0, y,
    0, 0, 1, z,
    0, 0, 0, 1,
}
local rows, columns = 4, 4
local transpose = false
gl.UniformMatrix(location, translation, rows, columns, transpose)
```

Reading from uniform variables

Uniform variables can be read from shader programs with the `gl.GetUniform` functions. There are four versions of this function. One for each type of value: integer, unsigned integer, float, and double. Each of these functions can return one or more variables as return values. This depends on whether the queried variable is a primitive type such as a float, an integer, or a vector. The following table lists all the versions of the `gl.GetUniform` function:

Function names	Return types
gl.GetUniformi	Integer
gl.GetUniformui	Unsigned integer
gl.GetUniformf	Float
gl.GetUniformd	Double

Generic function specification accepts two arguments:

```
gl.GetUniform(shader_program, location)
```

For example, if you'd want to obtain a 3D vector from the shader program, you'd use the following code:

```
local x,y,z = gl.GetUniformf(shader_program, location)
```

All three variables would be filled with vector variable content.

How it works...

Uniform variables are available for all parts of the shader program. For instance, you can access the same uniform variable from the vertex and fragment shaders. You should always try to minimize the amount of uniform variable updates. Every update consumes a small part of bandwidth between CPU memory and GPU memory.

Writing a vertex shader

Vertex shaders are programs that operate on vertices and their attributes. This stage is also used to apply matrix transformations as well. GLSL shader programs use input and output variables. In the case of a vertex shader, input variables are either uniforms or vertex buffer data. Output variables are passed to the next stage of rendering the pipeline. There are also special built-in variables such as `gl_Position`, `gl_PointSize`, and others. These are mostly used with fixed functionality and may not be redeclared.

All shaders use the entry point function—`main`. This function is applied on each element—vertex.

Getting ready

This recipe will use the GLSL shading language with version 3.3. It assumes that all the vertices are stored in **Vertex Buffer Object** (**VBO**). The vertex shader program is applied on every vertex that is contained within VBO.

To prepare the vertex shader, you'll need to create the shader object first:

```
local shader_stage = gl_enum.GL_VERTEX_SHADER
local shader_object = gl.CreateShader(shader_stage)
```

How to do it...

The shader programs code can be stored in a text file or you can submit it directly as a string value. This recipe will use the latter method. The following source code will define the basic vertex shader:

```
local shader_source = [[
//Requires GLSL 3.3 at least
#version 330

//Input variables - vertex attributes
layout (location = 0) in vec3 VertexPosition;
layout (location = 1) in vec4 VertexColor;
layout (location = 2) in vec2 VertexTexCoord;
```

```
//Output variables for later shader stages
out VertexData {
  vec4 Color;
  vec2 TexCoord;
} outData;

//Application variable
uniform mat4 matrix;

//Entry function for vertex shader
void main(){
  gl_Position = matrix * vec4(VertexPosition.xyz, 1.0);
  outData.Color = vec4(VertexColor.rgba);
  outData.TexCoord = vec2(VertexTexCoord.st);
}
]]
```

Now you can load and compile this source code into the shader object:

```
gl.ShaderSource(shader_object, shader_source)
gl.CompileShader(shader_object)
```

Be sure to always check for the compilation status. The production version of the game should use at least some kind of message logging mechanism, so you can store error messages into the bug report file, which is always handy. In order to store the messages, use the following code:

```
local status = gl.GetShaderiv(shader_object,
gl_enum.GL_COMPILE_STATUS)
if status == gl_enum.GL_FALSE then
  local compilation_status = gl.GetShaderInfoLog(shader_object)
  error("Vertex Shader compilation failed: "..compilation_status)
end
```

After these steps, you can finally link the vertex shader with the shader program.

How it works...

It's recommended to specify the required shader specification version at the beginning of the shader source code. This is done with preprocessor macro:

```
#version VERSION_NUMBER
```

The version number is always in the form of three digits. For example, for GLSL version 1.5, one would use a number 150. The good thing is that OpenGL shaders are backwards compatible. This way you can use older GLSL specifications even on newer graphic cards.

The input variables for the vertex shader can have two forms. You can use either the uniform variables or the vertex attributes stored in VBO. This recipe uses the vertex attributes with layout specification. Each vertex attribute layout number represents a VBO identifier. This way the GLSL shader knows what VBO to use:

```
layout (location = 0) in vec3 VertexPosition;
```

Optionally, layouts can be set explicitly in Lua with the following code:

```
local attribute_name = "VertexPosition"
gl.BindAttribLocation(shader_program, layout_index,
attribute_name)
```

The vertex shader has to pass results to the next stage. The output variables can be specified in two ways. The first one uses direct output variable specification:

```
out vec4 VertexColor;
```

The second way is more preferred as it offers a certain level of consistency:

```
out VertexData {
  vec4 Color;
  vec2 TexCoord;
} outData;
```

This is also called as an interface block. Interface blocks are shared between shader stages. However, this will work only if the interface block shares the same interface name, variable name, and also their order and types have to be the same. Notice that the interface block name `VertexData` is specified right after our qualifier. The local interface name `outData` is valid only in the local context. You can refer to these variables as if you were using C structures. Therefore, to set the vertex color, you would use the following code:

```
outData.Color = vec4(...);
```

You may also omit the local interface name. In that case, you can refer to the interface variables in this fashion:

```
Color = vec4(...);
```

The uniform variables are specified with the qualifier `uniform`:

```
uniform mat4 matrix;
```

The last and the most important part of vertex shader is the `main` function. This sample does simple matrix transformation on the vertex position:

```
gl_Position = matrix * vec4(VertexPosition.xyz, 1.0);
```

It takes three coordinates x, y, and z in the form of a vector with three elements. This vector is extended to contain four elements with the `vec4` type declaration. Notice that the forth element is set to 1. This is because the matrix multiplication rule must be applied. The A x B matrix can be multiplied only with matrix B x C. This will result in A x C matrix. In this case, you are using 4 x 4 matrix and you multiply it with the 4 x 1 matrix. Vectors with N elements can be seen as matrices with the size of N x 1. The result of this is a 4 x 1 matrix or a vector with four elements.

The other attributes such as the vertex color of texture coordinates are passed unchanged:

```
outData.Color = vec4(VertexColor.rgba);
outData.TexCoord = vec2(VertexTexCoord.xy);
```

There's more...

The vector data type in GLSL can contain 2, 3, or 4 components. As you've already seen, components are accessed by their names x, y, z and w. This is also called **swizzling**. That's because you can use any combination of components as long as you maintain the correct output data type. Therefore, the following code is completely valid:

```
vec2 vector1;
vec3 vector2 = vector1.xxy;
vec4 vector3 = vector2.zwyx;
vec4 vector4 = vector1.xxxx;
```

You can use swizzling even on the left side (also known as l-value) of the value assignment:

```
vec4 vector1;
vector1.xz = vec2(1.0, 2.0);
```

Alternatively, you can use color component names r, g, b, and a; or even texture coordinate names s, t, p, and q.

See also

- ► The *Loading and using GLSL shaders* recipe
- ► The *Using uniform variables with shaders* recipe
- ► The *Writing fragment (pixel) shader* recipe

Writing a fragment (pixel) shader

Fragment shader operates on pixel fragments from the rasterization process. The rasterizer transforms the whole graphical scene into a set of values that form fragments. A set of values that are related to one graphical primitive is called a fragment. These values may contain colors, alpha transparency, depth values, or even user supplied data. The fragment shader program might even decide whether to discard certain pixels from being drawn into the frame buffer.

Fragment shaders are often used in two-pass postprocessing. In the first pass, the whole scene is rendered into the texture or a buffer by using the first fragment shader. This shader renders primitives without postprocessing effects. In the second pass, this texture is used on a rectangle that covers the whole screen. This pass uses the fragment shader to control rendering of the texture on the rectangle. This way you can apply various effects such as High Definition Range transformation—HDR, screen distortions, and many others.

The other uses of the fragment shader may be per pixel lighting and shadows.

Keep in mind that fragment shaders usually use more iterations than vertex shaders. Therefore, always try to minimize the complexity of the fragment shader program.

Getting ready

The preparation of the fragment shader is fairly similar to the preparation of the vertex shader:

```
local shader_stage = gl_enum.GL_FRAGMENT_SHADER
local shader_object = gl.CreateShader(shader_stage)
```

This will create the shader object, which you can use to load and compile the shader source code.

How to do it...

This recipe will use the shader code stored in a string variable:

```
#version 330

in VertexData {
    vec4 Color;
    vec2 TexCoord;
} inData;

uniform sampler2D texID;
uniform int textured;
```

```
layout(location = 0) out vec4 diffuseColor;

void main() {
  if (textured>0){
    int LOD = 0;
    ivec2 texSize = textureSize(texID, LOD);
    ivec2 tc = ivec2(inData.TexCoord * texSize);

    vec4 texel0 = texelFetch(texID, tc, LOD);
    vec4 texel1 = texture(texID, inData.TexCoord);

    diffuseColor = inData.Color * texel1.rgba;
  }else{
    diffuseColor = inData.Color;
  }
}
```

This fragment shader doesn't do anything special. It can draw colored primitive on screen where the vertex colors are automatically interpolated. Optionally, you can switch uniform variable `textured` to draw textured primitive.

How it works...

Firstly, you should always set the required GLSL version. It's considered as a good practice because this way you can safely expect and use certain features that are available from this version of GLSL. If this version is not supported on the system, the compilation process will fail, and therefore, you can apply the fallback mechanism. To set the version use the following code:

```
#version 330
```

Another part is the interface block definition:

```
in VertexData {
  vec4 Color;
  vec2 TexCoord;
} inData;
```

Notice that this block contains the same variables as in the vertex shader interface block. This block is used as data input; therefore, the `in` qualifier comes before the block name. Every variable inside this block is accessible via the local block name `inData`, so to access vertex color, you'd use `inData.Color`. Another thing to mention as that these variables are linearly interpolated by default.

This shader makes use of uniform variables. This first one, called `texID` points, at one texture, which is two-dimensional, in this case, and uses float numbers. Therefore, it's defined to use the `sampler2D` type. As you already know, there are many types of textures. A list of the sampler types is shown in the following table:

Sampler type	OpenGL texture type	Description
gsampler1D	GL_TEXTURE_1D	This is a 1D texture
gsampler2D	GL_TEXTURE_2D	This is a 2D texture
gsampler3D	GL_TEXTURE_3D	This is a 3D texture
gsamplerCube	GL_TEXTURE_CUBE_MAP	This is a cubemap texture
gsampler2DRect	GL_TEXTURE_RECTANGLE	This is a rectangle texture
gsampler1DArray	GL_TEXTURE_1D_ARRAY	This is a 1D array texture
gsampler2DArray	GL_TEXTURE_2D_ARRAY	This is a 2D array texture
gsamplerCubeArray	GL_TEXTURE_CUBE_MAP_ARRAY	This is a cubemap array texture
gsamplerBuffer	GL_TEXTURE_BUFFER	This is a buffer texture
gsampler2DMS	GL_TEXTURE_2D_MULTISAMPLE	This is a multisample texture
gsampler2DMSArray	GL_TEXTURE_2D_MULTISAMPLE_ARRAY	This is a multisample texture array

You may wonder why all sampler types have a prefix g. This prefix specifies the element data type. If you omit this prefix, GLSL assumes that the texture contains float values.

Sampler type prefixes	Data types
sampler	float
isampler	int
usampler	unsigned int

The second uniform variable `textured` enables or disables texturing:

```
uniform int textured;
```

You can omit this variable if you don't need to control texturing in your fragment shader.

The last thing you'll need to specify is the output of the fragment shader. The shader in this recipe uses the color output only. The output variable at location 0 is reserved to diffuse the color output by default:

```
layout(location = 0) out vec4 diffuseColor;
```

On certain occasions, you might want to use multiple outputs in the fragment shader. Each output variable must have its own location, which in return can be used to bind the frame buffer. This is often used to split the output to color and the depth buffer.

As in the case of the vertex shader, the fragment shader also uses the main function. This function is divided into two modes of operation by the control variable textured. When texturing is enabled, you can access the texture elements—texels—in two ways. Either you use the normalized float texture coordinates that are within the range (0,1), or you use the exact texture coordinates specified as an integer's offset values from the origin point. The first way is used often as you can directly use texture coordinates produced by the vertex shader. With this method, you can also query subpixel values that are calculated with linear interpolation:

```
vec4 texel1 = texture(texID, inData.TexCoord);
```

The second method is more exact but you'll need to know the texture size in pixels:

```
vec4 texel0 = texelFetch(texID, tc, LOD);
```

The LOD or Level of Detail value is used in conjunction with mipmapping. It defines the mipmap level where the level 0 is a base texture. Be aware that the texelFetch function uses the ivec texture coordinates that use integer values. You can obtain the texture size with the textureSize function:

```
ivec2 texSize = textureSize(texID, LOD);
```

If you want to use the texture coordinates from the vertex shader with pixel perfect coordinates, you can use the following code:

```
ivec2 tc = ivec2(inData.TexCoord * texSize);
```

It uses float number coordinates that are in the range (0, 1) and multiplies them with texture dimensions. This will produce the vec2 type vector, which is not what you want to use in this case. Therefore, you'll need to cast the vec2 vector into the ivec2 vector. All values in the vector are truncated.

You can apply the texel value directly to the fragment shader output. Alternatively, you can combine it with vertex color—inData.Color. This value is obtained from the vertex shader and it's the only output variable if texturing is turned off.

The following code contains a complete example of the simple fragment shader program that fills the graphical primitive with the texture:

```
//this shader program requires as least OpenGL 3.3
#version 330
//diffuseTexture will contain texture unit identifier (integer)
uniform sampler2D diffuseTexture;

//structure contains values from previous stage (vertex shader)
//all values use linear interpolation by default
in VertexData {
  vec4 Color;     //vertex color value
  vec2 TexCoord; //texture coordinates
} inData;

//fragment shader output variable
layout(location = 0) out vec4 diffuseColor;

//main procedure will be called for each texel
void main() {
  //texel will be filled with color value from a texture
  vec4 texel = texture(diffuseTexture, inData.TexCoord);
  //texel value is multiplied with vertex color in this case
  diffuseColor = inData.Color * texel;
}
```

Texture rendering can be controlled by setting vertex colors. The original form of the texture will be rendered if you use white color on all vertices.

There's more...

If you're using the depth or depth-stencil texture format, you'll need to use a special kind of sampler. These are called **shadow samplers**. The following table shows the list of shadow samplers depending on the OpenGL texture type:

Show sampler type	OpenGL texture type
sampler1DShadow	GL_TEXTURE_1D
sampler2DShadow	GL_TEXTURE_2D
samplerCubeShadow	GL_TEXTURE_CUBE_MAP
sampler2DRectShadow	GL_TEXTURE_RECTANGLE
sampler1DArrayShadow	GL_TEXTURE_1D_ARRAY
sampler2DArrayShadow	GL_TEXTURE_2D_ARRAY
samplerCubeArrayShadow	GL_TEXTURE_CUBE_MAP_ARRAY

These textures use only float numbers that are on the range (0,1).

See also

▸ The *Using uniform variables with shaders* recipe

▸ The *Writing vertex shader* recipe

Drawing primitives using vertex buffers

VBO was, in the past, a part of an OpenGL as an extension. With the new OpenGL specification, the VBO mechanism is included in the GLSL specification. This means that you can reuse much of the existing functionality with small changes. VBOs present an opaque storage for data; therefore, they might contain the vertex positions, texture coordinates, colors or any other data. GLSL shaders can use these buffers but they must be differentiated so the shader program knows what data is stored inside of these buffers. That's where the **vertex array objects** or **VAO** come in. The vertex array object is a *structure* that merges VBOs for use in the shader program. They are used in GLSL shader programs as a main source of vertex attributes. Each of the attributes can be submitted in its own VBO. It ensures efficient upload of all vertices into graphic memory and you can easily add other vertices if needed.

You may find it desirable to use interleaved data format for VBO. It's a way to store all the vertex attributes into one vertex buffer. Examples of data layout are shown in the following diagram:

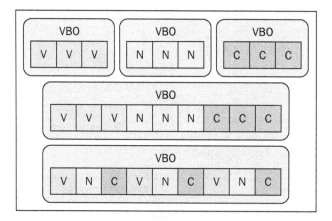

There are three cases of decisions on data layout:

▸ Each vertex attribute has its own VBO—vertices, normal vectors, and vertex colors.

▸ All the attributes are stored in one VBO. They are grouped by the attribute type.

▸ All the attributes are stored in one VBO. They are grouped by the vertex.

Note that if you plan on frequent updating of vertex attributes, it's better to reserve the whole VBO for this purpose. This way OpenGL can optimize memory access to vertex attributes.

Getting ready

This recipe will use data layout where each vertex attribute will use its own VBO. You'll be using the vertex position, the texture coordinates, and the vertex color. Therefore, you'll need to create three VBOs. You can create the vertex buffer objects with the `gl.GenBuffers` function:

```
local vertex_buffer_object = gl.GenBuffers(3)
```

It accepts one parameter that presents the number of vertex buffer objects to be created.

You'll also be using the vertex array object that specifies the vertex data layout and references to all used VBOs. The vertex array object can be created using the `gl.GenVertexArrays` function. This function accepts the number of vertex array objects to be reserved:

```
local vertex_array_object = gl.GenVertexArrays(1)
```

How to do it...

You'll need one vertex buffer object for each vertex attribute. In this case, you'll be using three vertex buffer objects for the vertex position, the vertex color, and the vertex texture coordinates. Now, you can fill each one with the corresponding vertex data.

Vertex positions

We will use four vertices to draw the rectangular polygon. The following code will define the vertex positions for one rectangle:

```
//vertex positions are specified by X, Y pairs
local vertex_positions = {
  -1, -1,
  1, -1,
  1, 1,
    -1, 1,
}
gl.BindBuffer(gl_enum.GL_ARRAY_BUFFER, vertex_buffer_object[1])
gl.BufferData(gl_enum.GL_ARRAY_BUFFER, vertex_positions,
gl_enum.GL_STATIC_DRAW)
```

Vertex colors

You can use this code to store the vertex colors:

```
//vertex colors use RGBA quadruplets
local vertex_colors = {
  1,0,0,1,
  0,1,0,1,
```

```
      0,0,1,1,
      1,1,0,1,
   }
   gl.BindBuffer(gl_enum.GL_ARRAY_BUFFER, vertex_buffer_object[2])
   gl.BufferData(gl_enum.GL_ARRAY_BUFFER, vertex_colors,
   gl_enum.GL_STATIC_DRAW)
```

Vertex texture coordinates

The following code will define the texture coordinates for vertices:

```
   //texture coordinates use U, V coordinate pairs
   local vertex_texcoords = {
      0, 0,
      1, 0,
      1, 1,
         0, 1,
   }
   gl.BindBuffer(gl_enum.GL_ARRAY_BUFFER, vertex_buffer_object[3])
   gl.BufferData(gl_enum.GL_ARRAY_BUFFER, vertex_texcoords,
   gl_enum.GL_STATIC_DRAW)
```

Now that you have data stored in VBOs, you'll have to bind them into VAO. The vertex array object contains data layout information. For instance, if the vertex position consists of three dimensions, each vertex will use three subsequent values from VBO that contains vertex positions.

Before using the vertex array object, you'll need to bind it with the `gl.BindVertexArray` function:

```
   gl.BindVertexArray(vertex_array_object[1])
```

Another step is enabling and mapping vertex attributes to buffers. In this recipe, each vertex contains three vertex attributes: the vertex position, the vertex color and the texture coordinate. Each vertex attribute will use different attribute index. This index will correspond to the location value in the shader source:

```
   layout (location = 0) in vec3 VertexPosition;
```

The vertex attribute is mapped by a pair of functions: `gl.BindBuffer` and `gl.VertexAttribPointer`. The first one prepares VBO to be used. The second command uses this function specification:

```
   gl.VertexAttribPointer(location_index, vertex_elements_count,
   normalized, stride)
```

The final code will look like this:

```
-- vertex position
gl.BindBuffer(gl_enum.GL_ARRAY_BUFFER, vertex_buffer_object[1])
gl.VertexAttribPointer(0, 2, false, 0)

-- vertex color
gl.BindBuffer(gl_enum.GL_ARRAY_BUFFER, vertex_buffer_object[2])
gl.VertexAttribPointer(1, 4, false, 0)

-- texture coordinates
gl.BindBuffer(gl_enum.GL_ARRAY_BUFFER, vertex_buffer_object[3])
gl.VertexAttribPointer(2, 2, false, 0)
```

Notice that the vertex position is specified by two elements (x, y), vertex color by four elements (r, g, b, a) and texture coordinates by two elements (s, t).

The last thing you'll need to do before drawing is enabling vertex attributes with the `gl.EnableVertexAttribArray` function.

```
gl.EnableVertexAttribArray(0)
gl.EnableVertexAttribArray(1)
gl.EnableVertexAttribArray(2)
```

Alternatively, you can disable certain vertex attributes with the `gl.DisableVertexArray` function:

```
gl.DisableVertexAttribArray(attribute_index)
```

After all these steps, you are ready to use VBOs and VAO to efficiently draw vertices. Don't forget to bind the currently used vertex array object before drawing. Otherwise, OpenGL wouldn't know what data to use and you could get unpredictable results.

Vertices can be drawn by using the `gl.DrawArrays` function:

```
gl.DrawArrays(gl_enum.GL_QUADS, 0, 4)
```

The first parameter specifies what graphic primitive will be used. It uses the same constants as were used in the `gl.Begin` function. The second parameter sets the vertex offset and the last one is a number of vertices to be used.

How it works...

Vertex buffer objects can contain arbitrary data. Vertex itself can use more than one vertex attribute. Attributes usually contain more than one element. For instance, the vertex position uses two coordinates in 2D space, but in 3D space there are three coordinates. OpenGL doesn't know how many coordinates you use for vertices. Therefore, vertex array objects are used to help with this issue. Vertex array object defines how to get attributes for each vertex. Keep in mind that it contains only references to VBOs, so you'll need to keep them.

LuaGL uses the float data type for VBO elements.

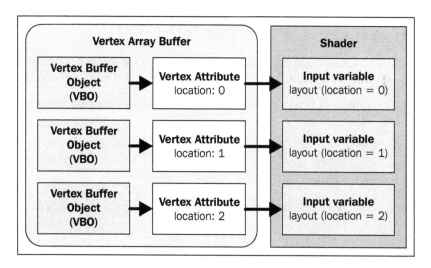

There's more...

VBO presents a common data storage. It provides limited storage depending on implementation and current machine. Some parts can be cached in system RAM and the currently used parts are in graphic memory.

Another thing is that the gl.BufferData function reserves a certain amount of memory to store data. You can use only a reserved range for data updates. There might be situations where you know exactly how much storage you'll need, but you don't want to upload data right away. For this case, you can use the gl.BufferData function, but instead of submitting data in a Lua table, you'll be using elements count:

```
local element_count = 12
gl.BufferData(gl_enum.GL_ARRAY_BUFFER, element_count,
gl_enum.GL_STATIC_DRAW)
```

This will reserve memory space for 12 elements, which you can update with the `gl.BufferSubData` function:

```
local offset = 0
local data = {1,2,3,4}
gl.BufferSubData(gl_enum.GL_ARRAY_BUFFER, offset, data)
```

The offset parameter presents a number of elements to be skipped.

See also

▸ The *Using uniform variables with shaders* recipe

▸ The *Writing a vertex shader* recipe

▸ The *Writing a fragment (pixel) shader* recipe

Rendering to texture

Rendering to texture technique is used whenever you need to apply some kind of postprocessing on screen or to produce dynamic textures in reflections.

Over the past few years, OpenGL introduced a number of ways to obtain screen content and transfer it to texture. You could read directly from the frame buffer and store all data in texture with `gl.TexSubImage2D` function. This approach is a slow process because all rendering must be stalled in order to obtain a copy of the whole frame. For this kind of operation, there was a P buffer introduced sometime in 2000. It presented a more efficient way of transferring larger blocks of pixel data. However, this kind of buffer wasn't available everywhere and what's more, it was hard to use. Later, it was deprecated in OpenGL 3.0 and subsequently removed from OpenGL 3.1. Currently, the standardized way of working with frame buffer is to work with Render Buffer. Render buffer objects have been available since OpenGL 3.0. They use native pixel format, which makes them optimized for offscreen rendering target. The older technique used a texture as a target and used the pixel format conversion in each update which is slow.

This recipe will show you how to prepare and use render buffer object.

Getting ready

You can attach render buffers to various kinds of data that frame buffer produces. Render buffer can store color data, depth information, or stencil data.

Each render buffer will need to know its dimensions. Let's assume that you have this information already since you need to have the application window in order to display anything. The size of the application window will be stored in these variables: `screen_width` and `screen_height`.

You'll also need a valid texture that will be used as a rendering target. This texture will contain screen content and it will use the texture identifier stored in the `screen_texture` variable. Note that this texture should be at least as big as the application window.

How to do it...

First, you'll need to create the frame buffer object or FBO:

```
local fbos = gl.GenFrameBuffers(1)
```

The next thing is to activate this frame buffer:

```
gl.BindFramebuffer(gl_enum.GL_FRAMEBUFFER, fbos[1])
```

With this set, you can proceed to individual render buffers. This recipe will show you how to create and use the render buffer for color data and depth information.

The render buffer with the color attachment

The render buffer with the color attachment is used often for offscreen rendering in order to do postprocessing effects. Render buffer will use all four color components, where each one will use 8 bits. This means that one color value will use 32 bits or 4 bytes:

```
local render_buffers = gl.GenRenderBuffers(1)
local internal_format = gl_enum.GL_RGBA8
local rb_target = gl_enum.GL_RENDERBUFFER
local fb_target = gl_enum.GL_FRAMEBUFFER
local attachment = gl_enum.GL_COLOR_ATTACHMENT0

gl.BindRenderBuffer(rb_target, render_buffers[1])
gl.RenderBufferStorage(rb_target, internal_format, screen_width,
screen_height)
gl.FramebufferRenderbuffer(fb_target, attachment, rb_target,
render_buffers[1])
```

The render buffer with the depth attachment

The render buffer with the depth data usage can be seen in deferred shading or depth of field effects. Deferred shading is a process where the graphical scene is rendered into separate parts—buffers. These buffers usually contain color information, map of normal vectors, and z depth. Basically, it skips all pixels that doesn't get to the screen (pixels that fail the Z test). This technique is used to save time spent by the fragment shader and it's used on complex scenes with a large number of lights:

```
local render_buffers = gl.GenRenderBuffers(1)
local internal_format = gl_enum.GL_DEPTH_COMPONENT16
local rb_target = gl_enum.GL_RENDERBUFFER
```

```
local fb_target = gl_enum.GL_FRAMEBUFFER
local attachment = gl_enum.GL_DEPTH_ATTACHMENT

gl.BindRenderBuffer(rb_target, render_buffers[1])
gl.RenderBufferStorage(rb_target, internal_format, screen_width,
screen_height)
gl.FramebufferRenderbuffer(fb_target, attachment, rb_target,
render_buffers[1])
```

You should always check the frame buffer has been prepared properly:

```
local status =
gl.CheckFramebufferStatus(gl_enum.GL_DRAW_FRAMEBUFFER)
if status ~= gl_enum.GL_FRAMEBUFFER_COMPLETE then
  error('Frame buffer is not complete!')
end
```

After this step, you can switch rendering to this frame buffer with the gl.BindFramebuffer function:

```
gl.BindFramebuffer(gl_enum.GL_FRAMEBUFFER, fbos[1])
```

Alternatively, you can turn off rendering to this frame buffer with the following code:

```
gl.BindFramebuffer(gl_enum.GL_FRAMEBUFFER, 0)
```

This will cause rendering to the default frame buffer—screen.

OpenGL offers a very powerful function, gl.CopyImageSubData. It allows you to copy data from one buffer to another. This can be used to copy render buffer content to texture:

```
local src_level = 0
local src_x, src_y, src_z = 0, 0, 0
local dest_level = 0
local dest_x, dest_y, dest_z = 0, 0, 0
local src_width, src_height = screen_width, screen_height
local src_depth = 1

gl.CopyImageSubData(
  render_buffers[1], gl_enum.GL_RENDERBUFFER,
  src_level,
  src_x, src_y, src_z,
  screen_texture, gl_enum.GL_TEXTURE_2D,
  dest_level,
  dest_x, dest_y, dest_z,
  src_width, src_height, src_depth
)
```

After this step, you can apply the `screen_texture` texture on polygons. Postprocessing is usually done by rendering this texture on one rectangular polygon that occupies the whole screen. This is shown in the following pseudo-code:

```
gl.BindFramebuffer(gl_enum.GL_FRAMEBUFFER, fbos[1])
  draw_scene()
gl.BindFramebuffer(gl_enum.GL_FRAMEBUFFER, 0)

gl.CopyImageSubData(...)
draw_textured_quad_on_whole_screen()
```

How it works...

OpenGL, by default, uses its own frame buffer. Frame buffer represents an abstract structure that sets the output for color data, depth information, and others. On the other hand, render buffer contains real data that has to be allocated in memory.

Render buffer uses native data format. Therefore, its content can be directly drawn on screen. Optionally, the render buffer content can be copied into the texture, which uses data format conversion. This approach is faster than rendering into texture first with each frame.

See also

▸   The *Writing a fragment (pixel) shader* recipe
▸   The *Drawing primitives using vertex buffers* recipe

Applying highlights and shadows to the scene

This recipe will deal with per-pixel lighting and simple shadowing. It will allow you to apply one or more lights in the 3D scene. There are two types of light sources: directional and positional light. Directional light doesn't have a position and it's used mostly for daylight. Positional light has a source at a certain position. This type of light can be divided to omnidirectional and spotlight. Omnidirectional light is used mostly with light bulbs. Spotlight is often used with reflectors. Light intensity decreases with increasing distance from the light source.

This recipe will use simple shadowing. This means that surfaces that aren't directly facing the light source will be in the shadow. However, this doesn't include real shadow casting as this is a more advanced topic that's beyond the scope of this book.

Getting ready

Before staring, you'll need to set up the camera position, object state in a scene, light sources, and materials. The camera position is stored in a structure, `cameraState`. It includes three matrices: position, rotation, and perspective correction. You could've multiplied these matrices into one but keep in mind that not every matrix is updated frame by frame. What's more, GPU can do matrix multiplication much faster than on CPU.

The object state is defined by object position. The position is computed from translation and rotation matrices stored in the `positionState` structure.

Light sources use a structure, `lightState`, that stores all the needed information about the light source such as light position, direction, attenuation, and spotlight parameters. The scene uses ambient light color, `sceneAmbient`, to emulate global illumination.

The last thing you'll need to set up is material parameters stored in the `materialState` structure.

You'll be setting uniform variables quite a lot. This means you'll be getting a uniform variable location on every access. To make uniform variable manipulation easier, you can bundle these operations into one function that stores location identifiers in a table:

```lua
local uniformLocations = {}
local uniformTypeFn = {
  f = gl.Uniformf, -- float number
  d = gl.Uniformd, -- double float number
  i = gl.Uniformi, -- integer number
  ui = gl.Uniformui, -- unsigned integer number
  m = gl.UniformMatrix, -- matrix
}

local function setUniform(var_type, name, ...)
  -- uniform variable location is cached to speed up process
  local location = uniformLocations[name]
  if not location then
    location = gl.GetUniformLocation(shader_program, name)
    uniformLocations[name] = location
  end
  local uniformFn = uniformTypeFn[var_type]
  if type(uniformFn) == "function" then
    uniformFn(location, ...)
  end
end
```

Do note that this function works on single shader programs. Each shader program must use its own `uniformLocation` table.

The last thing you'll need is a way to compute projection matrix for camera perspective correction. You can use the following example of a function to get the projection matrix based on the field of a view angle, the screen aspect ratio, and the depth parameters. The `projectionMatrix` function is based on the `computeFrustum` function from the *Setting up orthogonal and perspective camera* recipe in *Chapter 4, Graphics – Legacy Method with OpenGL 1.x-2.1*. The main difference is that, in this case, it results in a transformation matrix. You can find the whole derivation process of the projection matrix at `http://www.songho.ca/opengl/gl_projectionmatrix.html`.

The previous version relied on OpenGL to compute the matrix internally:

```lua
local function projectionMatrix(fov, aspect, znear, zfar)
    -- xymax variable refers to the coordinate
    -- of the right/bottom clip-plane
    local xymax = znear * math.tan(math.rad(fov/2))
    local ymin = -xymax -- top clip-plane
    local xmin = -xymax -- left clip-plane

    local width = xymax - xmin
    local height = xymax - ymin
    local depth = zfar - znear

    -- q and qn parameters are used to achieve
    -- perspective correction
    local q = -(zfar + znear) / depth
    local qn = -2 * (zfar * znear) / depth

    local w = 2 * znear / width
    w = w / aspect
    local h = 2 * znear / height

    -- transposed version of the projection matrix
    return {
        w, 0, 0, 0,
        0, h, 0, 0,
        0, 0, q, -1,
        0, 0, qn, 0,
    }
end
```

How to do it...

The first step is to supply the initial values to all uniform variables. This recipe will use one positional light source that is placed just next to the camera. The scene object is positioned in front of the camera:

```
-- camera parameters
setUniform('m', 'camera.translation', {
  1,0,0,0,
  0,1,0,0,
  0,0,1,0,
  0,0,0,1,
}, 4, 4, true)
setUniform('m', 'camera.rotation', {
  1,0,0,0,
  0,1,0,0,
  0,0,1,0,
  0,0,0,1,
}, 4, 4, true)
setUniform('m', 'camera.perspective', projectionMatrix(60, 1, 1,
10), 4, 4, true)

-- object parameters
setUniform('m', 'object.translation', {
  1,0,0,-0.5,
  0,1,0,-0.5,
  0,0,1,-0.5,
  0,0,0,1,
}, 4, 4, true)
setUniform('m', 'object.rotation', {
  1,0,0,0,
  0,1,0,0,
  0,0,1,0,
  0,0,0,1,
}, 4, 4, true)

-- light parameters
setUniform('f', 'lights[0].position', {-1, 0, -1, 1})
setUniform('f', 'lights[0].diffuse', {1, 0.8, 0.8, 1})
setUniform('f', 'lights[0].specular', {1, 1, 1, 1})
setUniform('f', 'lights[0].spotCutoff', 180.0)
setUniform('f', 'lights[0].spotExponent', 1.2)
setUniform('f', 'lights[0].constantAttenuation', 0)
```

```
setUniform('f', 'lights[0].linearAttenuation', 1)
setUniform('f', 'lights[0].quadraticAttenuation', 0)
setUniform('f', 'lights[0].spotDirection', {0, 0, 0})

setUniform('i', 'totalLights', 1)


-- material parameters
setUniform('f', 'material.ambient', {0.2, 0.2, 0.2, 1})
setUniform('f', 'material.diffuse', {1, 1, 1, 1})
setUniform('f', 'material.specular', {1, 1, 1, 1})
setUniform('f', 'material.shininess', 5.0)

-- scene ambient color
setUniform('f', 'sceneAmbient', {0.2, 0.2, 0.2, 1})

-- textures
setUniform('i', 'diffuseTexture', 0)
```

The next important thing is having correct vertex attributes. You'll need the vertex position, the vertex texture coordinates, and the vertex normal vector. Therefore, you'll need three vertex buffer objects. Each one for every vertex attribute:

```
local positionVBO = gl.GenBuffers(1)
local texcoordVBO = gl.GenBuffers(1)
local normalVBO = gl.GenBuffers(1)
local vertex_array_object = gl.GenVertexArrays(1)


-- vertex coordinates
gl.BindBuffer(gl_enum.GL_ARRAY_BUFFER, positionVBO)
gl.BufferData(gl_enum.GL_ARRAY_BUFFER, vertexPositions, gl_enum.GL_
STATIC_DRAW)
-- normal vector coordinates
gl.BindBuffer(gl_enum.GL_ARRAY_BUFFER
-- texture coordinates
gl.BindBuffer(gl_enum.GL_ARRAY_BUFFER, texcoordVBO)
gl.BufferData(gl_enum.GL_ARRAY_BUFFER, texcoords,
gl_enum.GL_STATIC_DRAW), normalVBO)
gl.BufferData(gl_enum.GL_ARRAY_BUFFER, normals,
gl_enum.GL_STATIC_DRAW)

-- setup vertex attributes
gl.BindVertexArray(vertex_array_object[1])

-- vertex position
```

```
gl.BindBuffer(gl_enum.GL_ARRAY_BUFFER, positionVBO)
gl.VertexAttribPointer(0, 3, false, 0)

-- vertex texture coordinates
gl.BindBuffer(gl_enum.GL_ARRAY_BUFFER, texcoordVBO)
gl.VertexAttribPointer(1, 2, false, 0)

-- vertex normal vector
gl.BindBuffer(gl_enum.GL_ARRAY_BUFFER, normalVBO)
gl.VertexAttribPointer(2, 3, false, 0)
```

Vertex shader

The vertex shader code would look like this:

```
#version 330

struct cameraState{
  mat4 perspective;
  mat4 translation;
  mat4 rotation;
};

struct positionState{
  mat4 translation;
  mat4 rotation;
};

layout (location = 0) in vec3 VertexPosition;
layout (location = 1) in vec2 VertexTexCoord;
layout (location = 2) in vec3 VertexNormal;

out VertexData {
  vec2 texCoord;
  vec3 normal;
  vec3 position;
} outData;

uniform float time;
uniform cameraState camera;
uniform positionState object;

void main(){
  // model-view matrix
  mat4 objMatrix = (object.translation * object.rotation);
```

```
    // vertex position in the world
    vec4 localPos = objMatrix * vec4(VertexPosition.xyz, 1.0);
    // final vertex position on screen
    gl_Position = (camera.perspective * camera.translation *
      camera.rotation) * localPos;
      // texture coordinates and original vertex position
      // for the next stage - fragment shader
    outData.texCoord = vec2(VertexTexCoord.st);
    outData.position = vertexPos.xyz;
    // normal vectors are adjusted to match object orientation
    vec4 tmpNormal = objMatrix * vec4(VertexNormal.xyz, 0.0);
    outData.normal = normalize(tmpNormal.xyz);
}
```

Fragment shader

The fragment shader code would contain these definitions:

```
#version 330
// a structure for light parameters
struct lightState {
  vec4 position;
  vec4 diffuse;
  vec4 specular;
  float constantAttenuation, linearAttenuation,
    quadraticAttenuation;
  float spotCutoff, spotExponent;
  vec3 spotDirection;
};
// structure with material properties
struct materialState {
  vec4 ambient;
  vec4 diffuse;
  vec4 specular;
  float shininess;
};
// camera position and orientation matrices
struct cameraState{
  mat4 perspective;
  mat4 translation;
  mat4 rotation;
};

// diffuseTexture contains texture unit identifier (integer)
uniform sampler2D diffuseTexture;
```

```
uniform cameraState camera;
uniform materialState material;
// ambient light color
uniform vec4 sceneAmbient;

//total number of lights, currently 8 is the maximum
uniform int totalLights;
uniform lightState lights[8];

in VertexData {
  vec2 texCoord;
  vec3 normal;
  vec3 position;
} inData;

layout(location = 0) out vec4 diffuseColor;
```

The whole light reflection algorithm is packed into one function, processLighting. It accepts three parameters: material parameters, the current point on surface, and the normal vector. This makes the entire code much easier to read. Note that the processLighting function operates on voxels—points in space:

```
/*
  Input:
    material - material type specification
    surface - voxel position in world space
    normalDirection - normal vector for current voxel
*/
vec4 processLighting(in materialState material, in vec3 surface,
  in vec3 normalDirection){
  // camera position in world space
  vec4 cam = camera.translation * vec4(0,0,0,1);
  // directional vector from the surface to the camera
  // it's used primarily to determine highlights
  vec3 camDirection = normalize(cam.xyz - surface);
  vec3 lightDirection;

  float attenuation;

  // ambient light
  vec3 ambientLighting = sceneAmbient.rgb * material.ambient.rgb;
  vec3 totalLighting = ambientLighting;

  // iterate over all lights on the scene
```

```
for (int index=0; index < totalLights; index++){
  lightState light = lights[index];

  // omni-directional light
  if (light.position.w == 0.0){
    lightDirection = light.position.xyz;
    attenuation = 1.0;
  }else{
  // directional light
    vec3 lightVector = light.position.xyz - surface.xyz;
    lightDirection = normalize(lightVector);
    float distance = length(lightVector);

    attenuation = 1.0 / (
      light.constantAttenuation +
      light.linearAttenuation * distance +
      light.quadraticAttenuation * (distance * distance)
    );

    /* spot-light
      Note: cut-off angle presents one half of
      light cone spatial angle
      A light with cut-off angle greater than 90 degrees
      is considered to be omni-light
    */
    if (light.spotCutoff <= 90.0){
      float spotAngle = max(0.0,
        dot(lightDirection, light.spotDirection)
      );
      // there's no light outside of light cone
      if (spotAngle < cos(radians(light.spotCutoff))){
        attenuation = 0.0;
      }else{
        attenuation *= pow(spotAngle, light.spotExponent);
      }
    }
  }

  /*
    Diffuse light is dependent only on the surface normal
    and light direction
  */
  vec3 diffuseReflection = attenuation *
    light.diffuse.rgb * material.diffuse.rgb *
    max(0.0, dot(normalDirection, lightDirection));
```

```
  /*
    Specular reflection is present only if the light ray
    reflects almost directly to camera lenses.
  */
  vec3 specularReflection;
  // There's no specular reflection on the dark side
  if (dot(normalDirection, lightDirection) < 0.0) {
    specularReflection = vec3(0.0, 0.0, 0.0);
  } else {
  // Specular reflection
    specularReflection = attenuation *
      light.specular.rgb * material.specular.rgb *
      pow(
        max(0.0,
          dot(reflect(-lightDirection, normalDirection),
            camDirection)
        ),
        material.shininess
      );
  }

  // Add to total lighting contribution
  totalLighting += diffuseReflection + specularReflection;
}
/*
  Material transparency is controlled by alpha channel
  of diffuse color
*/
return vec4(totalLighting, material.diffuse.a);
}
```

Now you can summarize everything in the `main` function for fragment shader.

```
void main() {
  vec4 texel = texture(diffuseTexture, inData.texCoord.st);
  materialState localMaterial = material;
  // Texel color is directly applied to current diffuse color
  localMaterial.diffuse *= texel;
  // Compute output color for current voxel
  diffuseColor = processLighting(
    localMaterial,
    inData.position,
    normalize(inData.normal)
  );
}
```

How it works...

The total light contribution is divided into three parts: ambient light, diffuse light, and specular light. Ambient light is a constant light produced by the surrounding environment. This lighting is simply added to the total light contribution. Diffuse lighting is produced by the lighting source. It's scattered in all directions in response to a rough material surface. Therefore, it mainly reflects the light that isn't absorbed by the material. In this case, the material color is reflected to the viewer. The specular light is a part of the lighting where the light directly reflects from the surface to the viewer with minimum scattering. This also means that specular reflection consists mainly of light color. You can observe this when you're looking at the water surface under low angle. The light reflection diagram is shown as follows:

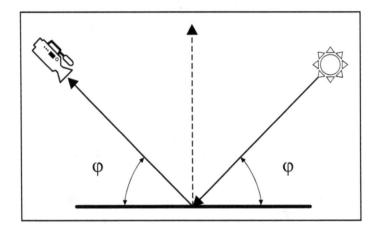

The light source position is defined by the vector with four components. If the last component equals 1, this vector defines the light position. Otherwise, this vector defines the orientation of directional light. Directional light doesn't have a source so the attenuation factor is 1.

The positional light uses the light source distance from the surface to adjust the light intensity. The light intensity can be described as the following attenuation formula:

$$\text{attenuation} = \frac{1}{C + L \times \text{distance} + Q \times \text{distance}^2}$$

This formula uses three parameters: *C*—constant attenuation, *L*—linear attenuation, and *Q*—quadratic attenuation.

The spotlight's cut-off value specifies the angular size of the light cone. The omnidirectional light has the spotlight's cut-off value greater than 90 degrees. The light spot intensity decreases with the second power of the angular distance from the light spot direction.

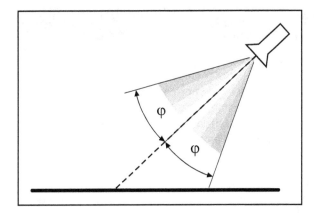

After these steps, you should have the final attenuation value, which will be used on diffuse and specular reflection.

Diffuse reflection uses the surface normal vector and light direction vector to calculate the amount of light reflected. Note that this type of reflection is independent of camera position. The final diffuse color is a result of multiplication of material color value with light color value and dot product of surface normal vector with the light direction vector. The dot product always produces values in a range (-1,1). If those two vectors are parallel, it results in a value 1. If they are perpendicular, it's 0. The negative values are produced when those two vectors enclose an angle greater than 90 degree. The final value of diffusion color is modified by attenuation value, so there are dark parts on the surface that are out of the light source range.

Specular reflection occurs only on surface parts that reflect light almost directly to the camera. The total amount of specular reflection is modified by the result of this formula:

```
spotLightModifier =
  (max (0, reflect (-lightDirection , normalDirection ) . camDirection ))^material_shininess
```

Finally, the diffuse and specular reflections are added to total light contribution on the selected part of the surface.

See also

> ▸ The *Bumpmapping* recipe

Bumpmapping

Bumpmapping presents a way to increase a detail level without increasing the total polygon count. This technique relies on using normal maps applied to surfaces. Without this, each surface or polygon would have only one normal vector, and therefore, it would look like a flat surface. It uses the term mapping because in addition to the basic texture map, it uses another texture that represents a normal map. A normal map contains normal vectors in tangent space and can be encoded as simple RGB texture, where each color component represents a normal vector component. It makes the surface look rough with bumps.

Bumpmap textures usually consist of grayscale image, where dark areas represent lower regions and lighter areas represent a higher region. Such images need to be converted into *colorful* normal map. You can use NVidia Texture Tools for Adobe Photoshop or a normal map plugin for the GIMP image editor. There's even a free online tool to do such conversion called NormalMap Online and it's available at the GitHub page `http://cpetry.github.io/NormalMap-Online/`.

Getting ready

This recipe uses a slightly modified version of shaders from the previous recipe. While the vertex shader is almost the same, the fragment shader uses two texture units instead of one. The first one is used for texture map and the second one is used for normal map. Therefore, you'll need to set up two texture units as follows:

```
local texture_target = gl_enum.GL_TEXTURE_2D
gl.ActiveTexture(gl_enum.GL_TEXTURE0)
gl.BindTexture(texture_target, texture_map)

gl.ActiveTexture(gl_enum.GL_TEXTURE1)
gl.BindTexture(texture_target, normal_map)

-- textures
setUniform('i', 'diffuseTexture', 0)
setUniform('i', 'normalTexture', 1)
```

You'll also need to prepare lights in your scene. You can copy the light setup from the previous recipe about lighting basics.

You could try to apply a normal map as an ordinal texture, but soon you would've discovered certain artifacts in normal vector orientations. That's why you'll need to know triangle tangent vectors additionally to existing vertex attributes, such as a normal vector. These vectors describe the direction of the triangle plane. You'll need these vectors to apply vector correction in a normal map. Otherwise, the normal map would cause distortions and incorrect light reflections. You can supply tangent vectors for each vertex by the vertex buffer.

How to do it...

First you'll have to prepare the vertex buffer objects and vertex attributes to prepare all data for shaders:

```lua
local positionVBO = gl.GenBuffers(1)
local texcoordVBO = gl.GenBuffers(1)
local normalVBO = gl.GenBuffers(1)
local tangentVBO = gl.GenBuffers(1)
local vertex_array_object = gl.GenVertexArrays(1)

-- vertex coordinates
gl.BindBuffer(gl_enum.GL_ARRAY_BUFFER, positionVBO)
gl.BufferData(gl_enum.GL_ARRAY_BUFFER, vertexPositions, gl_enum.GL_
STATIC_DRAW)
-- texture coordinates
gl.BindBuffer(gl_enum.GL_ARRAY_BUFFER, texcoordVBO)
gl.BufferData(gl_enum.GL_ARRAY_BUFFER, texcoords, gl_enum.GL_STATIC_
DRAW)
-- normal vector coordinates
gl.BindBuffer(gl_enum.GL_ARRAY_BUFFER, normalVBO)
gl.BufferData(gl_enum.GL_ARRAY_BUFFER, normals, gl_enum.GL_STATIC_
DRAW)
-- tangent vector coordinates
gl.BindBuffer(gl_enum.GL_ARRAY_BUFFER, tangentVBO)
gl.BufferData(gl_enum.GL_ARRAY_BUFFER, tangents, gl_enum.GL_STATIC_
DRAW)

-- setup vertex attributes
gl.BindVertexArray(vertex_array_object[1])

-- vertex position
gl.BindBuffer(gl_enum.GL_ARRAY_BUFFER, positionVBO)
gl.VertexAttribPointer(0, 3, false, 0)

-- vertex texture coordinates
gl.BindBuffer(gl_enum.GL_ARRAY_BUFFER, texcoordVBO)
gl.VertexAttribPointer(1, 2, false, 0)

-- vertex normal vector
gl.BindBuffer(gl_enum.GL_ARRAY_BUFFER, normalVBO)
gl.VertexAttribPointer(2, 3, false, 0)

-- vertex tangent vector
gl.BindBuffer(gl_enum.GL_ARRAY_BUFFER, tangentVBO)
gl.VertexAttribPointer(3, 4, false, 0)
```

You can get vertex positions, texture coordinates, and normal vectors easily. The difficult part is obtaining tangent vector.

Let's assume that you define each polygon with a triangle. Therefore, each triangle has three points: **A**, **B**, and **C** as shown in the following diagram:

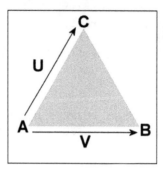

There are two vectors **U** and **V** that describe a plane defined by triangle points. You can compute these two vectors with the following code:

```
local U = {
    x = C.x - A.x,
    y = C.y - A.y,
    z = C.x - A.z
}
local V = {
    x = B.x - A.x,
    y = B.y - A.y,
    z = B.x - A.z
}
```

You'll need to do the same with texture coordinates as well. Texture coordinate vectors will use letters S and T:

```
local S = {
    x = C.tx - A.tx,
    y = C.ty - A.ty,
}
local T = {
    x = B.tx - A.tx,
    y = B.ty - A.ty,
}
```

Now that you have the U and V triangle edge vectors and texel direction vectors S and T, you can compute tangent and bi-tangent vectors with the following formula:

```
local r = 1/(S.x*T.y - S.y*T.x)
local tangent = {
  x = (T.y*U.x - S.y*V.x)*r,
  y = (T.y*U.y - S.y*V.y)*r,
  z = (T.y*U.z - S.y*V.z)*r
}
local bitangent = {
  x = (S.x*V.x - T.x*U.x)*r,
  y = (S.x*V.y - T.x*U.y)*r,
  z = (S.x*V.z - T.x*U.z)*r
}
```

Note that these tangent and bitangent vectors are related to the edge vectors and texture space vectors. You could use those vectors in normal mapping, but on certain occasions, you would get incorrect results. That's because these tangent space vectors aren't orthogonal or because they've got different orientation. You can solve these problems with Gram-Schmidt orthogonalization. For this operation, you'll need a normal vector N. The Gram-Schmidt orthogonalization formula looks like this:

$$\texttt{tangentOrthogonal = tangent} - \textbf{N} * (\textbf{N}.\texttt{tangent})$$

You can rewrite it in the Lua language with the following code:

```
local NdotS = N.x*tangent.x + N.y*tangent.Y + N.z*tangent.z
local tangentOrthogonal = {
  x = tangent.X - N.x*NdotS,
  y = tangent.y - N.y*NdotS,
  z = tangent.z - N.z*NdotS,
}
```

Now you're left with determining the triangle winding direction. Winding direction defines the order of triangle vertices. A visual representation of this triangle is regarded to be the front face. The back face of the triangle uses the opposite winding direction of vertices. The winding direction helps to determine the direction of the orthogonal tangent vector in the final step. The invalid (opposite) direction of the tangent vector would reverse a texture on the triangle.

In most cases, you'll be using counterclockwise winding, but this can differ if you're using triangle strips, where the triangle winding alternates and this can pose a problem. You can obtain winding direction from the following formula:

$$\texttt{winding} = (\textbf{N} \times \texttt{tangent}).\texttt{bitangent}$$

You'll need to rewrite this formula into the Lua language:

```
local NcrossS = {
  x = N.y * tangent.z - N.z * tangent.y,
  y = N.x * tangent.z - N.z * tangent.x,
  z = N.x * tangent.y - N.y * tangent.x,
}
local winding = NcrossS.x * bitangent.x +
  NcrossS.y * bitangent.y +
  NcrossS.z * bitangent.z
```

The last step in producing tangent vectors is to include the winding information in the tangent vector itself. You can store this information in the fourth element `w` of the tangent vector:

```
tangentOrthogonal.w = (winding < 0) and 1 or -1
```

Do note that this tangent vector has four elements: `x`, `y`, `z`, and `w`. The last one is used in the vertex shader to correct TBN matrix orientation. Fortunately, you only have to compute tangent vectors once.

To produce a bumpmapping effect, you can reuse the shader code introduced in previous samples with a few changes.

Vertex shader

The vertex shader code will need to include another vertex attribute that will contain the tangent vector for each vertex. You can do this by including this vertex layout specification code:

```
layout (location = 4) in vec4 VertexTangent;
```

After this step, you'll have to compute the so-called TBN matrix with the size of 3 x 3 elements. This matrix contains three columns, where the first contains the tangent vector, the second contains the bitangent vector and the last one contains the normal vector. This matrix represents a new vector space and is often known as the tangent space. The TBN matrix will be used in the fragment shader to correct the normal vector orientation. To build a TBN matrix, you'll need to know the bitangent vector as well. Fortunately, you can compute the bitangent vector from normal and tangent vectors. A bitangent vector is perpendicular to normal and tangent vectors. Note that it's important to adjust the vector orientation in this matrix to correspond with your coordinate system. OpenGL uses this coordinate system by default:

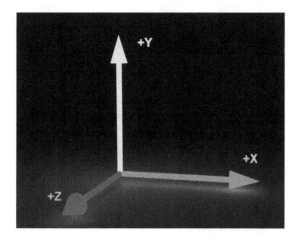

To produce the TBN matrix, you'll use the following code:

```
outData.tbn = mat3(
  normalize((objMatrix *
    vec4(VertexTangent.xyz, 0.0)).xyz),
  normalize((objMatrix *
    vec4(cross(VertexNormal, VertexTangent.xyz)*
      VertexTangent.w, 0.0)).xyz),
  normalize((objMatrix *
    vec4(VertexNormal.xyz, 0.0)).xyz)
);
```

The TBN matrix will be passed to the fragment shader by the modified VertexData structure:

```
out VertexData {
  vec2 texCoord;
  vec3 position;
  mat3 tbn;
} outData;
```

The final vertex shader code would be as follows:

```
#version 330

struct cameraState{
  mat4 perspective;
  mat4 position;
};
```

```
struct positionState{
  mat4 position;
};

layout (location = 0) in vec3 VertexPosition;
layout (location = 1) in vec3 VertexNormal;
layout (location = 2) in vec2 VertexTexCoord;
layout (location = 3) in vec4 VertexTangent;

out VertexData {
  vec2 texCoord;
  vec3 position;
  mat3 tbn;
} outData;

uniform cameraState camera;
uniform positionState object;

void main(){
  mat4 objMatrix = object.position;
  vec4 vertexPos = objMatrix * vec4(VertexPosition.xyz, 1.0);

  gl_Position = camera.perspective * camera.position * objMatrix *
  vec4(VertexPosition.xyz, 1.0);
  outData.texCoord = vec2(VertexTexCoord.st);
  outData.position = vertexPos.xyz;

  outData.tbn = mat3(
    normalize((objMatrix * vec4(VertexTangent.xyz, 0.0)).xyz),
    normalize((objMatrix * vec4(cross(VertexNormal,
    VertexTangent.xyz)*VertexTangent.w, 0.0)).xyz),
    normalize((objMatrix * vec4(VertexNormal.xyz, 0.0)).xyz)
  );
}
```

Fragment shader

First, you'll need to modify the fragment shader code to include the TBN matrix from the vertex shader:

```
in VertexData {
  vec2 texCoord;
  vec3 position;
  mat3 tbn;
} inData;
```

Now, you can read the normal map texel value from the `normalTexture` texture unit:

```
vec3 normalTexel = texture(normalTexture, inData.texCoord.st).xyz;
```

The `normalTexel` vector contains raw values of the normal vector from the normal map texture for the current texel. It means that all values are now in the range (0,1), which is the color component range in OpenGL as well. You need to convert these values into range (-1,1), so you can use them to produce a valid normal vector. You can do this with the following formula:

```
normalTexel = 2*normalTexel.xyz - vec3(1.0);
```

In addition to this conversion, you can apply the vector orientation correction by multiplying the `normalTexel` vector with the `vec3` vector.

```
normalTexel *= vec3(1, 1, 1);
```

Values in the vector multiplier are related to normal map values. Normal maps aren't standardized, so you'll need to find out what kind of normal map suits you the best. The normal maps that are generated from bumpmaps are usually fine. However, they are not very accurate for more complex 3D models. Such an example might be a 3D model with a low polygon count while using a normal map to define fine details. This is usually the result of using the sculpting tool in the Blender application. Fortunately, you can use the normal map baking tool to generate accurate normal maps from the sculpture.

Remember to always set up correct mapping of normal vector coordinates to color channels in a normal map. In most cases, normal maps use the blue color to represent the facing vector as you can see in the following screenshot:

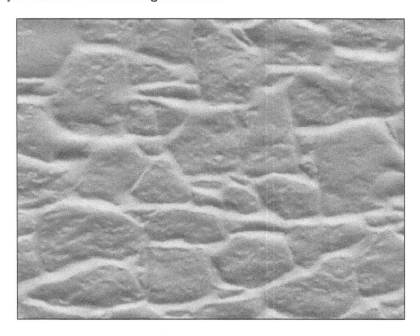

After all these steps, you can produce the final per-texel normal vector by converting the `normalTexel` vector into world space:

```
vec3 perTexelNormal = inData.tbn * normalize(normalTexel);
```

This vector can be used instead of the per-vertex normal vector in the `processLighting` function.

In the end, the fragment shader code would look like this:

```
#version 330

struct lightState {
  vec4 position;
  vec4 diffuse;
  vec4 specular;
  float constantAttenuation, linearAttenuation, quadraticAttenuation;
  float spotCutoff, spotExponent;
  vec3 spotDirection;
};

struct materialState {
  vec4 ambient;
  vec4 diffuse;
  vec4 specular;
  float shininess;
};

struct cameraState{
  mat4 perspective;
  mat4 translation;
  mat4 rotation;
};

uniform sampler2D diffuseTexture;
uniform sampler2D normalTexture;
uniform cameraState camera;
uniform materialState material;
uniform vec4 sceneAmbient;

uniform int totalLights;
uniform lightState lights[8];

in VertexData {
  vec2 texCoord;
```

```glsl
    vec3 normal;
    vec3 position;
} inData;

layout(location = 0) out vec4 diffuseColor;

vec4 processLighting(in materialState material, in vec3 surface, in
vec3 normalDirection){
    ...
}

void main() {
    //local copy of material
    materialState localMaterial = material;

    //texture texel
    vec4 texel = texture(diffuseTexture, inData.texCoord.st);
    localMaterial.diffuse *= texel;

    //normalmap texel
    vec3 normalTexel = texture(normalTexture, inData.texCoord.st).xyz;

    //normalize range
    normalTexel = (2*normalTexel.xyz - vec3(1.0));

    //change normal vector orientation
    normalTexel *= vec3(-1, -1, 1);

    //convert normal map vector into world space
    vec3 perTexelNormal = inData.tbn * normalize(normalTexel);

    diffuseColor = processLighting(
        localMaterial,
        inData.position,
        normalize(perTexelNormal)
    );
}
```

The result of the applied normal map on a 3D cube with a texture can be seen in the following screenshot:

How it works...

Bumpmapping affects the normal vector direction at each point of the polygon. Without it, normal vectors would use only linear interpolation between vertices and the surface would look smooth.

A normal map is usually represented by a 2D texture, where each pixel contains an encoded normal vector. A normal vector consists of three axes: *x*, *y*, and *z*, while in a normal texture map, they are mapped to R, G, and B color channels. A perfectly flat normal map would have a bluish look. That's because every pixel would use (128,128,255) RGB colors, which also means it will use a normal vector with XYZ coordinates (0,0,1).

The difficult part is to use these normal map values to produce a usable normal vector. You can't directly use a normal map as a simple texture because each polygon would have the same normal vectors. It would be as if all polygons were facing you, which is rare. Therefore, you'll need to rotate these normal vectors so that the normal vector (0,0,1) on the normal map would be the same as the normal vector of the polygon. You can achieve this by using the matrix multiplication on the vector from the normal map. This matrix will contain the tangent, bitangent, and normal vector values. Each one corresponds to the axis of the local coordinate system on each polygon:

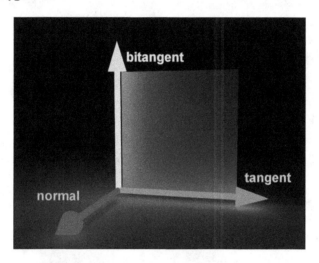

Therefore, this matrix is often called a TBN matrix:

$$TBN = \begin{pmatrix} tangent_x & bitangent_x & normal_x \\ tangent_y & bitangent_y & normal_y \\ tangent_z & bitangent_z & normal_z \end{pmatrix}$$

After multiplication with a normal vector from the normal map texture, you'll get the correct normal vector, which can be used with the lighting function.

There's more...

There's a simple way to debug normal vectors by using the `perTexelNormal` vector in place of the output color:

```
diffuseColor = vec4((normalize(perTexelNormal)+1.0)/2.0, 1);
```

Note that you'll need to adjust the value range of the vector because the normal vector can contain negative values and it would more often than not be black.

In this case, the blue color represents the facing direction, the red one is directed to the right, and the green one goes to the top:

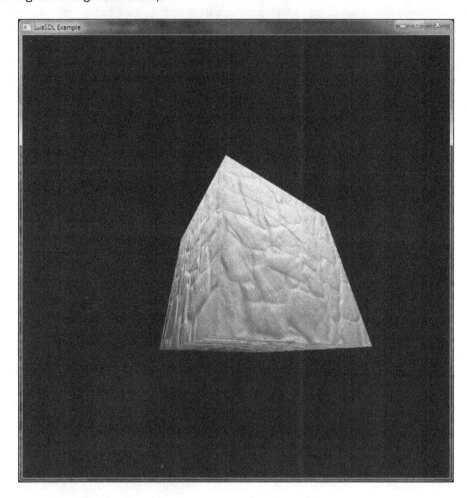

See also

▶   The *Applying highlights and shadows to the scene* recipe

6
The User Interface

This chapter will cover the following recipes:

- ▶ Drawing a simple window
- ▶ Moving the window
- ▶ Using the window hierarchy
- ▶ Showing the part of the window with the stencil test and window content scrolling
- ▶ Window controls and interaction

Introduction

What every game needs is an interface between a user and the game itself. In theory, a user interface should be able to provide two ways of interaction. This includes some form of status visualization and input controls. There's a part of computer science which deals with human-computer interaction or HCI in short.

This chapter will deal with a small part of HCI featuring a window as the basic element of interaction. This also means that a window can provide information to the user as well as taking input from the user. Windows plays a major role in the WIMP (windows, icons, menus, and pointer) interaction used in many modern operating systems.

Efficient text rendering will be important because it's the most used medium to display exact information.

Many ideas introduced in this chapter will be based on principles used in modern web browsers as they are most widely used applications in terms of HCI.

In the end, you'll be able to design any kind of user interface with ease.

Drawing a simple window

Drawing a window usually means drawing a rectangular region filled with information. This recipe will show you how to do this efficiently with new capabilities that OpenGL can offer, such as vertex buffers and shaders.

You could be tempted to put the window corner coordinates into the vertex buffer, which is fine for static windows. However, soon you would realize that it is harder to manipulate a window. To move your window, you'd need to change the window coordinates, which would mean changing the content of the vertex buffer. As you already know, moving data from CPU to GPU is a slow process and it basically halts the GPU processing for a while. A better solution to this would be putting static unit-sized window coordinates and transforming it with a model-view matrix. Matrices can be updated by using uniform variables as they tend to be much faster than doing buffer updates. This gives you an incredible amount of power for drawing a window because you can use those matrices in window positioning, hierarchy, and various visual effects.

Getting ready

This recipe will use a matrix manipulation library in the sample code for matrix operations. You can get one from the GitHub repository at `https://github.com/soulik/matrix`. A short introduction to this library is a part of the GitHub page as well.

You'll need to prepare at least two vertex buffers. One for vertex coordinates and one for texture coordinates. You'll also need the vertex array object, which will bind these buffers to your shader code. The good thing is that you can reuse this vertex buffer for all the windows you'll ever use.

The last thing you'll need are two matrices: the projection matrix and model-view matrix. The projection matrix will transform view space into a more suitable coordinate system. OpenGL uses coordinates within the range of (-1,1) for both horizontal and vertical directions. This might be valid in a case where you need your UI to scale with the screen resolution. If you want to render textured windows with pixel-perfect size, you'll need to transform the coordinate system into (0,`screen_width`) and (0,`screen_height`) respectively.

The model-view matrix will move and scale your rectangle into a desired position on the screen. This means that each window will have its own model-view matrix.

How to do it...

In the first step, you'll fill vertex buffers to create the basic window shape. The code you'll be using will look like this:

```
local vertex_buffer_object = gl.GenBuffers(2)
local vertex_array_object = gl.GenVertexArrays(1)

-- vertex coordinates
local vertex_positions = {
  -0.5, 0.5, 0,
  0.5, 0.5, 0,
  0.5, -0.5, 0,
  -0.5, -0.5, 0,
}
gl.BindBuffer(gl_enum.GL_ARRAY_BUFFER, vertex_buffer_object[1])
gl.BufferData(gl_enum.GL_ARRAY_BUFFER, vertex_positions,
gl_enum.GL_STATIC_DRAW)

-- texture coordinates
local vertex_texcoords = {
  0, 0,
  1, 0,
  1, 1,
  0, 1,
}
gl.BindBuffer(gl_enum.GL_ARRAY_BUFFER, vertex_buffer_object[2])
gl.BufferData(gl_enum.GL_ARRAY_BUFFER, vertex_texcoords,
gl_enum.GL_STATIC_DRAW)

-- bind vertex buffers to vertex array object
gl.BindVertexArray(vertex_array_object[1])

-- bind vertex coordinates
gl.BindBuffer(gl_enum.GL_ARRAY_BUFFER, vertex_buffer_object[1])
gl.VertexAttribPointer(0, 3, false, 0)

-- bind texture coordinates
gl.BindBuffer(gl_enum.GL_ARRAY_BUFFER, vertex_buffer_object[2])
gl.VertexAttribPointer(1, 2, false, 0)

-- enable vertex attributes in shader code
gl.EnableVertexAttribArray(0)
gl.EnableVertexAttribArray(1)
```

The second step will deal with the shader code for the UI. It's better to have one for each logic part of your application as it makes experimenting and spotting bugs easier in the future.

The shader code will consist of the vertex and fragment shader code. The vertex shader code will look like this:

```
#version 330

layout (location = 0) in vec3 VertexPosition;
layout (location = 1) in vec2 VertexTexCoord;

out VertexData {
  vec2 TexCoord;
} outData;

uniform mat4 projectionMatrix;
uniform mat4 modelviewMatrix;

void main(){
  gl_Position = projectionMatrix * modelviewMatrix *
  vec4(VertexPosition.xyz, 1.0);
  outData.TexCoord = vec2(VertexTexCoord.st);
}
```

To complete this part, you'll need the fragment shader code as well:

```
#version 330

uniform sampler2D diffuseTexture;
uniform mat3 UVmatrix;

in VertexData {
  vec2 TexCoord;
} inData;

layout(location = 0) out vec4 diffuseColor;

void main() {
  vec2 texSize = vec2(textureSize(diffuseTexture, 0));

  mat3 UV = matrixCompMult(UVmatrix, mat3(
    1/texSize.s, 1, 1/texSize.s,
    1, 1/texSize.t, 1/texSize.t,
    1/texSize.s, 1/texSize.t, 1
  ));
```

```
vec2 finalTexCoord = (vec3(inData.TexCoord.s, 1 -
inData.TexCoord.t, 1) * UV).st;

diffuseColor = texelFetch(diffuseTexture,
ivec2(finalTexCoord.s*texSize.s, finalTexCoord.t*texSize.t), 0);
}
```

Now, in the third step, you'll have to fill the content of uniform variables. For this task, you can use the `setUniform` function from the previous chapter, which will make setting uniform variables much easier. There are two matrices in the vertex shader code to be filled. The first one is for camera and second one is for a placement of your window. Fragment shader code uses the texture unit identifier and the UV mapping matrix. The UV mapping matrix can be set to identity, if you're not using a texture atlas. Remember that you don't have to set uniform variables in each drawing frame as they are stored in the GPU memory for each shader program. Also, don't forget to activate the shader program before setting up uniform variables:

```
setUniform('m', 'projectionMatrix',
  projectionMatrix, 4, 4, true)
setUniform('m', 'modelviewMatrix',
  modelviewMatrix, 4, 4, true)
setUniform('i', 'diffuseTexture', texture_unit)
setUniform('m', 'UVmatrix',{
  1,0,0,
  0,1,0,
  0,0,1,
  }, 3, 3, true)
```

The projection and model-view matrices will use the homogenous transformation matrix for affine transformation. There are four basic forms of transformation: translation, rotation, scale, and skew. These can be combined with multiplication to produce any desired transformation. Remember that the order of matrix multiplication is extremely important. For example, applying translation after rotation is different from translation followed by rotation.

The projection matrix can be obtained with this code:

```
local matrix = (require 'matrix')()
local T,S = matrix.translate, matrix.scale
local invW, invH = 1/screen_width, 1/screen_height
local invMaxDepth = 1/16378
projectionMatrix = T(-1, -1, 0.01)*S(2, 2, 1)*S(invW, intH, -
invMaxDepth)
```

This will transform screen space to match the screen resolution except that the (0,0) coordinate will correspond to the bottom-left corner.

The next and most important step is to generate the model-view matrix. This will determine the position of the resulting window. Depending on your needs, the model-view matrix will be constructed from translation and scaling transformations:

```
modelviewMatrix = T(window_x, window_y, 0)
   * S(window_width, window_height, 1)
   * T(window_origin_x, window_origin_y, 0)
```

The window position is set by the `window_x` and `window_y` variables. The window's and height use the `window_width` and `window_height` variables. The last two `window_origin_x` and `window_origin_y` variables present the coordinates of the window's origin point. The origin point is a basic element of positioning. With this point, you can set the window to be center or corner aligned. Another thing worth mentioning is that the window's position and size variables use pixel units, whereas the window's origin point uses the range (-0.5,0.5), where the value zero represents the center.

Now, in the final step, you'll draw the window with the `gl.DrawArrays` command:

```
gl.DrawArrays(gl_enum.GL_QUADS, 0, 4)
```

The resulting window will be drawn on the screen and it will look like the following screenshot:

How it works...

This recipe relies on drawing textured rectangles on your screen with GLSL. However, instead of drawing different sets of vertices for each window, it uses the same four vertices on all the windows.

Each window uses its own model-view matrix, which will transform vertex positions to match window-specific coordinates. To be specific, it's homogenous transformation, which means each transformation operates on the local coordinate system. If you use translation, you're applying the translation movement on the coordinate system. This approach is the basis of the hierarchical windowing system. This recipe uses translation and scaling transformation, as shown in the following diagram:

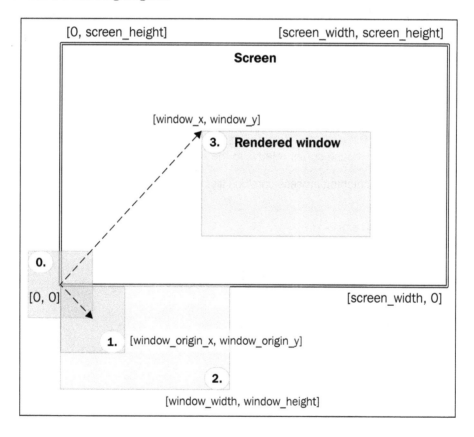

The first step consists of moving the basic rectangle to its origin point. This is followed by scaling, which will set the dimensions of the window. The final step is the translation to move the window to the desired position.

Moving the window

In some situations, it may be desirable for the user to be able to move the window to different places. There are many ways to achieve window movement. This recipe will show you how to use matrix operations to apply correct drag and drop movements in various situations.

Getting ready

First, you'll need to have the working event system from the LuaSDL library to catch the input from your mouse device. There are two kinds of events you'll want to detect: mouse movement and mouse button presses/releases. The most important part of this process is obtaining the mouse cursor position on the application window.

The last component of this recipe that you'll need is the window's model-view matrix. This will be used to determine the mouse cursor position on a window.

How to do it...

The first step of this recipe is to determine the current mouse cursor position. You can obtain its position by catching the SDL.SDL_MOUSEMOTION event, which returns the horizontal and vertical positions of the mouse cursor relative to the application window.

The code for the event catching process can look like the following sample code:

```lua
local running = true
local eventHandlers = {}

local function handleEvent(name, ...)
  local handlers = eventHandlers[name]
  if type(handlers)=="table" then
    for _, handler in ipairs(handlers) do
      if type(handler)=="function" then
        handler(...)
      end
    end
  end
end

local function addHandler(name, fn)
  local handlers = eventHandlers[name] or {}
  table.insert(handlers, fn)
  eventHandlers[name] = handlers
end
```

```
local events = {
  [SDL.SDL_MOUSEMOTION] = function(_event)
    local event = _event.motion
    handleEvent(SDL.SDL_MOUSEMOTION, event.x, event.y)
  end,
  [SDL.SDL_MOUSEBUTTONDOWN] = function(_event)
    local event = _event.button
    handleEvent(SDL.SDL_ MOUSEBUTTONDOWN, event.x, event.y,
    event.button)
  end,
  [SDL.SDL_MOUSEBUTTONUP] = function(_event)
    local event = _event.button
    handleEvent(SDL.SDL_ MOUSEBUTTONUP, event.x, event.y,
    event.button)
  end,
  [SDL.SDL_QUIT] = function(_event)
    running = false
  end,
}

local event = SDL.SDL_Event_local()
while (running) do
  if (SDL.SDL_PollEvent(event)~=0) then
    local event_fn = events[event.type]
      if type(event_fn)=='function' then
      event_fn(event)
    end
  end
  -- main application loop
  ...
end
```

Now, you'll need to obtain the inverse matrix to the model-view matrix of the window. If you have used only homogenous transformations on the model-view matrix, you can safely assume that the matrix is invertible. This matrix will be used to decide whether the mouse cursor is positioned on a window and to get mouse cursor position relative to the window. This will also work if the window has been rotated. By multiplying the inverted model-view matrix with the mouse cursor vector, you'll obtain the mouse cursor coordinates relative to the window. If these coordinates are in range (-0.5,0.5) in both dimensions, the mouse cursor is over the window. Otherwise, the mouse cursor is outside the window:

```
local relativeMouseCoords = modelviewMatrix.inv()
  * {mouse_x, mouse_y, 0, 1}
```

You can convert these coordinates to pixels with this formula:

```
local T,S = matrix.translate, matrix.scale
local originMatrix = T(window_origin_x, window_origin_y, 0)
local scaleMatrix = S(window_width, window_height, 1)
local mouseCoordsOnWindow = scaleMatrix * originMatrix
    * relativeMouseCoords
```

Note that you have to put the mouse cursor coordinates into the vector with four elements. The last element must be set to 1 to obtain the cursor position.

Now, you can use relativeMouseCoords to determine whether the mouse cursor is over the current window:

```
local wx,wy = relativeMouseCoords[1], relativeMouseCoords[2]
local isMouseCursorOverWindow = (wX<=0.5 and wX>=-0.5 and wY<=0.5
and wY>=-0.5)
```

To make further operations easier, you can turn the previous lines into functions:

```
local function projectMouseCursorToWindow(mouse_x, mouse_y)
  local relativeMouseCoords = modelviewMatrix.inv()
  * {mouse_x, mouse_y, 0, 1}
  local T,S = matrix.translate, matrix.scale
  local originMatrix = T(window_origin_x, window_origin_y, 0)
  local scaleMatrix = S(window_width, window_height, 1)
  local mouseCoordsOnWindow = scaleMatrix * originMatrix
    * relativeMouseCoords
  return mouseCoordsOnWindow[1], mouseCoordsOnWindow[2]
end

local function isMouseOverWindow(mouse_x, mouse_y)
  local relativeMouseCoords = modelviewMatrix.inv()
  * {mouse_x, mouse_y, 0, 1}
  local wx,wy = relativeMouseCoords[1], relativeMouseCoords[2]
  return (wX<=0.5 and wX>=-0.5 and wY<=0.5 and wY>=-0.5)
end
```

To achieve window movement with the mouse cursor, you'll need to process the mouse button and cursor movement events. This type of interaction usually consists of three steps:

▶ The pressed mouse button determines which window is under the cursor, set it into a focused state and store the mouse cursor position.

▶ The mouse cursor movement computes the movement of the vector for a selected window and move focused window

▶ The released mouse cursor clears the focused status of the selected window

In the first step of window movement, you'll have to add an event handler for pressing the mouse button:

```
local windowMovementStatus = {
  start_mouse_x = 0, start_mouse_y = 0,
  focused_window = false,
}
addHandler(SDL.SDL_MOUSEBUTTONDOWN, function(x, y, button)
  -- left mouse button uses number 1 identifier
  if button==1 and isMouseOverWindow(x, y)
    and not windowMovementStatus.focused_window then

    local projected_x, projected_y =
      projectMouseCursorToWindow(x, y)
    windowMovementStatus.start_mouse_x = projected_x
    windowMovementStatus.start_mouse_y = projected_y
    windowMovementStatus.focused_window = true
  end
end)
```

The second step is the most important one as it results in window movement. Therefore, you'll have to add the mouse movement event handler:

```
addHandler(SDL.SDL_MOUSEMOTION, function(x, y)
  if windowMovementStatus.focused_window then
    local projected_x, projected_y =
      projectMouseCursorToWindow(x, y)
    local movementMatrix = T(
      projected_x - windowMovementStatus.start_mouse_x,
      projected_y - windowMovementStatus.start_mouse_y,
      0
    )
    local newWindowPosition = movementMatrix
      * {window_x, window_y, 0, 1}
    window_x = newWindowPosition[1]
    window_y = newWindowPosition[2]
    -- update modelview matrix for selected window
  end
end)
```

And the final step will clear the focus status of the window to prevent further movement:

```
addHandler(SDL.SDL_MOUSEBUTTONUP, function(x, y, button)
  if button==1 and windowMovementStatus.focused_window then
    windowMovementStatus.focused_window = false
  end
end)
```

How it works...

Affine transformations allow you to manipulate with coordinates in various ways. Common window managers assume that windows are always perpendicular to screen edges. In this case, windows can be rotated, scaled, or skewed and you'll still be able to move them in the correct way. What's more, you can apply these techniques in sprite rendering and you can select them with your mouse cursor. Without affine transformations, correct object selection could be achieved with offscreen scene rendering to the frame buffer, where each object would be rendered with a unique opaque color. The object would be identified by its color value at the mouse cursor position in the frame buffer. After this, you'd need to redraw the whole scene. This was often used in the past and it wasn't as efficient. Remember that transferring data from CPU to GPU is a slow process.

As you already know, window placement is defined by the transformation matrix. In general, the inverse of this transformation matrix will produce a reverse transformation. In this case, the model-view matrix of a window transforms window vertices into a screen coordinate system. The inverse of the model-view matrix is used to produce coordinates in window space from the coordinates on screen.

Window movement relies on mouse cursor coordinates in window space. This approach uses two coordinates to produce a movement vector. The starting point of this vector is the mouse cursor coordinate in the moment of pressing the mouse button. The ending point of this vector uses the current mouse cursor position. This way you can move windows or any other objects in an easy manner.

Using the window hierarchy

A basic game UI can be constructed with a bunch of windows that are on the same level. There might be occasions where you'll need more complex UI with layered windows. You can observe this kind of UI in many modern window managers or web browsers. Windows can contain other windows or user controls. If you move the main window, it will also move inner elements with it. This behavior is done with the window hierarchy.

Getting ready

Implementing the window hierarchy system requires a well-defined data structure design, as well as correct use of matrix transformations.

This recipe will use a simple graph structure that consists of nodes and a list of child nodes. You can implement this structure in the Lua language with tables:

```
local main_window = {
  properties = {},
  children = {
```

```
    {
      properties = {},
      children = {},
    },
    -- ...
  },
}
```

In this case, each node contains window properties and a list of children windows. With this design, you can traverse all windows in one direction—from parent windows to child windows.

How to do it...

In this recipe, you'll be using a combination of tables and closures to define the window hierarchy. Every window functionality will be defined inside the window object closure. This will make things easier to maintain in further steps. The following code shows an example of the window hierarchy with two levels defined by the table structure:

```
--[[ gui table contains all functions to create
window object closures --]]
local gui = {}
local main_window = gui.window {
  properties = {
    width = 128,
    height = 128,
    x = 0, y = 0, z = 0,
  },
  children = {
    gui.window {
      properties = {
        width = 128,
        height = 128,
        x = 32, y = 0, z = 0,
      },
      children = {},
    },
  },
}
```

There are several points of view in window hierarchy implementations. The first one deals with drawing child windows correctly. Also, if the parental window is invisible, child windows should be invisible too.

Another point of view addresses event propagation to child windows.

Child window rendering

Each window uses its own model-view matrix to draw the window on screen at the desired position. From this point, window rendering is fairly easy to implement. The only problem is how to obtain the correct form of model-view matrix so that the child window is always relative to its parent window. This can be solved by a hierarchically propagated update of the model-view matrix of children windows when you update the parent windows' parameters. This way you can assure that each child window honors the model-view matrix of its parent window and it prevents the application of unwanted side effects such as child window stretching when you resize its parent window.

This might seem to be an expensive operation but take into account that it uses the tree structure to eliminate unnecessary updates and additionally, such window updates do not occur very often.

The following sample code uses the object closure approach so that each window object can be constructed with a single function call and a single table that contains the initial window parameters. You'll see the benefits of this later in the code:

```
-- def - window definition
gui.window = function(def)
  -- window object instance
  local obj = {}
  local prop = def.properties
  obj.properties = props
  local children = def.children

  -- computed model-view matrix
  local modelViewMatrix
  -- window visibility property
  if type(def.visible)=="boolean" then
    obj.visible = prop.visible
  else
    obj.visible = true
    end
    -- event propagation for window
    if type(def.enabled)=="boolean" then
    obj.enabled = prop.enabled
  else
    obj.enabled = true
  end

  --[[ updates model-view matrices - function parameters are
  expected to be matrices, these will be also used in addition to
  local model-view matrix
  --]]
```

```lua
obj.update = function(...)
  local outermatrices = {...}
  -- reset model-view matrix to identity
  modelViewMatrix = matrix.dup()

  local scaleMatrix = S(prop.width or 1, prop.height or 1, 1)
  -- invScaleMatrix prevents of unwanted side-effect propagation
  local invScaleMatrix =  scaleMatrix.inv()

  table.insert(outerMatrices,
    T(prop.x or 0, prop.y or 0, prop.z or 0)
    * R(prop.rotateX or 0, prop.rotateY or 0, prop.rotateZ or 0,
      prop.rotateAngle or 0)
    * scaleMatrix
    * T(prop.originX or 0, prop.originY or 0, prop.originZ or 0)
  )

  for _, m in ipairs(outerMatrices) do
    modelViewMatrix = modelViewMatrix * m
  end

  for i, child in ipairs(children) do
    local prop = child.properties
    child.update(modelViewMatrix, T((prop.relativeX or 0),
    (prop.relativeY or 0), (prop.relativeZ or 0)),
    invScaleMatrix)
  end

  obj.modelViewMatrix = modelViewMatrix
end

obj.draw = function()
  if obj.enabled then
    -- apply shader program for GUI if it's not already used
    if obj.visible then
      -- draw window with current model-view matrix
      -- ...window rendering code...
      for _, child in ipairs(children) do
        child.draw()
      end
    end
  end
end
-- prepare model-view matrix before first use
```

```
      obj.update()
      return obj
   end
```

Notice that window rendering relies on two functions, `update` and `draw`. The `update` function generates the model-view matrix for the window and its children. The `draw` function simply draws the current window and the same process is recursively repeated on the child windows.

Event propagation

Windows and user controls need some form of interaction. This is usually achieved with the event system. This recipe will use the so-called signal slots. Each signal slot represents a specific type of the event and it consists of a list of functions that will be called consecutively. You can implement this by extending the window creation routine with signal storage and three functions, namely, `propagateSignal`, `addSignal`, and `callSignal`. The following sample code shows the basis of this implementation:

```
gui.window = function(def)
   -- ...previous code for window object initialization
   local signals = {}
   --[[ list of events are invoked only
if mouse cursor is over window --]]
   local onWindowEvents = {
      SDL.SDL_MOUSEMOTION,
      SDL.SDL_MOUSEBUTTONDOWN,
      SDL.SDL_MOUSEBUTTONUP,
   }
   -- does this window have a focus?
   obj.focused = false

   obj.propagateSignal = function(name, ...)
     if obj.enabled then
       local propagate, callSignal = true, true
    for _, eventName in ipairs(onWindowEvents) do
         if eventName == name then
           local mouse_x, mouse_y = unpack {...}
           if obj.isMouseOverWindow(mouse_x, mouse_y) then
             propagate = false
           else
             callSignal = false
           end
           break
         end
       end
```

```lua
      for _, child in ipairs(children) do
        if not child.propagateSignal(name, ...) then
          return false
        end
      end

      if callSignal then
        obj.callSignal(name, ...)
      end
      return propagate
    else
      return false
    end
end

obj.callSignal = function(name, ...)
  local list = signals[name]
  if type(list)=="table" then
    for i, action in ipairs(list) do
      if type(action)=="function" then
        if not action(obj, ...) then
          return false
        end
      end
    end
  end
  return true
end

obj.addSignal = function(name, fn)
  if not signals[name] then
    signals[name] = {}
  end
  local list = signals[name]
  if type(list)=="table" and type(fn)=="function" then
    table.insert(list, fn)
  end
end

obj.projectMouseCursorToWindow = function(mouse_x, mouse_y)
  local relativeMouseCoords = modelviewMatrix.inv()
  * {mouse_x, mouse_y, 0, 1}
  local T,S = matrix.translate, matrix.scale
```

```
      local originMatrix = T(prop.originX or 0, prop.originY or 0,
      0)
      local scaleMatrix = S(prop.width or 0, prop.height or 0, 1)
      local mouseCoordsOnWindow = scaleMatrix * originMatrix
        * relativeMouseCoords
      return mouseCoordsOnWindow[1], mouseCoordsOnWindow[2]
    end

    obj.isMouseOverWindow = function(mouse_x, mouse_y)
      local relativeMouseCoords = modelviewMatrix.inv()
      * {mouse_x, mouse_y, 0, 1}
      local wx,wy = relativeMouseCoords[1], relativeMouseCoords[2]
      return (wX<=0.5 and wX>=-0.5 and wY<=0.5 and wY>=-0.5)
    end

    -- handle window focus state
    obj.addSignal(SDL.SDL_MOUSEBUTTONUP,
      function(self, x, y, button)
        if button==1 then
          if gui.focusedWindow then
            gui.focusedWindow.callSignal('lostFocus')
            gui.focusedWindow.focused = false
          end
          gui.focusedWindow = obj
          gui.focusedWindow.callSignal('focus')
          obj.focused = true
        end
      end)

    -- ...window object finalizer code
    return obj
  end
```

Note that the `callSignal` function expects the signal functions to return a Boolean value. This helps to determine whether further signal functions should be called. This behavior allows you to literally consume the signal, if further processing of the event is not necessary.

However, for this to work, you'll need to modify the `handleEvent` function to route the event into the main window:

```
local function handleEvent(name, ...)
  main_window.propagateSignal(name, ...)
end
```

How it works...

The window hierarchy is based on the tree structure. Each node is represented by the window or control elements. Each node can contain a list of children windows.

Note that window definitions use table structures. Each one consists of window properties and a list of children elements.

The drawing process paints the windows from the top to the bottom level. Each window has two Boolean flags that define the painting behavior. If the window has the `enabled` flag set to false, it's invisible along with the children windows. On the other hand, if the window has the visible flag set to false, it's `invisible` but the drawing process continues on its children windows. This way you can create window containers that aren't visible to the user but they can override the behavior of its children windows. This is useful for making window element groups or scrollable window content.

The good thing is that you can draw each window with the same set of vertices. The only thing that changes for each window is its model-view matrix. This allows you to avoid unnecessary CPU/GPU data transfer, which will slow down your game. However, this approach is valid only for windows that share the same window shape. This recipe uses a simple rectangular shape.

Events are defined by simple structures represented by signals. Each signal uses its own ordered list of functions. Signal functions return a Boolean value that determines whether the signal should be propagated further.

The `propagateSignal` function is a bit more complex. It uses a list of events that are invoked only if the mouse cursor is over the current window. You must have noticed that it uses depth-first node traversal. This is especially useful when you click on a child window and you don't want the event to be propagated to parent windows. This will also ensure correct handling of the drag and drop feature for Windows.

See also

▶ The *Drawing a simple window* recipe

Showing the part of the window with the stencil test and window content scrolling

Sometimes you'll need to draw only a part of the window content inside the closed region. In this case, you could have used the scissor test to define the rectangular region. Pixels would be drawn only inside this region. The downside of this approach would be that this region is strictly rectangular and each side of the region would be parallel with the corresponding screen side.

In this recipe, you'll learn how to use stencil test, which provides a more general solution to this problem. Stencil test defines a bit mask with any shape.

Getting ready

Before getting started, make sure you have the stencil buffer available on your graphic card. Nowadays, almost any graphic card allows you to use stencil buffer with at least 8 bits per pixel depth. This will provide enough space to draw 255 masked layers of windows.

Be sure to initialize the stencil buffer before setting up the graphic mode with this code:

```
SDL.SDL_GL_SetAttribute(SDL.SDL_GL_STENCIL_SIZE, 8)
```

Note that the LuaSDL library doesn't use the stencil buffer by default.

How to do it...

To enable content slipping inside a window, you'll have to modify the window drawing function:

```
local stencilEnabled = false

gui.window = function(def)
  -- ...existing code of window object closure
  -- window content clipping
  obj.clip = def.clip
  -- model-view matrix for children elements
  obj.childMatrix = function(...)
    local outerMatrices = {...}
    local localMatrix = modelViewMatrix
    local scaleMatrix = S(def.width or 1, def.height or 1, 1)

    for _, m in ipairs(outerMatrices) do
      localMatrix = localMatrix * m
    end
```

```
      return localMatrix * scaleMatrix.inv()
end
-- modified window drawing function
obj.draw = function(parentData)
  if obj.enabled then
    local parentData = parentData or {}
    local parentStencilValue = parentData.stencilValue or 0x00
    local parentStencilMask = parentData.stencilMask or 0xFF
    local currentStencilValue = parentStencilValue
    local currentStencilMask = parentStencilMask

    -- apply shader program for GUI if it's not already used
    if obj.visible then
      if obj.clip then
        if not stencilEnabled then
          gl.Enable(gl_enum.GL_STENCIL_TEST)
          stencilEnabled = true
        end
        currentStencilValue = currentStencilValue + 1
        if currentStencilValue == 1 then
         gl.StencilOp(
            gl_enum.GL_REPLACE,
            gl_enum.GL_REPLACE,
            gl_enum.GL_REPLACE)
          gl.StencilFunc(
            gl_enum.GL_ALWAYS,
            currentStencilValue,
            currentStencilMask)
       else
          gl.StencilOp(
            gl_enum.GL_KEEP,
            gl_enum.GL_KEEP,
            gl_enum.GL_INCR)
          gl.StencilFunc(
            gl_enum.GL_EQUAL,
            parentStencilValue,
            parentStencilMask)
        end
        gl.StencilMask(0xFF)
      end
      -- draw window with current model-view matrix
      -- ...window rendering code...
      --[[ disable further writes to stencil buffer
```

```
                    and allow children elements to be rendered
          --]]
          if obj.clip then
            gl.StencilOp(
              gl_enum.GL_KEEP,
              gl_enum.GL_KEEP,
              gl_enum.GL_KEEP)
            gl.StencilFunc(
              gl_enum.GL_EQUAL,
              currentStencilValue,
              currentStencilMask)
            gl.StencilMask(0x00)
          end

          -- call custom drawing function
          callSignal('draw', obj.childMatrix())

          for _, child in ipairs(children) do
            child.draw({
              stencilValue = currentStencilValue,
              stencilMask = currentStencilMask,
            })
          end
          -- revert previous state of stencil buffer
          if obj.clip then
            gl.StencilOp(
              gl_enum.GL_KEEP,
              gl_enum.GL_KEEP,
              gl_enum.GL_KEEP)
            gl.StencilFunc(
              gl_enum.GL_EQUAL,
              parentStencilValue,
              parentStencilMask)
          end
          if stencilEnabled and currentStencilValue == 1 then
            gl.Disable(gl_enum.GL_STENCIL_TEST)
            stencilEnabled = false
          end
        end
      end
    end
```

```
    -- prepare model-view matrix before first use
    obj.update()
    return obj
end
```

There's one more thing left to do. You'll have to clear the stencil buffer before rendering the next frame. Otherwise, the stencil test will have unexpected results. Before clearing the stencil buffer, you'll need to set the current stencil bit mask to a `0xFF` value:

```
gl.StencilMask(0xFF)
gl.Clear(gl_enum.GL_STENCIL_BUFFER_BIT)
gl.StencilMask(0x00)
```

The following screenshot shows the result of the window content clipping on the scene with one main window and two inner windows:

How it works...

Masking with the stencil buffer usually consists of drawing a mask shape followed by object rendering. In this case, you can use a rendered window to produce a mask at the same time. Every window that applies clipping has its own stencil buffer value that represents the mask level.

The stencil test uses a reference value for testing, as well as for writing into the stencil buffer. This is set by the gl.StencilFunc function, where the first parameter presents a comparator function, the second is a reference value, and the third one is a bit mask. The behavior of the stencil test is set by the gl.StencilOp function, where this first parameter sets an action if the stencil test fails. The second parameter presents the operation if the depth buffer test fails, and the third one influences the operation if both the depth test and stencil test pass. Keep in mind that you can't write to the stencil buffer directly. Writing to the stencil buffer uses a bit mask defined by the gl.StencilMask function. This is also used when clearing the content of the stencil buffer. The stencil test affects rendering only if the GL_STENCIL_TEST flag is set.

This recipe uses the following approach. The stencil test is turned on the first window with content clipping. In this stage, the stencil test always passes so the first mask with value 1 is rendered into the stencil buffer. Every following window uses a different configuration, where, in the first step, OpenGL tests which parts of the window will be visible. In the next step, values in the stencil buffer that correspond to all the visible parts of the window are incremented by one. This procedure is repeated for each child window that has the clipping enabled.

Keep in mind that the stencil buffer clamps values to prevent the value overflow. Therefore, the maximum depth of the clipping is 255 with an 8-bit stencil buffer.

The following screenshot shows the content of a stencil buffer to get a better idea of how it works. The black color represents the stencil buffer value of 0, the gray color has a value of 1, and the white parts have a value of 2:

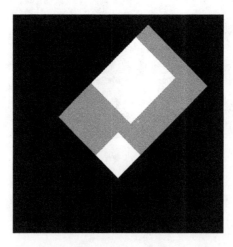

As you may have noticed, the sample code in this recipe calls the custom drawing function with the signal draw. This signal also receives a single parameter that contains the model-view matrix applicable for child elements. It can be used to draw more complex windows such as buttons with captions or edit boxes.

See also

▶ The *Drawing a simple window* recipe

Window controls and interaction

Now that you've got the basic functionality to draw and manipulate windows, you can design your own control elements such as buttons, edit boxes, and many other.

This recipe will show you how to create buttons and edit boxes that users can interact with. There will be three subsections where each one will deal with one king of control element.

Getting ready

This recipe will use the concepts of the previous window element to create window controls. You should be able to create and draw a window and handle input events. You'll be using mouse and keyboard events primarily.

First, you should extend the applicable event types with keyboard operations. You can do this by adding two event handlers, as shown in the following code:

```
events[SDL.SDL_KEYDOWN] = function(_event)
  local event = _event.key
  local key = event.keysym.sym
  local mod = event.keysym.mod
  if gui.focusedWindow then
    gui.focusedWindow.callSignal(SDL.SDL_KEYDOWN, key, mod)
  end
end
events[SDL.SDL_KEYUP] = function(_event)
  local event = _event.key
  local key = event.keysym.sym
  local mod = event.keysym.mod
  if gui.focusedWindow then
    gui.focusedWindow.callSignal(SDL.SDL_KEYUP, key, mod)
  end
end
```

For edit box control, you'll also need functions for bit operations from the `bit` library. You can include it with the following line:

```
local bit = require 'bit'
```

From now on, you can capture and process the keyboard input, which will be important to edit box user control.

How to do it...

The following lines will show you how to create user controls by extending the capabilities of basic windows.

Button

One of the most important user controls is a button. It's a specialized type of window that invokes a procedure on mouse button release. Buttons usually contain caption text or an image that describes the button action.

You can divide buttons into three groups by their behavior:

▸ **The momentary button**: Pressing this button down will perform an action

▸ **The toggle button**: Each press of this button will change the state of the action

▸ **The click button**: This action is performed when you press and release the button

The button object can be defined as an extension of the basic window object. The following code shows you how to implement the click button:

```
gui.clickButton = function(def)
   local obj = gui.window(def)
   local prop = obj.properties
   prop.caption = prop.caption or "Default button caption"

   obj.addSignal('draw', function(self, modelViewMatrix)
     local textPosition = modelViewMatrix * {0,0,0,1}
     -- draw caption text at position specified by textPosition
   end)

   obj.addSignal(SDL.SDL_MOUSEBUTTONUP,
     function(self, x, y, button)
       if button==1 then
         -- code to be invoked on button click
       end
     end)
   return obj
end
```

As you can see, extending the window object is a simple process because all the necessary handlers are already implemented in the base object.

You can implement other types of buttons in this fashion as well. The following sample code shows the implementation of the toggle button:

```
gui.toggleButton = function(def)
  local obj = gui.window(def)
  local prop = obj.properties
  prop.state = false

  -- code for custom drawing function...

  obj.addSignal(SDL.SDL_MOUSEBUTTONUP,
    function(self, x, y, button)
      if button==1 then
        prop.state = not prop.state
        -- code to be invoked on button state change
      end
    end)
  return obj
end
```

The following sample code shows the implementation of the momentary button:

```
gui.momentaryButton = function(def)
  local obj = gui.window(def)
  local prop = obj.properties
  prop.state = false

  -- code for custom drawing function...

  obj.addSignal(SDL.SDL_MOUSEBUTTONDOWN,
    function(self, x, y, button)
      if button==1 then
        prop.state = true
        -- code to be invoked on button press
      end
    end)
  obj.addSignal(SDL.SDL_MOUSEBUTTONUP,
    function(self, x, y, button)
      if button==1 then
        prop.state = false
        -- code to be invoked on button release
      end
    end)
  return obj
end
```

Edit box

Creating the edit box user control is a bit more complex mainly because you need to solve keyboard input handling. This user control usually uses caret cursor to visualize the current editing position in text. However, this recipe will deal mainly with keyboard input handling and virtual caret that's invisible to the user. That's because the correct positioning of the caret on screen needs to know the width of each letter, its exact position, and an amount of font kerning. This information is also vital to selecting a part of text using the mouse cursor. The problems of caret positioning exceed the scope of this book and it's not necessary to create fully working edit box controls.

If you're interested in correct caret cursor rendering, you can refer to *Chapter 3, Text Components with Custom Views* in the book *Core Swing: Advanced Programming* by *Kim Topley*. Alternatively, you can use the online reference manual to the Text API for the Java programming language at `https://docs.oracle.com/javase/tutorial/2d/text/index.html`.

The edit box implementation is shown in the following sample code:

```
gui.editbox = function(def)
  local obj = gui.window(def)
  local prop = obj.properties

  -- default values for selected properties
  prop.caption = prop.caption or "Default caption"
  prop.maxLength = prop.maxLength or 8
  prop.locale = prop.locale or os.setlocale()
  -- key repetition uses ms unit
  prop.keyRepeatDelay = prop.keyRepeatDelay or 500
  prop.keyRepeatInterval = prop.keyRepeatInterval or 100

  local caret = {
    pos = 0,
    visible = false,
  }; obj.caret = caret

  -- functions for caret movement and text deletion
  local keyboardFn = {
    [SDL.SDLK_LEFT] = function()
      if caret.pos>0 then
        caret.pos = caret.pos - 1
      end
    end,
    [SDL.SDLK_RIGHT] = function()
      if caret.pos<#prop.caption then
        caret.pos = caret.pos + 1
      end
```

```lua
    end,
    [SDL.SDLK_HOME] = function()
      caret.pos = 0
    end,
    [SDL.SDLK_END] = function()
      caret.pos = #prop.caption
    end,
    [SDL.SDLK_DELETE] = function()
      if caret.pos < #prop.caption then
        local tmpCaption = {}
        table.insert(tmpCaption, string.sub(prop.caption, 1,
        caret.pos))
        table.insert(tmpCaption, string.sub(prop.caption,
        caret.pos+2))
        prop.caption = table.concat(tmpCaption)
      end
    end,
    [SDL.SDLK_BACKSPACE] = function()
      if caret.pos > 0 then
        print('Backspace')
        local tmpCaption = {}
        table.insert(tmpCaption, string.sub(prop.caption, 1,
        caret.pos-1))
        table.insert(tmpCaption, string.sub(prop.caption,
        caret.pos+1))
        prop.caption = table.concat(tmpCaption)
        caret.pos = caret.pos - 1
      end
    end,
}

local keycodeTranslations = {
  -- standard locale for en-US keyboard layout
  ['C'] = {
    shift = {
      [0x31] = 0x21, [0x32] = 0x40, [0x33] = 0x23,
      [0x34] = 0x24, [0x35] = 0x25, [0x36] = 0x5E,
      [0x37] = 0x26, [0x38] = 0x2A, [0x39] = 0x28,
      [0x30] = 0x29, [0x60] = 0x7E, [0x2D] = 0x5F,
      [0x3D] = 0x2B, [0x5B] = 0x7B, [0x5D] = 0x7D,
      [0x5C] = 0x7C, [0x3B] = 0x3A, [0x27] = 0x22,
      [0x2C] = 0x3C, [0x2E] = 0x3E, [0x2F] = 0x3F,
    },
    keypad = {
```

```
            [SDL.SDLK_KP_DIVIDE] = 0x2F,
            [SDL.SDLK_KP_MULTIPLY] = 0x2A,
            [SDL.SDLK_KP_MINUS] = 0x2D,
            [SDL.SDLK_KP_PLUS] = 0x2B,
            -- period character on numpad is locale-dependent!
            [SDL.SDLK_KP_PERIOD] = 0x2E,
        },
    },
}


local band = bit.band

--[[ determine if pressed key is printable along with
      optional translation
--]]
local function isPrintable(key, mod)
  local key0 = key
  local keycodeTranslation = keycodeTranslations[prop.locale]
  -- defaults to C locale
  if not keycodeTranslation then
    keycodeTranslation = keycodeTranslations['C']
  end

  if key0 >= 0x20 and key0 < 0x7F then
    if band(mod, SDL.KMOD_SHIFT)>0 or band(mod, SDL.KMOD_CAPS)>0
    then
      -- big letters
      if key0>=0x61 and key0<= 0x7A then
        key = key0 - 0x20
      -- alternative characters for various keys
      elseif keycodeTranslation.shift[key0] then
        key = keycodeTranslation.shift[key0]
      end
    end
    return key
  elseif key0 >= 0x100 and key0 <= 0x10E and band(mod,
SDL.KMOD_NUM)>0 then
    -- numpad number keys
    if key0 <= 0x109 then
      return key0 - 0xD0
    -- numpad operator keys
    elseif keycodeTranslation.keypad[key0] then
      return keycodeTranslation.keypad[key0]
    end
```

```lua
    end
    return false
  end

local function processKeyboard(key, mod)
  local key0 = isPrintable(key, mod)
  -- insert character into caption at caret position
  if key0 then
    local tmpCaption = {}
    table.insert(tmpCaption, string.sub(prop.caption, 1,
    caret.pos))
    table.insert(tmpCaption, string.char(key0))
    table.insert(tmpCaption, string.sub(prop.caption,
    caret.pos+1))
    prop.caption = table.concat(tmpCaption)
    caret.pos = caret.pos + 1
  else
    -- caret movement
    local kFn = keyboardFn[key]
    if type(kFn)=="function" then
      kFn()
    end
  end
end

obj.addSignal('draw', function(self, modelViewMatrix)
  -- don't call font rendering if the caption is empty
  if #prop.caption>0 then
    local textPosition = modelViewMatrix * {0,0,0,1}
    -- draw caption text at position specified by textPosition
  end
end)

obj.addSignal(SDL.SDL_MOUSEBUTTONUP,
  function(self, x, y, button)
    if button==1 then
      -- code to be invoked on button click
    end
  end)

obj.addSignal('focus',
  function(self)
    caret.pos = 0
    caret.visible = true
```

```
          -- tunrn on key repetition
        SDL.SDL_EnableKeyRepeat(
          prop.keyRepeatDelay,
          prop.keyRepeatInterval)
      end)

    obj.addSignal('lostFocus',
      function(self)
        caret.visible = false
        -- disable key repetition
        SDL.SDL_EnableKeyRepeat(0, 0)
      end)

    obj.addSignal(SDL.SDL_KEYDOWN,
      function(self, key, mod)
        if obj.focused then
          processKeyboard(key, mod)
        end
      end)
    return obj
  end
```

Such an edit box is able to handle simple text editing with caret movement.

How it works...

As you have already noticed, apart from only using mouse events, this recipe deals with keyboard input events. Almost all events are propagated along with window hierarchy except for keyboard events. These are sent directly to the focused window. This is the known behavior of most window managers.

This recipe uses two user-defined events called `focus` and `lostFocus`. These events handle getting and losing window focus when clicking. You can use them to highlight specific user control as well.

The button user control primarily uses mouse button events. The action is performed only if certain conditions are met depending on the button type.

The edit box user control is much more complex as it requires you to handle the locale-specific text input. Unfortunately, older versions of the LibSDL library provide low-level keyboard input only. You can write your own keyboard handler to fit your needs or use the one provided with this recipe.

Keyboard inputs are divided into two categories. The first one represents key presses that write down printable characters. The second one deals with caret movement and text deletion.

The first case uses the `isPrintable` function to determine whether the pressed key is printable. On success, it returns the character code. There's also a shift key translation process that turns letters to uppercase if the *Shift* key is pressed or if the *Caps Lock* key is pressed, which sets the modifier. The translation process is used on other keys such as numbers, square braces, and others as well. The numeric keyboard block has numbers and mathematic operators as well so these keys are processed only if the num lock modifier is set.

A new character is put right at the caret position, which, by default, is positioned at the beginning of the caption text.

Notice that keyboard input uses the locale name obtained by the `os.setlocale()` function.

The caret movement is achieved with left and right cursor keys, the *Home* and *End* keys. The *Delete* and backspace keys present a special case where you have to take care to delete only the desired part of text. The *Delete* key maintains the caret position and deletes only the character in front of the caret. On the other hand, the backspace key deletes the character on the left of the caret position and moves the caret to the left. Both cases make sure that you won't delete the character or move outside the caption text.

The last thing that edit box handles are key repetitions, that is, if a key on the keyboard is pressed longer than a specified amount of time. This recipe uses the `SDL.SDL_EnableKeyRepeat` function provided by LuaSDL. You can set a delay before the first repetition and an interval for all succeeding repetitions with it. You can turn it off by setting both parameters to 0. The key repetition feature is useful only on text input. Otherwise it would make in-game movement with the keyboard rather strange. The following screenshot shows a scene with one parent window, one edit box control, and one button:

There's more...

You can add a special keystroke handler for certain key combinations such as *Ctrl + C*, *Ctrl + V*, and so on. This can be achieved by adding the following lines of code before the isPrintable function:

```
local band, bor = bit.band, bit.bor

local keystrokes = {
  [0x63] = {
    [SDL.KMOD_CTRL] = function()
    end,
  },
  [0x76] = {
    [SDL.KMOD_CTRL] = function()
    end,
  }
}

local function handleKeystroke(key, mod)
  local keyFns = keystrokes[key]
  if type(keyFns)=="table" then
    for modMask, keystrokefn in pairs(keyFns) do
      if band(mod, modMask)>0 then
        keystrokeFn()
        return true
      end
    end
  end
  return false
end
```

To make keystrokes work, you'll need to use handleKeystrokes in the processKeyboard function, resulting in the following code:

```
local function processKeyboard(key, mod)
  if handleKeyStrokes(key, mod) then
    --[[ you don't want further processing
        after successful keystroke
    ]]--
    return
  end
  local key0 = isPrintable(key, mod)
  -- ... previous code
end
```

The edit box control can be extended with clipboard capabilities with a newer version of the libSDL Lua binding called LuaSDL2. There are three clipboard functions: `hasClipboardText`, `getClipboardText`, and `setClipboardText`. You can find more information about this function at the libSDL2 wiki page at `https://wiki.libsdl.org/CategoryClipboard`.

The LuaSDL2 library obeys function specifications used in the plain libSDL2 library, so using them should be straightforward.

This way you can create fully operating edit box controls that are able to interact with shared content from other applications.

See also

- ► The *Drawing a simple window* recipe
- ► The *Displaying the text* recipe
- ► The *Using the window hierarchy* recipe

7
Physics and Game Mechanics

This chapter will cover following topics:

- ▶ Using Box2D with Lua
- ▶ Using vector math
- ▶ Choosing the correct vector scaling for the physics engine
- ▶ Creating static and dynamic objects
- ▶ Setting up object properties
- ▶ Moving objects
- ▶ Setting up bullets
- ▶ Running the physics simulation
- ▶ Detecting object collision
- ▶ Setting up object collision filtering
- ▶ Setting up object joints

Introduction

Physics simulation plays an important role in modern games. The first generation of games often used simplified math in a physics simulation to accommodate the CPU power at those times. Usually, it relied on the assumption that each frame took approximately the same time to render. This caused some games to run sluggishly or too fast on certain occasions. Another problem that arose from those simplifications was collision detection. The physical movement of an object isn't a continuous process. Instead, physical simulation uses small steps. The fast movement of objects results in larger steps and on certain occasions, the step might be large enough to skip a wall. For instance, you can shoot or run through a wall in some action games.

A good physical engine tries to eliminate most of these problems. This chapter will use the Box2D library for physical simulation in a 2D space.

Using Box2D with Lua

The Box2D library is a physical simulation engine developed in the C++ language. Fortunately, there's a binding to the Lua language called LuaBox2D. This recipe shows you how to prepare the LuaBox2D library for use in case there's no binary package available for your platform.

Getting ready

The LuaBox2D library uses the CMake building system to accommodate different platform needs. This also makes the preparation process almost painless and automatic. However, there are certain requirements to make this possible.

You'll will need the following:

- A C++11 standard compliant C++ compiler
- The CMake build system
- The Git versioning system
- The Lua 5.1 development package with header files and linkable libraries

After these requirements are satisfied, you can start building the LuaBox2D library.

How to do it...

First, you'll have to download the LuaBox2D repository content to your computer with the following Git command:

```
git clone --recursive https://github.com/soulik/LuaBox2D.git
```

This will create the LuaBox2D directory with the source files. In the next step, you'll need to prepare a working directory that will contain project files, as well as compiled binaries. This directory will be called `build` and can be created with the `mkdir` command:

```
mkdir LuaBox2D/build
```

You can move into the working directory with the following command:

```
cd LuaBox2D/build
```

Now, it's time to use CMake to prepare project building files. The easiest way to use CMake is to run the following command in the current directory:

```
cmake ..
```

Depending on the currently used platform, this will locate the Lua 5.1 header files and libraries and set up the building environment without the use of an intervention. This is mostly true on Unix-based systems where every file has its place. In case you're using the Windows operating system, you'll need to set the correct paths for the Lua 5.1 header and library files.

To make this easier, there's a graphical frontend for the CMake building system called `cmake-gui`. You can use it by issuing a similar command to the LuaBox2D directory:

```
cmake-gui ..
```

This will open up a CMake application window with the dialog window asking for your building environment type. Unix-based systems usually provide the `cmake` tool with a similar interface to `cmake-gui`, but it uses the `gui` console instead. The usage of this tool is exactly the same as in previous cases.

On the Windows operating system, you'll probably want to use Microsoft Visual Studio. The only settings you'll need to change are LUA_INCLUDE_DIR, LUA_LIBRARIES, and LUA_LIBRARY. The first one should point to the directory with header files from the Lua development package ending with .h. The other two should point to the Lua 5.1 library file ending with the .lib or .a extensions.

You can validate the settings by pressing the **Configure** button. If requirements are satisfied, all parts marked in the color red will turn white.

Clicking on the **Generate** button will complete the preparation for building the environment:

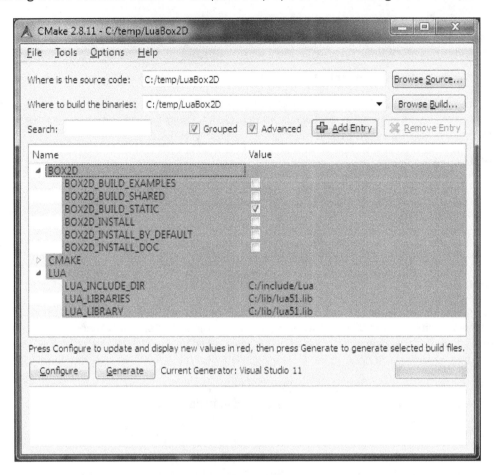

Now, you can use the building tool to actually build the LuaBox2D library. On the Windows operating system, you'll need to open the Microsoft Visual Studio solution file ending with the `.sln` extension and build it. On the Unix-based system, you can use the `make` command in the LuaBox2D directory.

If everything went well, you should be left with the LuaBox2D library file ending with the `.dll` or `.so` extensions inside the `build/bin` directory.

From this point, you can use the LuaBox2D library in your Lua scripts with the following line:

```
local box2d = require 'LuaBox2D'
```

How it works...

LuaBox2D presents an interface between the Lua language and the Box2D library, which is written in the C++ language.

The main issue is correct memory management of the Box2D objects to prevent application crashes and other unexpected behavior. LuaBox2D tries to elevate those concerns by doing all the hard work behind the scenes. Lua developers are presented with an easy-to-use interface and all the features that the Box2D library provides.

Most of this work is done with the next generation of the Lutok2 middleware library that connects the C++ language with Lua language environment. There are many other alternatives to this middleware library. Each one has its pros, cons, and limitations. This one tries to offer a full set of functions that the Lua language provides with certain perks the newest C++ language standard provides.

Using vector math

The Box2D library uses two-dimensional vectors in a form of its own native data type called b2Vec2. It's used in many places of the Box2D library so it's better to stick with this one.

This data type can be used to specify the position in a 2D space, directional vector with unit size or a speed vector. Keep in mind that Box2D doesn't know the difference between the uses of this vector.

Getting ready

This recipe expects the user to have a basic knowledge of vector math.

The LuaBox2D library contains the b2Vec2 object interface called Vec2. You can create one simply by calling its constructor function. Almost all object constructors are available via the LuaBox2D interface:

```lua
local box2d = require 'LuaBox2D'
local Vec2 = box2d.Vec2
```

This will define a shortcut for the Vec2 object constructor.

How to do it...

You can create a new `Vec2` vector object by calling the constructor in one of the following ways:

```
-- create zero vector
local vector1 = Vec2()
-- create a vector with x=1 and y=2
local vector2 = Vec2(1, 2)
```

The first case uses the `Vec2` object constructor without a parameter that will create a vector with both coordinates set to zero. This is also known as a zero vector. The second case uses the constructor parameters to set initial coordinate values.

Each `Vec2` vector object contains two coordinates: `x` and `y`. You can access and modify them directly as shown in the following sample code:

```
local vector = Vec2(1, 2)
vector.x = 10.5
vector.y = 13.25 + vector.x
```

The `Vec2` object provides the following set of mathematical operations: addition, subtraction, negation, scalar multiplication, dot product, and cross product. All operations are immutable, which means that each mathematical operation on vectors results in a new `Vec2` object. Unused vector objects are automatically cleaned with a garbage collection mechanism. This behavior is a part of the Lua language design.

The following table will show the usage of basic mathematical operations on the `Vec2` object where `v1` and `v2` variables present valid `Vec2` objects:

Operation	Lua notation
The addition of two Vec2 vectors	`v1 + v2`
The addition of the Vec2 vector with a scalar number	`v1 + 5.5`
The subtraction of two Vec2 vectors	`v1 - v2`
The subtraction of the Vec2 vector with a scalar number	`v1 - 5.5`
The Vec2 vector negation	`-v1`
The scalar multiplication of the Vec2 vector	`v1 * 5.5`
The dot product of two Vec2 vectors	`v1 * v2`
The cross product of two Vec2 vectors	`v1 % v2`

There are other operations available on vectors such as: vector equality comparison, the minimum and maximum of two vectors, vector normalization, vector length determination, the distance between two positional vectors, and the clamping of a vector.

Operation	Lua notation
Compare two vectors	`(v1 == v2)`
Get a minimum of two vectors	`v1.min(v2)`
Get a maximum of two vectors	`v1.max(v2)`

Get the vector length	`v1.length`
	or
	`#v1`

Obtain a distance between two positional vectors	`v1.distanceFrom(v2)`
Clamp a vector	`v1.clamp(Vec2(0,0),` `Vec2(1,1))`

How it works...

The `Vec2` object presents an interface between the Lua and Box2D world for the `b2Vec2` object. Its purpose is to make using 2D vectors easier.

Keep in mind that the `Vec2` object adds a small overhead because it must create the `b2Vec2` object before use, and with each call of the mathematical operator, it has to do an input validation.

Choosing the correct vector scaling for the physics engine

The Box2D library uses floating numbers to represent numerical values. The problem with these kind of numbers is that they offer limited precision. This limitation often results in various artefacts such as players walking right above the ground or boxes that can't remain in one place. Box2D uses the **MKS** (**meters**, **kilograms**, and **seconds**) system to represent the basic units. You should never use a pixel as a base unit. Therefore, you are expected to use the scaling factor to convert Box2D coordinates to pixels on the screen.

Getting ready

First, you should decide what scaling factor you will use. If you decide that 100 pixels will represent 1 meter, the scaling factor will be 100. You can define this factor as a global constant in the Lua language:

```
box2dScalingFactor = 100
```

How to do it...

When converting pixel-sized objects or vectors to the Box2D system, the scaling factor will be used to scale down by dividing all those values. The following pseudo code shows how to use scaling when you want to create a new Box2D object with pixel units:

```
-- definition of crate box dimensions
local crate_box = {
  width = 50,
  height = 50,
}
-- create a crate box physical object in Box2D system
local box2d_crate = box2d_create_box(
  crate_box.width / box2dScalingFactor,
  crate_box.height / box2dScalingFactor
)
```

The other situation is when you're rendering physical objects on the screen. You'll need to use the scaling factor to multiply the object's dimensions and its world position. The following pseudo code shows how to scale up physical objects from the Box2D system to match pixels and render it on the screen:

```
local box_position = box2d_crate.body.position *
  box2dScalingFactor

draw_box(box_position.x, box_position.y,
  crate_box.width, crate_box.height)
```

Notice that the `box2dScalingFactor` value was used on a `Vec2` vector object that represents the physical object's position in a world. This way, you use the Vec2 operators to convert a position based on the MKS unit system to pixels. You already know the crate box size in pixels, so you can use that in the `draw_box` function that draws a nice box in your game.

How it works...

The correct use of the floating point numbers comes from the fact that floating numbers offer a limited precision. The Box2D library uses a 32-bit floating number mainly due to performance reasons. However, you can't express every real number in a floating point variable. Therefore, a floating point math uses rounding to get an approximate value.

The creator of Box2D knows a great deal about this issue and empirically set the usable range of floating point numbers that can be used to simulate the physical environment and object interactions within certain limits. This is true not only for object coordinates but for movement vectors as well.

This is why you should appropriately scale your game world to match this range. Your objects should be within the range of 0.1 and 10 meters in size. This will guarantee a good level of simulation quality.

Creating static and dynamic objects

The Box2D library uses its own special representation of physical objects to achieve the simulation of physics. It's often desirable that some objects are fixed in place and other objects move after physical interaction.

This recipe will show you how to prepare physical objects with the LuaBox2D library in an environment of the Lua language.

Getting ready

First of all, you'll need to set up the world environment where all the physical objects will reside. To do this, you'll have to create a `World` object, as shown in the following sample code:

```
local gravity = Vec2(0, -10)
local world = box2d.World(gravity)
```

You'll often need to have only one `World` object. The `World` object constructor accepts one `Vec2` vector object to set the `gravity` vector. You can change it later with the following code:

```
world.gravity = Vec2(0, -5) -- uses unit m/s^2
```

Do note that the Box2D library uses metric units. The vector for gravitational acceleration uses *m*s-2*. However, you can change the overall scale of all the units to suit your game.

From this point , you've got the `World` object ready and you can create bodies of physical objects.

How to do it...

The Box2D library was designed with efficiency in mind. Therefore, initial body properties are defined in the `BodyDef` object that acts as a template for body objects. The `BodyDef` object contains initial properties of the body object such as the body type, position, angle, and damping. Box2D assumes that all objects are static by default. If you want the physical object to be dynamic, you'll have to set this property in the `BodyDef` object. The following lines show how to create a static object from the `BodyDef` definition:

```
local body_def = box2d.BodyDef()
body_def.type = 'static'
body_def.position = Vec(0,0)
-- angle uses radian units
```

```
body_def.angle = 0

local body = world.createBody(body_def)
```

This will create a body of physical objects. However, this object doesn't have a shape or size. To fix this, you'll need to create a fixture:

```
-- definition of crate box object
local crate_box = {
  width = 50,
  height = 50,
  density = 1,
}

local box_shape = box2d.PolygonShape()
box_shape.setAsBox(
  crate_box.width/box2dScalingFactor,
  crate_box.height/box2dScalingFactor)
local box_fixture = body.createFixture(box_shape,
  crate_box. density)
```

Now you have created a static box object that can act as a wall because no matter what you'll do, this box will stay in its place.

In contrast to static objects, dynamic objects can move and they are affected by forces. Creating a dynamic object is not much different from creating static ones. The following code shows you how to do it:

```
local body_def = box2d.BodyDef()
body_def.type = 'dynamic'
body_def.position = Vec(0,20)
-- angle uses radian units
body_def.angle = 0

local body = world.createBody(body_def)
-- definition of crate box object
local crate_box = {
  width = 50,
  height = 50,
  density = 1,
  friction = 0.1,
}

local box_shape = box2d.PolygonShape()
box_shape.setAsBox(
```

```
   crate_box.width/box2dScalingFactor,
   crate_box.height/box2dScalingFactor)

-- fixture definition
local fixture_def = box2d.FixtureDef()
fixture_def.shape = box_shape
fixture_def.density = crate_box.density
fixture_def.friction = crate_box.friction

local box_fixture = body.createFixture(fixture_def)
```

You can see that instead of using the shape and density as a parameter in the `createFixture` function, you can use the `FixtureDef` object as well. This way you can set all the important fixture parameters in a fixture definition object and reuse this definition later.

How it works...

Each physical object consists of a body and its fixture. The body of the object contains the position of the object's origin point, angle, damping values, and many other parameters. On the other hand, a fixture defines the physical properties of an object and its shape.

This library divides the physical object types into two main categories: static and dynamic objects. However, there's a third kind of objects called kinematic. Kinematic objects behave as if they have an indefinite mass and they don't respond to forces.

There's more...

The body object can contain more fixtures to achieve more complex object shapes. To create a new one, simply call the `createFixture` function. The Box2D library knows three more shapes you can use: `CircleShape`, `EdgeShape`, and `ChainShape`.

`CircleShape` represents a circle with a radius and a position of central point. `EdgeShape` can be used to define a line segment with two points. This one is often used on simple platforms but it's not that great on terrain. `ChainShape` can be used to create variously shaped terrains. You can see these shapes in the following code:

```
local circle_shape = box2d.CircleShape()
circle_shape.radius = 1
-- central point
circle_shape.m_p = Vec2(0,0)

local edge_shape = box2d.EdgeShape()
edge_shape.vertex1 = Vec2(-1, 0)
edge_shape.vertex2 = Vec2(1, 0)
```

```
local chain_shape = box2d.ChainShape()
chain_shape.createChain({
  Vec2(-1,0), Vec2(1,1), Vec2(2,1), Vec2(4, 0)
})
```

The body object can contain more than one fixture. You can cycle over the body object fixtures using the following code:

```
local current_fixture = body.fixture
while current_fixture do
  -- do something with Fixture object
  current_fixture = current_fixture.next
end
```

Setting up object properties

Physical objects in the Box2D simulation environment contain many customizable properties. You can use this to adapt object behavior to suit your needs.

Getting ready

First of all, you'll need an object to set properties on. For all properties to be effective, you can use a dynamic object:

```
local body_def = box2d.BodyDef()
body_def.type = 'dynamic'
body_def.position = Vec(0,0)
body_def.angle = 0

local body = world.createBody(body_def)
local shape = box2d.CircleShape()
shape.radius = 1

local fixture_def = box2d.FixtureDef()
fixture_def.shape = box_shape
fixture_def.density = 1

local fixture = body.createFixture(fixture_def)
```

Now that you've got everything prepared, you can set up physical object properties. Keep in mind that you should never change object properties during a simulation cycle as it will lead to simulation errors. You can determine this situation by querying the World object world. locked. The world object is locked when you're in the middle of the simulation process.

How to do it...

The body object offers parameters such as linear, angular damping, gravity scale, rotation locking, and many others.

Movement damping

Damping leads to the gradual slowing of object movement and it approximates the movement friction in the real world. Otherwise, the object would move indefinitely. While linear damping applies to linear motion, angular damping applies to rotational movement. You can access these parameters in a form of the body object properties:

```
body.linearDamping = 0
body.angularDamping = 0.1
```

Object gravity scale

Another parameter accessible on the body object is the gravity scale factor. This can be used to artificially decrease or increase the object's weight or make objects float:

```
-- normal gravity scale is equal to 1, floating objects can use 0
body.gravityScale = 1
```

Fixed rotation

When simulating the player's body, it's often desirable to lock object rotation. This is achievable by setting the `fixedRotation` property to `true`:

```
body.fixedRotation = true
```

Object sleeping

When simulation takes place, Box2D determines what objects are currently moving or interacting with other objects. Such objects are awake. Other objects are in a resting (idle) state. These are turned into a sleeping state when they are not moving at all or there are no other objects touching them for a certain period of time. This period of time is defined in the Box2D source code, and you should not change it unless you know what you're doing. This feature can greatly increase the physical engine performance.

You can obtain the object awake state with the `awake` property:

```
if not body.awake then
    -- do something
end
```

The object sleeping can be manually disabled with the `allowSleeping` property:

```
body.allowSleeping = true
```

Object mass and rotational inertia

Each body object contains information about its mass value in kilograms and inertia in the *kg*m2* unit. Body mass affects the object's ability to move in a linear movement. On the other hand, rotational inertia determines the ability to rotate. For instance, figure skaters can decrease their rotational inertia by pulling their arms. This allows them to spin faster.

You can't change these properties directly from the body object. However, these properties are indirectly accessible from the `massData` object that you can obtain with the `massData` property. The following lines of code will show you how to access and modify these properties:

```
local object_mass = body.mass
local object_inertia = body.inertia
local mass_data = body.massData
massData.center = Vec2(0, 0)
massData.mass = 10.0
massData.inertia = 0.9
```

So far, you've seen the use of properties that are accessible directly from the body objects. For physical properties of the object material, you'll have to use the `fixture` object. You can access the `fixture` object from the body object or use the object reference obtained from the `createFixture` function:

```
local fixture = body.fixture
```

The `fixture` object contains properties such as friction, restitution, and density.

Friction

Friction determines how much an object will move when its surface is in contact with another object. Objects with friction 1 will glide until damping slows them down:

```
body.fixture.friction = 0.5
```

Restitution

The restitution property affects the object elasticity on impact. For instance, you can use this property to simulate inflatable balls:

```
body.fixture.restitution = 0.6
```

Density

Density is usually set in the `BodyDef` object during the object's creation. It might be desirable to change this value as part of the object's heating simulation or size expansion:

```
body.fixture.density = 0.8
```

When you change the object's density, it's good to call `resetMassData` as well. This will apply the density property to the object mass and rotational inertia:

```
body.resetMassData()
```

How it works...

LuaBox2D contains interfaces for each Box2D object. This gives you the ability to experiment with various types of bodies and settings without much trouble as if you've used the Box2D C++ interface. The LuaBox2D library uses `UpperCamelCase` for object constructors. All object properties use `lowerCamelCase`.

For a more detailed description of all the available object properties, you can refer to the Box2D manual, which you can find online at `http://box2d.org/manual.pdf`.

Moving objects

Dynamic objects can be moved primarily by using forces. Moving objects by setting their position manually is not recommended because you can easily miss an object collision this way. However, you can set an object's position at the start of your game to adjust the initial object location.

Getting ready

For this recipe, you'll need a dynamic object with a nonzero mass and density:

```
local body_def = box2d.BodyDef()
body_def.type = 'dynamic'
body_def.position = Vec(0,0)
body_def.angle = 0

local body = world.createBody(body_def)
local shape = box2d.CircleShape()
shape.radius = 1

local fixture_def = box2d.FixtureDef()
fixture_def.shape = shape
fixture_def.density = 1.5
fixture_def.friction = 0.3
fixture_def.restitution = 0.2

local fixture = body.createFixture(fixture_def)
```

How to do it...

In the real world, you have to use a force to move objects. There are two ways in which you can apply a force to move objects in Box2D—the continual force and impulses.

The continual force

The continual force affects object movement gradually for a longer time. Depending on the previous state of an object's movement, this can take some time for the object to achieve the desired speed. You can either choose to apply force to certain points of an object or use the object's center. If you choose other to apply a force on a point other than the object's center, it will generate a torque and the object will rotate:

```
local point_on_object = Vec2(0.5, 0.5)
local linear_force = Vec2(1, 0)
local rotational_moment = 20

body.applyForce(linear_force, point_on_object, true)
body.applyForceToCenter(linear_force, true)
```

You can use the `applyTorque` function to change the angular velocity. The base unit for the rotational moment is *N*m*:

```
body.applyTorque(rotational_moment, true)
```

The last parameter of this function determines whether to wake the body object after the force has been applied. This is usually set to `true`.

Impulses

Impulses result in a sudden change of movement direction or speed. An impulse, in general, is a force applied over a time interval. They are usually used with a very large force over a very short time span. When the time is short enough, it can be approximated as an instantaneous change of velocity. Similarly, as in a case with the continual force, you can apply an impulse to a certain point of the object:

```
body.applyLinearImpulse(linear_force, point_on_object, true)
body.applyAngularImpulse(rotational_moment, true)
```

Object velocity information

Sometimes you'll need to get the current object velocity. For instance, this information is useful in the motion blur effect for fast moving objects. There are two types of velocity you can use: linear and angular velocity. Linear velocity is used for translation movement and it's represented by the `Vec2` vector.

Angular velocity tells you how fast the object rotates and uses units of radians per second:

```
local linear_velocity = body.linearVelocity
local angular_velocity = body.angularVelocity
```

You can use these properties to set the current object velocity as well but it results in unnatural movement. However, it can be useful when setting up an initial object velocity:

```
body.linearVelocity = Vec2(1, 0)
body.angularVelocity = 2
```

How it works...

Movement in Box2D is simulated in small discreet steps. The size of these steps varies with the time spent on frame rendering.

There are a few problems that a rise from discrete physics simulation. The most notable one is object tunneling when an object moves so fast that it literally teleports through the wall. Box2D eliminated this problem with continuous collision detection or CCD. Because CCD increases the processing time for each frame, it's turned off by default for all objects.

The maximum velocity of objects is 2 meters per time-step. This might seem small but take in to account that you usually use from 30 to 60 time-step frames per second, which gives you a maximum object speed from 60 to 120 meters per second or from 216 to 432 kms per hour. This limit exists to achieve better accuracy. To get greater speeds, you'll need to lower your physical world scale.

Setting up bullets

Objects usually move slow enough to stop before passing through walls. However, some objects might move so fast that they teleport through obstacles. This is especially true for bullet type objects. You can eliminate this problem by letting Box2D know that these objects should be treated as bullets. Some games use a ray-casting technique where you basically determine the point of the bullet's impact on a wall or another object. This usually assumes a bullet trajectory in a straight line, which is not very accurate when compared to the real world.

Getting ready

For this recipe, you'll need to have one dynamic object, bullet, and one static object, wall to build a sample scene. For this purpose, you can use the following code:

```
local function createBullet(position, radius)
  local body_def = box2d.BodyDef()
  body_def.type = 'dynamic'
```

```
        body_def.position = position * box2dScalingFactor
        body_def.angle = 0

        local body = world.createBody(body_def)
        local shape = box2d.CircleShape()
        shape.radius = radius * box2dScalingFactor

        local fixture_def = box2d.FixtureDef()
        fixture_def.shape = shape
        fixture_def.density = 1.5
        fixture_def.friction = 0.3
        fixture_def.restitution = 0.2

        body.createFixture(fixture_def)
        body.bullet = true
        return body
    end

    local function createWall(position, size)
        local size = size * box2dScalingFactor
        local body_def = box2d.BodyDef()
        body_def.type = 'static
        body_def.position = position * box2dScalingFactor
        body_def.angle = 0

        local body = world.createBody(body_def)choose
        local shape = box2d.PolygonShape()
        shape.setAsBox(size.x, size.y)

        body.createFixture(shape, 0)
        return body
    end
```

How to do it...

Now, with the basic function set, you can create a model scene with one bullet and four walls that enclose the space around the bullet so it won't escape to the outside world:

```
    local walls = {
        createWall(Vec2(0, -5), Vec2(10, 1)),
        createWall(Vec2(5, 0), Vec2(1, 10)),
        createWall(Vec2(0, 5), Vec2(10, 1)),
        createWall(Vec2(-5, 0), Vec2(1, 10)),
    }
```

```
local bullets = {
  createBullet(Vec2(0, 0), 0.5),
}
```

Bullet behavior for the body object is set by its property `bullet` to true. You can notice this in the `createBullet` function near the end. With this, bullet objects can run really fast and they will still collide with walls. Without this, the bullet would most probably run through the wall and into outer space.

How it works...

Box2D uses two phases for object collision detection: a broad phase and a narrow phase. A broad phase uses an internal dynamic tree structure to determine what objects will collide at a certain point in time. On the other hand, a narrow phase is used to denote the collision of two objects.

A bullet simulation takes collision detection further by using continuous collision detection or CCD for short. On each time-step, it sweeps objects along the path it took and tries to detect collisions with a time of impact. Do note that all collision detection uses the body shape of the object! After collision is detected, it moves an object to a location where these two objects nearly collide. After this, there might be another substep and time of impact events to complete object collision.

Running the physics simulation

The Box2D library uses the physics simulation divided into time steps. You can think of it as a world where you can control time. The Box2D library offers you two modes: the fixed-time step and the dynamic time step. It uses the fixed-time step by default, which is fine for accurate and stable simulation. This mode assumes that your game will have a constant frame-rate.

With the second simulation mode using the dynamic-time step, the world time doesn't flow continuously but rather in small steps with varying durations. The Box2D library can simulate object movement and collisions with relatively high accuracy regardless of the size of time steps, although the accuracy might suffer. However, this mode might sometimes be accompanied by sudden jumps between object positions. This issue can be remedied with the interpolation of object transformations between the previous and current state of the physical simulation. The interpolation code isn't included in this recipe but you can find inspiration from a great article, *Fix your timestep!*, by Glenn Fiedler. It's available at `http://gafferongames.com/game-physics/fix-your-timestep/`.

This recipe will show you how to use both modes with a fixed or dynamic time step.

Getting ready

This recipe will require you to have at least one `World` object. You can prepare one with the gravity vector set to match a value of the real-world gravitational acceleration approximated at *9.81 m*s2*:

```
local gravity = Vec2(0, -9.81)
local world = box2d.World(gravity)
```

Another thing to consider is the size of the time step in your game. This is related to the used rate of frames that is usually 30 or 60 frames per second or fps in short. Lower values of frames per second tend to make games more stuttering, but you'll have more time to process the game logic. Most of the movies use frame rates below 30 fps, 24 fps to be precise. This is what makes movies seem like movies. Higher frame rates make motion in movies look more lifelike. You can notice this difference between movies and some TV shows.

The size of the time step should be constant and should not relate directly to the current game frame-rate. This leads to more predictable results in simulation.

How to do it...

You can run one step of the physics simulation by using the `step` function in the World object. This function accepts three parameters: the size of a time step, number of iterations for the velocity constraint solver, and a number of iterations for the position constraint solver:

```
local desired_fps = 60
local time_step = 1/desired_fps
local velocity_iterations = 8
local position_iterations = 3

world.step(time_step, velocity_iterations, position_iterations)
```

A greater number of iterations increases the simulation stability and it's independent of the time step duration. Therefore, you should never compensate for larger time step durations with a larger number of iterations.

During the time step, some Box2D library processes: velocity, position, constraints, and collisions for each object if needed.

Usually, you'll want to use the `step` function periodically in each frame.

The fixed-time step

The following pseudo code shows the typical usage simulation stepping with the fixed-time step:

```lua
local function game_loop()
  while (game_running) do
    process_user_input()

    world.step(time_step,
      velocity_iterations,
      position_iterations)

    draw_objects_on_screen()
  end
end
```

The dynamic-time step

Physical simulation with the dynamic-time step assumes that you use an accurate source for the current time. For the sake of code simplicity, you'll be using the `os.clock` function which is available in plain Lua language:

```lua
local clock = os.clock -- returns approx. time used in seconds
local currentTime, timeAccum = 0, 0

local function game_loop()
  while (game_running) do
    process_user_input()
    local newTime = clock()
    -- incorporate maximum time for the simulation is the game
    -- runs too slow - less than 4fps
    local frameTime = math.min(newTime - currentTime, 0.25)
    currentTime = newTime
    -- timeAccum contains time spent by game logic and renderer
    timeAccum = timeAccum + frameTime
    -- loop to accommodate simulation with slower frame rate
    -- it'll advance simulation to match the time lost
    -- by the renderer if it takes more time than time_step
    while (timeAccum >= time_step) do
      world.step(time_step,
        velocity_iterations,
        position_iterations)
      timeAccum = timeAccum - time_step
    end
    draw_objects_on_screen()
  end
end
```

How it works...

Physical simulation problems are hard to solve accurately in general. Solving object position, movement, and collisions usually needs the use of differential equations. There are many methods for solving these equations. Each solver is better suited to different situations. Therefore, there's no best solver for differential equations.

The Box2D library uses the Symplectic Euler's integration method, which provides great performance with relatively good accuracy and stability with fewer time steps. This method is used to solve an ordinary differential equation, or ODE for short. It uses one independent variable (time) and its derivatives (position and velocity) to determine object location.

There's more...

The Box2D library supports a more advanced method of solving simulation with the fixed-time step duration and variable game frame rate. This method is called substepping.

Detecting object collision

The basic set of features that the Box2D library offers might be sufficient for simple games. However, sometimes you need to know when objects collide. For instance, in action games you usually shoot things and need to know what object was hit by your projectile.

Fortunately, the Box2D library offers an interface for collision detection in the form of callbacks. Using callbacks in the Lua language might not be straightforward because of the Lua language design. LuaBox2D contains a simple interface to set up callback functions for collision detection.

This recipe shows you how to define your own callback function in the Lua environment and how to process events when collision occurs.

Getting ready

First of all, you'll need a World object, some static walls, and at least one dynamic object. You can use the `createWall` and `createBullet` functions from the *Setting up bullets* recipe.

How to do it...

Object collision can be detected with the `ContactListener` object. It provides a simple interface to a set of callback functions that are called in various stages of collision. To be precise, there are four callback functions you can override: `beginContact`, `endContact`, `preSolve`, and `postSolve`.

First, you'll have to create the `ContactListener` object. After this step, you can set one of these callback functions to point to your function in the Lua environment.

The last step consists of setting a current contact listener in the World object to your new `ContactListener` object. The following sample code sets a new contact listener with callback functions:

```
local contact_listener = box2d.ContactListener()
contact_listener.beginContact = function(contact)
end
contact_listener.endContact = function(contact)
end
contact_listener.preSolve = function(contact, oldManifold)
end
contact_listener.postSolve = function(contact, contactImpulse)
end
world.contactListener = contactListener
```

How it works...

The Box2D library allows you to observe and analyze various stages of the object collision test. An important thing to remember is that callback functions are called during the time step. All the objects are in a locked state during this stage and you shouldn't change the objects' properties. This would lead to computational errors and instability. Now, because all the callback functions are defined in the Lua environment, it's fairly easy to postpone such changes on objects until the current time step is complete.

The beginContact callback

This function is called before fixtures begin to touch. Although this function gives you only one parameter in the form of a `Contact` object, it offers you everything you'll need.

The Contact object consists of many properties, but most notable among them are `manifold`, `isTouching`, `enabled`, `fixtureA`, `fixtureB`, and `next`.

The manifold contains a list of contact points between two fixtures. A property `isTouching` tells you if these two fixtures are actually touching. You can disable further collision testing for these two fixtures by setting the `enabled` property to false. Both fixtures are available from the `fixtureA` and `fixtureB` properties. You can access respective body objects for each of these two fixtures, and it's often used in conjunction with user data to get information about which game objects have collided.

Don't forget that there might be more than one contact. You can get the next `Contact` object with the `next` property.

The endContact callback

This function is used when two objects cease to collide. Similarly, as with the `beginContact` callback function, you've got only one parameter—the `Contact` object.

The preSolve callback

The Box2D library calls this function whenever contacts are updated. This gives you a chance to inspect a contact just before it's used in the solver. This function gives you two parameters: the `Contact` object and the `oldManifold` object. This way, you detect changes in contact points.

This function is rarely used in games.

The postSolve callback

This function lets you inspect resulting contacts after the solver has finished its job. This is particularly useful if you want to inspect contact impulses. Contact impulses can help you determine the outcome of the collision response after the solver has processed all the contacts.

The `PostSolve` callback accepts two parameters—the `Contact` object and the `ContactImpulse` object, which contains a list of contact impulses.

Do note that Box2D might call the `preSolve` and `postSolve` callbacks many times even when there's only one collision. This is a result of approximation in the solver.

There's more...

The following sample code shows how to use `ContactListener` with user data to know exactly which game objects did collide:

```
local wall = createWall(Vec2(0,0), Vec2(5,1))
local bullet = createBullet(Vec2(0, 5), 1)
wall.userData = {
  name = 'Wall'
}
bullet.userData = {
  name = 'Bullet'
}

local contact_listener = box2d.ContactListener()
contact_listener.beginContact = function(contact)
  local bodyA = contact.fixtureA.body
  local bodyB = contact.fixtureB.body
  local dataA = bodyA.userData
```

```
    local dataB = bodyB.userData
    if type(dataA)=="table" and type(dataB)=="table" then
      print(dataA.name, 'has collided with', dataB.name)
    end
  end
```

As you can see, the `userData` property can refer to any Lua value. This value is bound to the Body object and if you destroy the Body object, you'll lose the reference to the `userData` value as well. Therefore, it's always better to store the object data somewhere in your Lua environment and use `userData` only to store references in it.

You can use `userData` on the `Fixture` object as well to store fixture-specific information.

Setting up object collision filtering

Object collision might not be always desirable. For example, if your game allows multiplayer, it can be frustrating when another player blocks your movement right in front of doors and you can't get past them. The Box2D library solves this problem with the binary mask for collisions.

Getting ready

This recipe will require a basic understanding of bitwise operations. You'll need at least two `FixtureDef` or `Fixture` objects.

How to do it...

The Box2D library uses a pair of two 16-bit binary masks to determine whether two objects should collide. The first one is called `categoryBits` and it indicates the object category. The second one uses the name `maskBits` and it indicates what object categories are allowed to collide with the current object. The following sample code shows the typical uses of these bit-masks in the `FixtureDef` object:

```
    local fixture_def = box2d.FixtureDef()
    fixture_def.shape = shape
    fixture_def.density = 1.5
    fixture_def.friction = 0.3
    fixture_def.restitution = 0.2

    fixture_def.filter.maskBits = 0x0001
    fixture_def.filter.categoryBits = 0x0002
```

Usually, you set these bit masks in the `FixtureDef` object before actually creating the `Fixture` object. However, you may change filtering settings later with a small overhead as this will automatically call the `refilter` function in the fixture object to update Box2D's internal state.

The following sample code shows how to update fixture masks on the go:

```
local new_filter = box2d.Filter()
new_filter.maskBits = 0x0000
new_filter.categoryBits = 0x0002
body.fixture.filter = new_filter
```

This will cause the fixture to not collide with anything because `maskBits` is set to a zero value.

How it works...

The Box2D library uses 0xFFFF masks and 0x0001 category bits by default for every Fixture object you've created. This leads to a situation where every object can collide with other objects.

Before the collision occurs, the Box2D library tests if such a collision is allowed by using the AND binary operation. If the result is nonzero it means that the collision is allowed. The following pseudo code shows how this binary test looks:

```
result = (current_object.categoryBits & other_object.maskBits)
if result > 0 then
  -- collision allowed
else
  -- skip collision
end
```

The advantage of using bit-masks in collision detection is that it can skip the whole process of computing collision points and you can save a bit of performance in your game.

There's more...

For special situations where objects are somehow related, you can use the `groupIndex` property on the Filter object. The same positive numbers mean that these two objects should always collide. On the other hand, the same negative numbers indicate that these two objects should never collide. This property has a higher precedence over mask and category bits. If this property is set to zero or the `groupIndex` values don't match, collision testing will use mask and category bits:

```
local FD = box2d.FixtureDef
local f1,f2,f3,f4 = FD(), FD(), FD(), FD()
f1.filter.groupIndex = 42
f2.filter.groupIndex = 42
```

```
f3.filter.groupIndex = -3
f4.filter.groupIndex = -3
```

Fixtures `f1` and `f2` can always collide, but fixtures `f3` and `f4` will never collide.

Setting up object joints

Joints present a way of two or more connected objects with a certain type of constraint. The Box2D library offers several types of joints between objects. This type of object connection is useful when simulating arms, wheels, or more complex objects such as cars, robots, and so on.

Getting ready

You'll need at least two dynamic objects to use joints. This recipe will use two rectangular bodies that will be used with various types of joint connections. To make things easier, the following sample code offers a simple function that prepares a rectangular body that will be used many times in this recipe:

```
local makeBox = function(position, size, angle)
  local size = size * box2dScalingFactor
  local bodyDef = box2d.BodyDef()
  bodyDef.type = 'dynamic'
  bodyDef.position = position * box2dScalingFactor
  bodyDef.angle = math.rad(a)

  local body = world.createBody(bodyDef)
  local box = box2d.PolygonShape()
  box.setAsBox(size.x, size.y)

  local fixtureDef = box2d.FixtureDef()
  fixtureDef.shape = box
  fixtureDef.density = 0.1
  fixtureDef.friction = 0.3
  fixtureDef.restitution = 0.2
  body.createFixture(fixtureDef)
  return body
end
```

Now, you can create two rectangular bodies that will be used for each joint type:

```
local bodyA = makeBox(Vec2(0, 50), Vec2(2, 2))
local bodyB = makeBox(Vec2(10, 50), Vec2(2, 2))
```

The following screenshot shows a scene with two red boxes next to each other. There are four static green walls around the scene to keep the red boxes inside. This scene will be used as a base for each type of joint between those two red boxes.

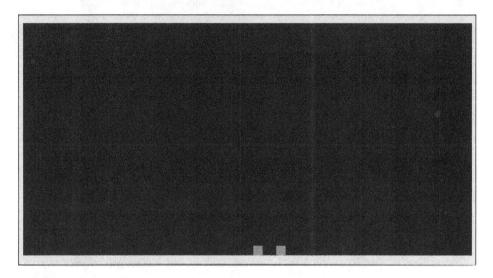

The Box2D library offers 11 types of joints. Each creation of a joint is preceded by the joint definition object that is used in a similar fashion to the `BodyDef` and `FixtureDef` objects.

The following sections will show you how to prepare the joint definition object and use it to create respective Joint objects.

Revolute joint

This type of joint is one of the most used joints in games mainly because of its versatility. You can use it to simulate arms, worms, trap doors, and many others.

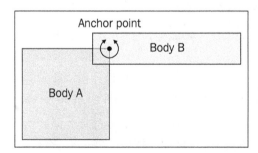

First, prepare the joint definition object. Revolute joint types use `RevoluteJointDef`:

```
local anchorA = Vec2(5, 0)
local anchorB = Vec2(0, 0)

local jd = box2d.RevoluteJointDef()
jd.bodyA = bodyA
jd.bodyB = bodyB
jd.collideConnected = false
jd.localAnchorA = anchorA
jd.localAnchorB = anchorB
```

This is the simplest form of the definition object for revolute joint types. Note that this joint uses one anchor point for each body. The anchor point uses relative coordinates from the origin point of the body and defines a local point of rotation axis.

Now you can create the `RevoluteJoint` object by calling the `createJoint` function on the `World` object:

```
local joint = world.createJoint(jd)
local revolute_joint = box2d.RevoluteJoint(joint)
```

After you create the revolute joint, it tries to merge anchor points into one. Also, notice that there's the `box2d.RevoluteJoint` constructor used to actually convert generic joint type to `RevoluteJoint`. You only have to show this if you want to change joint properties over time.

You can define limits for angular motion such as the maximum angle and minimum angle:

```
jd.enableLimit = true
jd.lowerAngle = math.rad(-45)
jd.upperAngle = math.rad(45)
```

The revolute joint can be used as a motor joint if you wish, where speed uses rad/s units:

```
jd.enableMotor = true
jd.motorSpeed = math.pi*2
jd.maxMotorTorque = 10
```

Motor should always have a reasonable limit for torque defined by the `maxMotorTorque` property. This property uses *N*m* units.

The prismatic joint

The prismatic or slider joint is used commonly for elevators, moving platforms, sliding doors, and pistons. This joint fixes the angle between two bodies and moves them along a specified axis.

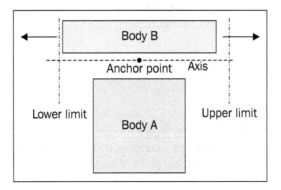

Joint definition for the prismatic joint can look like the following:

```
local anchorA = Vec2(5, 0)
local anchorB = Vec2(0, 0)
local axisA = Vec2(1,0)

local jd = box2d.PrismaticJointDef()
jd.bodyA = bodyA
jd.bodyB = bodyB
jd.collideConnected = false
jd.localAnchorA = anchorA
jd.localAnchorB = anchorB
jd.lowerTranslation = -10
jd.upperTranslation = 10
jd.enableLimit = true
jd.axisA = axisA
```

There are additional parameters for this joint. You can motorize this joint with these three parameters:

```
jd.enableMotor = true
jd.maxMotorForce = 1
jd.motorSpeed = math.pi/4
```

You can create the `PrismaticJoint` object with the `createJoint` function in the World object:

```
local joint = world.createJoint(jd)
local prismatic_joint = box2d.PrismaticJoint(joint)
```

This joint uses anchor points for each body object, as well as axis vector for translation movement. You can set up additional constrains to limit translation movement by using the `lowerTranslation`, `upperTranslation`, and `enableLimit` properties.

The movement axis is set by the `axisA` property and its position is set by the anchor point of the first body.

The distance joint

The distance joint is used when you need to maintain a constant distance between two bodies or anchor points, to be precise.

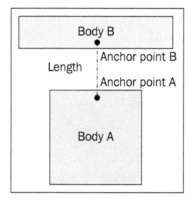

Definition for this type of joint can look like the following code:

```
local anchorA = Vec2(5, 0)
local anchorB = Vec2(0, 0)
local distance = 20

local jd = box2d.DistanceJointDef()
jd.bodyA = bodyA
jd.bodyB = bodyB
jd.collideConnected = false
jd.localAnchorA = anchorA
jd.localAnchorB = anchorB
jd.length = distance
```

This joint can behave like a spring to a certain measure. You can set this with these two properties—`frequencyHz` and `dampingRatio`:

```
jd.frequencyHz =5
jd.dampingRatio = 0.8
```

The `DistanceJoint` object is created with the `createJoint` function in the `World` object:

```
local joint = world.createJoint(jd)
local distance_joint = box2d.DistanceJoint(joint)
```

The rope joint

The rope joint works in a very similar fashion to the distance joint with one exception. Instead of maintaining a constant distance from the other object, this one uses the maximum distance constraints. As the name suggests, the rope joint is great for rope simulation like in the *Tarzan* movie:

The `RopeJoint` definition looks like the following code:

```
local anchorA = Vec2(5, 0)
local anchorB = Vec2(0, 0)
local max_length = 20

local jd = box2d.RopeJointDef()
jd.bodyA = bodyA
jd.bodyB = bodyB
jd.collideConnected = false
jd.localAnchorA = anchorA
jd.localAnchorB = anchorB
jd.maxLength = max_length
```

The only difference between the `DinstanceJointDef` object is in the `maxLength` property. This will set the length of a rope.

The rope joint is created with the following code:

```
local joint = world.createJoint(jd)
local rope_joint = box2d.RopeJoint(joint)
```

The weld joint

The weld joint is the simplest type of joint that connects two bodies. It is very similar to the distance joint, but it locks the body rotation as well. With this joint, two bodies behave as if they are one body. Therefore, bodies keep the same orientation and constant distance.

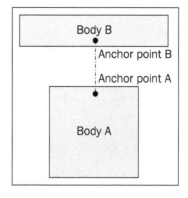

You can define this joint with the following lines of code:

```
local anchorA = Vec2(5, 0)
local anchorB = Vec2(0, 0)
local referenceAngle = 0

local jd = box2d.DistanceJointDef()
jd.bodyA = bodyA
jd.bodyB = bodyB
jd.collideConnected = false
jd.localAnchorA = anchorA
jd.localAnchorB = anchorB
-- mass-spring-damper frequency
jd.frequencyHz = 0
jd.dampingRatio = 0
jd.referenceAngle = referenceAngle
```

The weld joint can have a certain amount of stiffness set by the `frequencyHz` and `dampingRatio` properties. You can disable damping completely by setting `dampingRatio` to 0. Another thing is the `referenceAngle` property. This one is used to set the initial angle between two bodies. Usually, this angle is set to zero, which means that bodies manage the angle as they did before the joint application.

You can create the `WeldJoint` object with the following two lines:

```
local joint = world.createJoint(jd)
local weld_joint = box2d.WeldJoint(joint)
```

The pulley joint

The pulley is a special type of joint where two bodies are attached to a virtual rope and this rope hangs in the air. This can be useful to simulate various traps or hanging platforms.

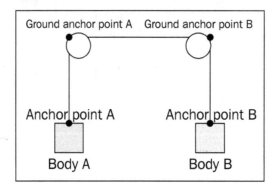

The following sample code contains the definition for the pulley joint. Notice that you can set the pulley ratio to simulate, block, and tackle:

```
local anchorA = Vec2(0, 0)
local anchorB = Vec2(0, 0)
local groundAnchorA = Vec2(-10, 40)
local groundAnchorB = Vec2(10, 40)
local lengthA = 20
local lengthB = 20
local ratio = 1

local jd = box2d.PulleyJointDef()
jd.bodyA = bodyA
jd.bodyB = bodyB
jd.collideConnected = false
jd.localAnchorA = anchorA
jd.localAnchorB = anchor
jd.groundAnchorA = groundAnchorA
jd.groundAnchorB = groundAnchorB
jd.lengthA = lengthA
jd.lengthB = lengthB
jd.ratio = ratio
```

In this situation, each body is attached to the rope at a local anchor point. The rope hangs at one or two places in the air, set by the ground anchor point. Be sure to set up the rope length at each side. It's recommended to place static objects around the ground anchor point to prevent bodies from being pulled out of the pulley. In reality, this can't happen but it can cause inconsistencies in the pulley simulation.

The pulley joint is created after the `createJoint` function call in the World object:

```
local joint = world.createJoint(jd)
local pulley_joint = box2d.PulleyJoint(joint)
```

The wheel joint

The wheel joint is a renamed version of the so-called line joint that was used in earlier versions of the Box2D library. This one behaves like a combination of the prismatic joint for spring and shock absorber and the revolute joint for a wheel. It is commonly used when simulating cars.

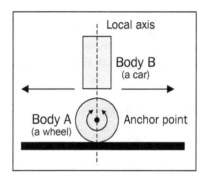

You can define the wheel joint with the following code:

```
local anchorA = Vec2(0, 0)
local anchorB = Vec2(0, -5)
local axisA = Vec2(0, 1)

local jd = box2d.WheelJointDef()
jd.bodyA = bodyA
jd.bodyB = bodyB
jd.collideConnected = false
jd.localAnchorA = anchorA
jd.localAnchorB = anchorB
jd.axisA = axisA
```

You can set a hardness of wheel hinge with the `frequencyHz` and `dampingRatio` properties:

```
jd.frequencyHz = 5
jd.dampingRatio = 0.8
```

Now you can use this joint definition to create the `WheelJoint` object:

```
local joint = world.createJoint(jd)
local wheel_joint = box2d.WheelJoint(joint)
```

The wheel joint can rotate a wheel by itself. You'll just have to set the motor parameters and enable the motor by setting the `enableMotor` property:

```
-- one rotation over 4 seconds
wheel_joint.motorSpeed = math.pi/4
-- max torque is 10 Nxm
wheel_joint.maxMotorTorque = 10
wheel_joint.enableMotor = true
```

After this, you can easily notice that the wheel is slowly rotating.

The gear joint

The gear joint connects the other two joints to the virtual gear. However, this type of joint works only with revolute and prismatic joints. There are three possible variations: two revolute joints, two prismatic joints, and one revolute with the prismatic joint. In any case, the gear joint uses a ratio to measure the movement of the other joint. This is the type of joint that can be used, for example, on cog-wheels, platforms on wheels, or hydraulic lifts. You can see these three scenes in the following three diagram.

The first one shows a scene with cog-wheels:

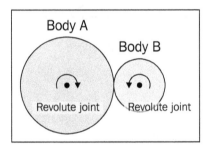

The second one illustrates a platform on wheels:

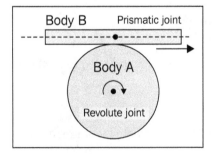

The last one contains a scene with hydraulic lifts:

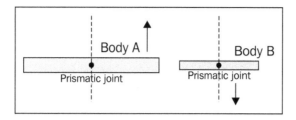

The gear joint definition will look like this:

```
local jd = box2d.GearJointDef()
jd.bodyA = bodyA
jd.bodyB = bodyB
jd.collideConnected = false
jd.joint1 = revolute_joint1
jd.joint2 = revolute_joint2
jd.ratio = 1
```

Keep in mind that movable objects should always be set in the `bodyB` property for each of these two joints: `joint1` and `joint2`. Otherwise, it won't be moving objects you expected.

You can change the movement direction of the other object with a negative ratio.

Now you can finalize this joint by calling the `createJoint` function in the World object:

```
local joint = world.createJoint(jd)
local gear_joint = box2d.GearJoint(joint)
```

The motor joint

Sometimes you need to control the movement of the body relative to the other body. The motor joint is designed exactly for this task. This can be used to push the body to always be next to another object at a certain relative position. You can use this to create interactive popups or icons that hover above the player's head.

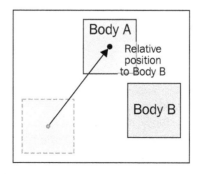

You can define the motor joint with the following code:

```
local jd = box2d.MotorJointDef()
jd.bodyA = bodyA
jd.bodyB = bodyB
jd.collideConnected = true
jd.linearOffset = Vec(0, 5)
jd.angularOffset = 0
jd.maxForce = 1
jd.maxTorque = 1
jd.correctionFactor = 0.3
```

As you can there, there are many options to set. For instance, you can set a relative position with the `linearOffset` property. You can also set a relative angle with the property `angularOffset` so the object will try to be at a certain angle relative to the other one. Sometimes, you might want to slow down hovering over the object. To do this, you can experiment with different values for the `maxForce` and `maxTorque` properties. The final option you can use is `correctionFactor`, which sets the measure of how much will hovering object try to accommodate with a new position.

The `MotorJoint` object can be finalized with the following two lines:

```
local joint = world.createJoint(jd)
local motor_joint = box2d.MotorJoint(joint)
```

The mouse joint

This type of joint works in a similar way to the `MotorJoint` object, but instead of using the relative position to the other object, this one uses world coordinates.

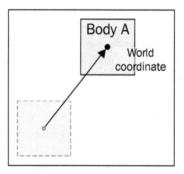

The `MouseJoint` object is used primarily in the Box2D TestBed application to test out the model situations with various objects and constraints. Even when this joint isn't included in the Box2D documentation, you can certainly find its use for special cases. For instance, if you've got a space simulator game, you can move your ship by clicking with your mouse button somewhere in the space. The ship will slowly follow the destination specified in the world coordinates.

The `MouseJoint` object definition can look like the following code:

```
local target_x = 0
local target_y = 0

local jd = box2d.MotorJointDef()
jd.bodyA = bodyA
jd.bodyB = bodyB
jd.collideConnected = true
jd.target = Vec(target_x, target_y)
jd.maxForce = 1
jd.frequencyHz = 5
jd.dampingRatio = 0.7
```

Target coordinates use world space coordinates and they are set in the `target` property. You can maximize the speed of the ship by changing the `maxForce` property. You can take a measure of the movement elasticity with the `frequencyHz` and `dampingRatio` properties.

The `MouseJoint` object is created with the following code:

```
local joint = world.createJoint(jd)
local mouse_joint = box2d.MouseJoint(joint)
```

The friction joint

The friction joint is used mostly as the name suggests, to add friction to the movement at certain places. For instance, it you're making a platform game, the player can sometimes jump from heights. If you've implemented a fall damage, this type of joint can come in handy. You can create special landing platforms that add friction to the player's falling movement, and therefore, save them from breaking their bones. Other examples of use can be found in the wind simulation where the friction joint slows down the player when running.

The friction joint can be defined as follows:

```
local anchorA = Vec2(0, 0)
local anchorB = Vec2(0, 0)
local max_force = 0.8
local max_torque = 0.9

local jd = box2d.FrictionJointDef()
jd.bodyA = bodyA
jd.bodyB = bodyB
jd.collideConnected = false
jd.localAnchorA = anchorA
jd.localAnchorB = anchorB
jd.maxForce = max_force
jd.maxTorque = max_torque
```

Greater values of `maxForce` and `maxTorque` have a greater damping effect on objects. Do note that anchor points might not have any significant effect on the friction of movement.

You can complete the friction joint with the following two lines:

```
local joint = world.createJoint(jd)
local friction_joint = box2d.FrictionJoint(joint)
```

How it works...

The Box2D objects usually have three degrees of movement freedom; these are horizontal movement, vertical movement, and rotation around the *z* axis (out of your screen's direction). This might not be desirable for certain cases. Joints limit object movement specifically to used joint types.

However, these movement constraints might not always be exact mainly due to computational and rounding errors. Even with these inaccuracies, you should be fine as long as you're not doing 100 percent physically correct simulations or using inappropriate values for world scaling.

Each joint is created in two steps. First, you have to create a joint definition, and after this step you can use this joint definition as many times as you desire. The last step is joint creation with the `createJoint` function in the `World` object.

The joint object needs to be contained within your Lua environment because the `Joint` object can be garbage collected when unused. After this process, your Joint object will no longer exist. It's better to put the Joint object into the Lua table, which will keep the Joint object alive. This table should exist at least until the scene finishes.

See also

▶   The *Choosing the correct vector scaling for the physics engine* recipe

8
Artificial Intelligence

This chapter will cover the following recipes:

- ▸ A simple pathfinding algorithm for a maze
- ▸ Pathfinding for tile-based environments with obstacles
- ▸ Using a fuzzy logic for decision making

Introduction

This chapter will show you how to add a bit of intelligence into your game. However, this does not mean that your game characters will be able to behave like real-life people. Instead, they will be able to handle specific situations with a predefined set of rules. This adds a realistic-looking behavior to the game characters.

The earlier games used a simple mechanism with static environment and static movement paths. Nonplayer characters or NPCs could move only along certain paths and couldn't handle changes in the game environment. You could see this in the *Super Mario Bros* series.

The next step in artificial intelligence was introduced in 3D action games such as *Doom*. NPCs always try to approach the player character after they've been alarmed about the player's presence. But still, they can't handle the simplest obstacles. A certain level of intelligence is emulated with special skills to make the games more challenging.

Modern games use a static or dynamic set of paths to move from one point to another. The advantage of static paths is that these are usually well designed within certain game environments and allow NPCs to move to other locations even if there are obstacles. The downside of this approach is that this set of paths must be prepared by game developers and it usually can't be changed during gameplay. What's more, it can't respond to dynamic changes in the environment.

Dynamic paths are used in some games today to incorporate intelligent movement in changing game environments. This consists of graph-like structures, where significant locations are marked as graph nodes and paths between these nodes can contain a set of instructions to successfully move between these two locations. However, this approach is the hardest to implement and it's more computationally intensive as well.

Artificial intelligence in games is used not only for pathfinding, but also for NPC behavior. This kind of AI can be divided into two categories: static and dynamic. Most games use static behavioral AI with a set of rules that define NPC actions on certain inputs. The downside of static AI is that it can't learn new things. Dynamic behavioral AI usually uses neural network expert systems with a feedback loop (observation) to generate a set of rules on top of predefined static rules. A typical example of such a system is the H.A.L. 9000 computer in *A Space Odyssey* or a robot in the *Terminator* movie series.

A simple pathfinding algorithm for a maze

Maze pathfinding can be used effectively in many types of games, such as side-scrolling platform games or top-down, gauntlet-like games. The point is to find the shortest viable path from one point on the map to another. This can be used for moving NPCs and players as well.

Getting ready

This recipe will use a simple maze environment to find a path starting at the start point and ending at the exit point. You can either prepare one by yourself or let the computer create one for you. A map will be represented by a 2D-map structure where each cell will consist of a cell type and cell connections. The cell type values are as follows:

- 0 means a wall
- 1 means an empty cell
- 2 means the start point
- 3 means the exit point

Cell connections will use a bitmask value to get information about which cells are connected to the current cell. The following diagram contains cell connection bitmask values with their respective positions:

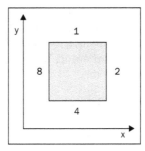

Now, the quite common problem in programming is how to implement an efficient data structure for 2D maps. Usually, this is done either with a relatively large one-dimensional array or with an array of arrays. All these arrays have a specified static size, so map dimensions are fixed. The problem arises when you use a simple 1D array and you need to change the map size during gameplay or the map size should be unlimited. This is where map cell indexing comes into place. Often you can use this formula to compute the cell index from 2D map coordinates:

```
local index = x + y * map_width
map[index]  = value
```

There's nothing wrong with this approach when the map size is definite. However, changing the map size would invalidate the whole data structure as the map_width variable would change its value. A solution to this is to use indexing that's independent from the map size. This way you can ensure consistent access to all elements even if you resize the 2D map.

You can use some kind of hashing algorithm that packs map cell coordinates into one value that can be used as a unique key. Another way to accomplish this is to use the Cantor pairing function, which is defined for two input coordinates:

$$\pi(k_1, k_2) := \frac{1}{2}(k_1 + k_2)(k_1 + k_2 + 1) + k_2$$

Index value distribution is shown in the following diagram:

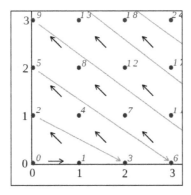

The Cantor pairing function ensures that there are no key collisions no matter what coordinates you use. What's more, it can be trivially extended to support three or more input coordinates. To illustrate the usage of the Cantor pairing function for more dimensions, its primitive form will be defined as a function `cantor(k1, k2)`, where `k1` and `k2` are input coordinates. The pairing function for three dimensions will look like this:

```
local function cantor3D(k1, k2, k3)
   return cantor(cantor(k1, k2), k3)
end
```

Keep in mind that the Cantor pairing function always returns one integer value. With higher number of dimensions, you'll soon get very large values in the results. This may pose a problem because the Lua language can offer 52 bits for integer values. For example, for 2D coordinates (83114015, 11792250) you'll get a value `0x000FFFFFFFFFFFFF` that still can fit into 52-bit integer values without rounding errors. The larger coordinates will return inaccurate values and subsequently you'd get key collisions. Value overflow can be avoided by dividing large maps into smaller ones, where each one uses the full address space that Lua numbers can offer. You can use another coordinate to identify submaps.

This recipe will use specialized data structures for a 2D map with the Cantor pairing function for internal cell indexing. You can use the following code to prepare this type of data structure:

```
function map2D(defaultValue)
   local t = {}
   -- Cantor pair function
   local function cantorPair(k1, k2)
      return 0.5 * (k1 + k2) * ((k1 + k2) + 1) + k2
   end
   setmetatable(t, {
      __index = function(_, k)
         if type(k)=="table" then
            local i = rawget(t, cantorPair(k[1] or 1, k[2] or 1))
            return i or defaultValue
         end
      end,
      __newindex = function(_, k, v)
         if type(k)=="table" then
            rawset(t, cantorPair(k[1] or 1, k[2] or 1), v)
         else
            rawset(t, k, v)
         end
      end,
   })
   return t
end
```

The maze generator as well as the pathfinding algorithm will need a stack data structure. For more information, refer to the *Making a stack* recipe from *Chapter 1, Basics of the Game Engine*.

How to do it...

This section is divided into two parts, where each one solves very similar problems from the perspective of the maze generator and the maze solver.

Maze generation

You can either load a maze from a file or generate a random one. The following steps will show you how to generate a unique maze.

First, you'll need to grab a maze generator library from the GitHub repository with the following command:

`git clone https://github.com/soulik/maze_generator`

This maze generator uses the depth-first approach with backtracking.

You can use this maze generator in the following steps. First, you'll need to set up maze parameters such as maze size, entry, and exit points.

```
local mazeGenerator = require 'maze'
local maze = mazeGenerator {
  width = 50,
  height = 25,
  entry = {x = 2, y = 2},
  exit = {x = 30, y = 4},
  finishOnExit = false,
}
```

The final step is to iteratively generate the maze map until it's finished or a certain step count is reached. The number of steps should always be one order of magnitude greater than the total number of maze cells mainly due to backtracking. Note that it's not necessary for each maze to connect entry and exit points in this case.

```
for i=1,12500 do
  local result = maze.generate()
  if result == 1 then
    break
  end
end
```

Now you can access each maze cell with the `maze.map` variable in the following manner:

```
local cell = maze.map[{x, y}]
local cellType = cell.type
local cellConnections = cell.connections
```

Maze solving

This recipe will show you how to use a modified Trémaux's algorithm, which is based on depth-first search and path marking. This method guarantees finding the path to the exit point if there's one. It relies on using two keys in each step: current position and neighbors.

This algorithm will use three state variables—the current position, a set of visited cells, and the current path from the starting point:

```
local currentPosition = {maze.entry.x, maze.entry.y}
local visistedCells = map2D(false)
local path = stack()
```

The whole maze solving process will be placed into one loop. This algorithm is always finite, so you can use the infinite `while` loop.

```
-- A placeholder for neighbours function that will be defined
later
local neighbours

-- testing function for passable cells
local cellTestFn = function(cell, position)
  return (cell.type >= 1) and (not visitedCells[position])
end

-- include starting point into path
visitedCells[currentPosition] = true
path.push(currentPosition)

while true do
  local currentCell = maze.map[currentPosition]
  -- is current cell an exit point?
  if currentCell and
    (currentCell.type == 3 or currentCell.type == 4) then
    break
  else
    -- have a look around and find viable cells
    local possibleCells = neighbours(currentPosition, cellTestFn)
    if #possibleCells > 0 then
      -- let's try the first available cell
```

```
          currentPosition = possibleCells[1]
          visitedCells[currentPosition] = true
          path.push(currentPosition)
        elseif not path.empty() then
          -- get back one step
          currentPosition = path.pop()
        else
          -- there's no solution
          break
        end
      end
    end
  end
```

This fairly simple algorithm uses the `neighbours` function to obtain a list of cells that haven't been visited yet:

```
-- A shorthand for direction coordinates
local neighbourLocations = {
  [0] = {0, 1},
  [1] = {1, 0},
  [2] = {0, -1},
  [3] = {-1, 0},
}

local function neighbours(position0, fn)
  local neighbours = {}
  local currentCell = map[position0]
  if type(currentCell)=='table' then
    local connections = currentCell.connections
    for i=0,3 do
      -- is this cell connected?
      if bit.band(connections, 2^i) >= 1 then
        local neighbourLocation = neighbourLocations[i]
        local position1 = {position0[1] + neighbourLocation[1],
        position0[2] + neighbourLocation[2]}
        if (position1[1]>=1 and position1[1] <= maze.width and
        position1[2]>=1 and position1[2] <= maze.height) then
          if type(fn)=="function" then
            if fn(map[position1], position1) then
              table.insert(neighbours, position1)
            end
          else
            table.insert(neighbours, position1)
          end
        end
      end
```

```
        end
      end
    end
    return neighbours
  end
```

When this algorithm finishes, a valid path between entry and exit points is stored in the `path` variable represented by the stack data structure. The path variable will contain an empty stack if there's no solution for the maze.

How it works...

This pathfinding algorithm uses two main steps. First, it looks around the current maze cell to find cells that are connected to the current maze cell with a passage. This will result in a list of possible cells that haven't been visited yet. In this case, the algorithm will always use the first available cell from this list. Each step is recorded in the stack structure, so in the end, you can reconstruct the whole path from the exit point to the entry point. If there are no maze cells to go, it will head back to the previous cell from the stack.

The most important is the `neighbours` function, which determines where to go from the current point. It uses two input parameters: current position and a cell testing function. It looks around the current cell in four directions in clockwise order: up, right, down, and left. There must be a passage from the current cell to each surrounding cell; otherwise, it'll just skip to the next cell. Another step determines whether the cell is within the rectangular maze region. Finally, the cell is passed into the user-defined testing function, which will determine whether to include the current cell in a list of usable cells.

The maze cell testing function consists of a simple Boolean expression. It returns true if the cell has a correct cell type (not a wall) and hasn't been visited yet. A positive result will lead to inclusion of this cell to a list of usable cells.

Note that even if this pathfinding algorithm finds a path to the exit point, it doesn't guarantee that this path is the shortest possible.

Pathfinding for tile-based environments with obstacles

This recipe will show you how to solve the pathfinding problem in your game by using the A* algorithm. You can use this whenever you need to move from one point to another in an unknown environment. It uses heuristics to improve the search speed and efficiency. The good thing is that you can use it with any shape of tile. The most common use of the A* search algorithm can be found in strategic games, many action games, and tower defense games. Its use can be extended beyond pathfinding problems to adapt AI decisions to the environment or to make a dynamic liquid-like environment.

Getting ready

The A* searching algorithm makes extensive use of the priority queue data structure and it needs to access map cells quite frequently. For this purpose, you'll be using a slightly modified version of the priority queue and map2D structure.

You can use the following code to define the priority queue object:

```
-- useful shortcuts
local ti = table.insert
local tr = table.remove
-- remove table element by its value
local tr2 = function(t, v)
  for i=1,#t do
    if t[i]==v then
      tr(t, i)
      break
    end
  end
end

function pqueue()
  local t = {}
  -- a set of elements
  local set = {}
  -- a set of priorities paired with a elements
  local r_set = {}
  -- sorted list of priorities
  local keys = {}
  -- add element into storage and set its priority and sort keys
  local function addKV(k, v)
        set[k] = v
    if not r_set[v] then
      ti(keys, v)
      table.sort(keys)
      local k0 = {k}
      r_set[v] = k0
      setmetatable(k0, {
        __mode = 'v'
      })
    else
      ti(r_set[v], k)
    end
  end
```

```lua
-- remove element from storage and sort keys
local remove = function(k)
      local v = set[k]
      local prioritySet = r_set[v]
      tr2(prioritySet, k)
      if #prioritySet < 1 then
        tr2(keys, v)
    r_set[v] = nil
    table.sort(keys)
    set[k] = nil
      end
end; t.remove = remove
-- returns an element with the lowest priority
t.min = function()
  local priority = keys[1]
  if priority then
    return r_set[priority] or {}
  else
    return {}
  end
end
-- returns an element with the highest priority
t.max = function()
  local priority = keys[#keys]
  if priority then
    return r_set[priority] or {}
  else
    return {}
  end
end
-- is this queue empty?
t.empty = function()
  return #keys < 1
end

setmetatable(t, {
  __index = set,
  __newindex = function(t, k, v)
    if not set[k] then
      -- new element
      addKV(k, v)
    else
      -- existing element, change its priority
      remove(k)
      addKV(k, v)
```

```
        end
      end,
   })

   return t
end
```

In contrast to the previous version of priority queue in the first chapter, this one allows you to obtain elements with the lowest or highest priority as well as test their existence in the queue.

How to do it...

The A* searching algorithm in this recipe will use the priority queue to define the frontier of the observed region. It will also need access to map cell data and also access to both the starting and ending points of the pathfinding process.

You can enclose the whole pathfinding solver into one function with three parameters—a list of map cells defined by the map2D data structure, the starting, and the ending point:

```
function solver(mapCells, startPoint, endPoint)
   ...
end
```

This recipe will use the tuple data structure to define the point position. However, the Lua language doesn't offer a real tuple data structure, where each tuple element is uniquely defined by its content. The easiest way to achieve tuple uniqueness is to cache tuples by their values.

The following lines of code will show you how to use the Cantor pairing function in tuple caching:

```
local cellCache = {}
local function cantorPair(k1, k2)
   return 0.5 * (k1 + k2) * ((k1 + k2) + 1) + k2
end
local function storeCells(...)
   for _, elm in ipairs {...} do
      cellCache[cantorPair(elm[1], elm[2])] = elm
   end
end
local function queryCell(p)
local cp = cantorPair(p[1], p[2])
   local cell = cellCache[cp]
   if not cell then
      cell = p
      cellCache[cp] = cell
   end
   return cell
end
```

Note that these functions should be inside the `solver` function to make the whole solving process independent of the current Lua state.

The next thing you'll need is a way to obtain the neighbor cell around the current map cell. You can implement this function as an iterator:

```lua
local directionSet = {
  {-1,-1}, { 0, 1}, { 1, 1},
  {-1, 0},          { 1, 0},
  { 1,-1}, { 0,-1}, {-1, 1},
}
-- general form of neighbour iterator
local function neighboursFn(p0)
  local list = {}
  for _, direction in ipairs(directionSet) do
    local p1 = queryCell({p0[1] + direction[1],
     p0[2] + direction[2]})
    coroutine.yield(p1)
  end
  coroutine.yield()
end
-- returns specialized parametrical iterator
local function neighbours(p0)
  return coroutine.wrap(function()
    return neighboursFn(p0)
  end)
end
```

Another important point of this algorithm is path reconstruction. The pathfinding solver uses a graph-like data structure, where the starting point is at the root of the graph and the ending point is at one of the leaf nodes. Path reconstruction goes from the leaf node—ending point back to the root while storing the whole path in a list data structure:

```lua
local function reconstructPath(cameFrom, goal)
  local totalPath = {current}
  local current = cameFrom[goal]
  while current do
    table.insert(totalPath, current)
    current = cameFrom[current]
  end
  return totalPath
end
```

The pathfinding algorithm uses simple heuristic functions to estimate which path is the best to take. You can use the Manhattan distance function to obtain the path cost estimation. The good thing is that it's easier to solve than the usual distance function with a square root.

```
local function heuristicCostEstimate(p0, p1)
   return math.abs(p0[1] - p1[1]) + math.abs(p0[2] - p1[2])
end
```

You'll need to get the cost of stepping to the neighbor cell as well. This can be determined by the cost function that looks at the target map cell to check whether there's a passage or a wall:

```
local function cost(p0, p1)
   local cell = mapCells[p1]
   -- map cell with 0 value is a wall
   if cell == 0 then
     return math.huge -- impassable wall cost
   else
     return 1 -- normal step cost
   end
end
```

Now, with all the necessary helping functions, you put them together with the A* searching algorithm implementation.

The code for the whole pathfinding solver will look like this:

```
function solver(mapCells, startPoint, endPoint)
   ... helping functions from above
   -- initial state
   local frontier = pqueue()
   local cameFrom = {}
   local costSoFar = {
     [start] = 0,
   }
   frontier[start] = 0
   storeCells(start, goal)

   while not frontier.empty() do
     local current = assert((frontier.min())[1])
     -- are we at goal?
     if current == goal then
       return reconstructPath(cameFrom, goal)
     end
     -- remove current position from the frontier
     frontier.remove(current)
     -- look at neighbours
```

```
        for neighbour in neighbours(current) do
          local newCost = costSoFar[current] +
          cost(current, neighbour)
          if not costSoFar[neighbour]
            or (newCost < costSoFar[neighbour]) then
            costSoFar[neighbour] = newCost
            frontier[neighbour] = newCost +
            heuristicCostEstimate(goal, neighbour)
            cameFrom[neighbour] = current
          end
        end
    end
end
```

The solver function can be used in the following manner:

```
mapCells = map2D(1)
local startPosition = {1, 1}
local endPosition = {10, 5}
local path = solver(mapCells, startPosition, endPosition)
```

How it works...

The A* search algorithm uses a best-first search approach, where it looks for a least-cost path from the starting point to the ending point. During path traversal, it looks for a path with the lowest expected cost. A set of possible path segments is stored in a priority queue sorted by the path segment cost. In a tiled environment, this priority queue can be imagined as a frontier.

This algorithm can be viewed as a combination of Dijkstras's and a greedy best-first algorithm by taking the best of both worlds. The heuristic function can help to quicken this process by adjusting the cost of the expected path so that path searching will lead in a direction closer to the goal. This heuristic function is a part of greedy best-first search algorithms and might not always lead to the best `solution.Path` cost.

This recipe uses two functions to measure the path cost. The immediate path cost to the neighbor cell is determined by the cost function, which will return step cost 1 if you can pass to the next cell. Otherwise, it will return a huge number or infinity, indicating that there's a wall and you can't walk through it no matter what. An important point to note about this function is that you can customize it to simulate passable but costly environment, such as water pools, grass, or a bush. You'll just need to set the cost number to be higher than 1.

Heuristic

A frontier ring of observed cells usually expands evenly in all directions. With the heuristic function, the shape of a frontier ring is formed differently. The ring expands more in the direction to the goal point. You can imagine the heuristic function as a hint that tells you what direction will probably be cheaper. This probability comes from the heuristic estimate that uses the Manhattan distance between the current and a goal point without taking obstacles into account. This distance function is based on the grid-like street geography of the New York borough of Manhattan.

There's more...

Note that the A* searching algorithm performs well in a static environment. It can be used in dynamic environments as well, but the observed area must be reasonably small to keep performance impact at minimum. What's more, the A* searching algorithm can't reuse search data from previous runs.

In general, the D* searching algorithm is more suited to be used in dynamic environments mainly because it can reuse its search data. If you add changes to the environment, it will recompute only a small fragment of search data.

This algorithm works in the same fashion as the A* algorithm when there are no changes in the observed environment. Other than that, it keeps path costs between each node and their parent node. This way, it can detect environment inconsistencies and adjust the corresponding path costs.

See also

► The *Simple pathfinding algorithm for a maze* recipe

Using a fuzzy logic for decision making

Fuzzy logic presents a way to move from exact reasoning of Boolean logic to an approximation of a truth value, whereas Boolean logic uses a binary set of true or false values; fuzzy logic can operate anywhere between these two values.

This can be used to deal with situations where you can't be 100 percent sure about the result. Many modern games use this to make autonomous NPCs or intelligent enemies that can accommodate their actions to the current situation or environment.

This recipe will use a simplistic version of the fuzzy inference system with a fixed number of value points. It's not as precise as the professional grade fuzzy inference systems, but still performs well enough to be used in games.

The FIS solver is designed in a way to make its configuration as simple as possible.

Fuzzy sets are often used with neural networks, mainly because neurons operate on various levels at synapses.

Getting ready

First, you'll need to prepare a special version of the mathematical and geometric functions in the form of function templates. These functions form the basic building blocks for fuzzy logic.

The following code contains basic mathematical functions capable of operating on fuzzy sets:

```lua
-- minimum of a fuzzy set
local function min(a, b)
  return function(x, y)
    return math.min(a(x), b(y))
  end
end
-- maximum of a fuzzy set
local function max(a, b)
  return function(x, y)
    return math.max(a(x), b(y))
  end
end
-- negation of a fuzzy set
local function neg(a)
  return function(x)
    return 1.0 - a(x)
  end
end
-- crop values of a fuzzy set
local function crop(rangeMin, rangeMax)
  return function(x)
    return math.min(math.max(x, rangeMin), rangeMax)
  end
end
-- merge two fuzzy sets
local function mergeSets(a, b)
  local out = {}
  for k, _ in pairs(a) do
    out[k] = true
  end
  if type(b)=='table' then
    for k, _ in pairs(b) do
```

```
        out[k] = true
      end
    end
    return out
  end
```

You'll need functions to define truth values in fuzzy sets as well. The truth value is a part of the fuzzy set and can be represented by continuous membership functions. It maps lexical value into a set of numerical values or vice versa. To get a better idea, see the following diagram showing truth values in a fuzzy set to map the temperature from word expressions into numerical values:

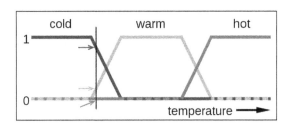

Truth values usually take one of these three shapes: triangle, trapezoid, or gauss curve:

```
    local function triangle(a, b, c)
      return function(_x)
        return function()
          local x = _x()
          if x>=a and x<b then
            return (x - a)/(b-a)
          elseif x>=b and x<c then
            return (c - x)/(c-b)
          else
            return 0
          end
        end
      end
    end

    local function trapezoid(a, b, c, d)
      return function(_x)
        return function()
          local x = _x()
          if x>=a and x<b then
            return (x - a)/(b-a)
          elseif x>=b and x<c then
```

```
            return 1
         elseif x>=c and x<d then
            return (d - x)/(d-c)
         else
            return 0
         end
      end
   end
end

local function gauss(deviation, mean)
   return function(_x)
      return function()
         local x = _x()
         return math.exp( -((x - mean)^2)/(2*deviation^2))
      end
   end
end
```

Each of these shapes uses a set of control points to define its position or to modify the shape itself.

How to do it...

The hardest part will be the fuzzy inference system or FIS solver. The whole code for the solver will be in the form of closure, so you can create the FIS solver just by using the constructor function.

FIS will consist of the objects' fuzzy sets, linguistic variables, and rules. A fuzzy set can represent input or output values with a specified numerical range. A fuzzy set is filled with at least one linguistic variable. Linguistic variables are also used in rules either in the form of a predicate or implication. The FIS solver will use these rules to produce numerical variables in the output.

The following code shows the basic FIS solver skeleton:

```
local function solver()
   local rules = {}
   local fuzzySets = {}
   local outputFuzzySets = {}

   local obj = {
      rules = rules,
      settings = {
         implicationOperator = math.min,
         aggregationOperator = math.max,
```

```
        step = 0.01,
      },
    }
    -- fuzzy set
    obj.F = function(def)
    end
    -- linguistic variable
    obj.L = function(def)
    end
    -- rule
    obj.R = function(factor)
    end

    local function computeImplication(rule)
    end
    local function aggregateResults(ruleResults)
    end
    local function defuzzifyResult(fuzzyResult)
    end
    -- the first parameter can be omitted as is contains a reference
    to the object itself
    local function solve(_, inputs)
    end

    setmetatable(obj, {
      __call = solve,
    })
    return obj
  end
```

In the next step, you'll need to implement the FIS elements—a fuzzy set, a linguistic variable, and a rule.

A fuzzy set

A fuzzy set object constructor will accept one parameter in the form of a table to define the fuzzy set name and a range of fuzzy set values.

```
    obj.F = function()
      assert(type(def)=='table')
      local name, range = unpack(def)
      assert(type(name)=='string' and type(range)=='table')

      local out = {}
      local range = {_min(unpack(range)), _max(unpack(range))}
```

```lua
    out.range = range
    out.name = name
    local langValues = {}; out.langValues = langValues
    fuzzySets[name] = {
      value = 0,
      range = range,
    }

    local crop = M.crop(unpack(range))
    local cropValue = M.crop(0, 1)
    local min, max, neg = M.min, M.max, M.neg

    local function getFuzzyValueFunctor()
      return function()
        return crop(fuzzySets[name].value)
      end
    end
    -- prepare fuzzy set object
    local function prepareFuzzySet(fn)
      local var = {
        fn = fn,
        crop = crop,
        fuzzySets = {
          [out] = true,
        },
      }
      -- define fuzzy set operators
      setmetatable(var, {
        -- OR
        __add = function(a, b)
          local fs = prepareFuzzySet(max(a.fn, b.fn))
          fs.fuzzySets = mergeSets(a.fuzzySets, b.fuzzySets)
          return fs
        end,
        -- AND
        __mul = function(a, b)
          local fs = prepareFuzzySet(min(a.fn, b.fn))
          fs.fuzzySets = mergeSets(a.fuzzySets, b.fuzzySets)
          return fs
        end,
        -- NOT
        __unm = function(a)
          local fs = prepareFuzzySet(neg(a.fn))
```

```
            fs.fuzzySets = mergeSets(a.fuzzySets)
            return fs
        end,
        __call = function(a)
            return cropValue(fn())
        end,
    })
    return var
end

    setmetatable(out, {
        __index = function(_, name)
            return langValues[name]
        end,
        __newindex = function(_, name, fuzzySetFn)
            assert(type(fuzzySetFn)=='function')
            langValues[name] = prepareFuzzySet(
                -- prepare elementary fuzzy set
                fuzzySetFn(getFuzzyValueFunctor())
            )
        end,
    })
    return out
end
```

A linguistic variable

Each fuzzy set must contain at least one linguistic variable. The linguistic variable object describes the truth value with the membership function. This object uses one parameter in the constructor to define the linguistic variable function shape:

```
obj.L = function(def)
    assert(type(def)=='table')
    local fnGen, parameters = unpack(def)
    assert(type(fnGen)=='function' and type(parameters)=='table')
    return fnGen(unpack(parameters))
end
```

A rule

FIS uses a set of rules to evaluate input variables into output variables. All rules consist of premise and implication. They are always in the following form:

```
IF premise THEN implication
```

You may use Zadeh operators in premises to specify more complex conditions. Zadeh operators AND, OR, and NOT are special types of Boolean operators and are defined as minimum, maximum, and complement:

```
obj.R = function(factor)
  local out = {
    premise = false,
    implication = false,
      factor = factor or 1,
  }
  table.insert(rules, out)
  return out
end
```

The `rules` parameter can use the `factor` value to modify the scale of rule impact on output variables. This is used mostly with more than one output variable.

The third step is the implementation of three functions `computeImplication`, `aggregateResults`, and `defuzzifyResult`. These functions are used in individual parts of the fuzzy inference evaluation process as follows:

```
local function computeImplication(rule)
  local premiseResult = rule.premise()
  local implication = rule.implication
  local factor = rule.factor or 1

  local out = {
  }

  local implicationFuzzySets = implication.fuzzySets
  local langValues = implication.langValues
  local implicationOperator = obj.settings.implicationOperator
  local oldValues = {}
  local range = {0, 0}

  -- store current values and obtain maximum range
  for fs, _ in pairs(implicationFuzzySets) do
    oldValues[fs.name] = fuzzySets[fs.name].value
    range[1] = _min(range[1], fs.range[1])
    range[2] = _max(range[2], fs.range[2])
  end

  -- compute values for each implication conclusion
  for x = range[1], range[2], obj.settings.step do
    for fs, _ in pairs(implicationFuzzySets) do
```

```
      fuzzySets[fs.name].value = x
    end
    local result = implicationOperator(implication(),
    premiseResult)
    table.insert(out, {x, result*factor})
  end

  -- restore old value
  for fs, _ in pairs(implicationFuzzySets) do
    fuzzySets[fs.name].value = oldValues[fs.name]
  end
  return out
end

local function aggregateResults(ruleResults)
  local aggregatedResult = {}
  local ruleResult1 = ruleResults[1]
  local aggregationOperator = obj.settings.aggregationOperator

  if #ruleResults > 1 then
    for i, point in ipairs(ruleResult1) do
      local values = {point[2]}
      for j=2,#ruleResults do
        table.insert(values, ruleResults[j][i][2])
      end
      aggregatedResult[i] = {point[1],
        aggregationOperator(unpack(values))}
    end
  else
    aggregatedResult = ruleResults[1]
  end
  return aggregatedResult
end

-- compute centroid point from fuzzy result
local function defuzzifyResult(fuzzyResult)
  local accumXY, accumY = 0, 0
  for i, point in ipairs(fuzzyResult) do
    if point[2] > 0 then
      accumXY = accumXY + point[1]*point[2]
      accumY = accumY + point[2]
    end
  end
  if accumY > 0 then
```

```
      return accumXY/accumY
   else
      return (fuzzyResult[1][2]-fuzzyResult[#fs][2])/2
   end
end
```

A solver

The final step in FIS implementation is the `solver` function. It will accept a table of input variables. Input variables are specified by a fuzzy set name as a key paired with numerical values.

```
local solve = function(_, inputs)
   for name, value in pairs(inputs) do
      fuzzySets[name].value = value
   end
   --outputFuzzySets
   local partialResults = {}
   for i, rule in ipairs(rules) do
      local implicationFSs = rule.implication.fuzzySets
      for FS, _ in pairs(implicationFSs) do
         local result = partialResults[FS.name]
         if not result then
            result = {}; partialResults[FS.name] = result
         end
         table.insert(result, computeImplication(rule))
      end
   end
   for name, results in pairs(partialResults) do
      local aggResult = aggregateResults(results)
      outputFuzzySets[name] = defuzzifyResult(aggResult)
   end
   return outputFuzzySets
end
```

A usage

The following example uses the FIS solver object to obtain the recommended tip amount in a restaurant depending on the food quality and the level of service:

```
local FIS = solver()
local F,L,R = FIS.F, FIS.L, FIS.R

local service = F {'service', {0, 10}}
service['poor'] = L {gauss, {1.5, 0}}
```

```
service['good'] = L {gauss, {1.5, 5}}
service['excellent'] = L {gauss, {1.5, 10}}

local food = F {'food', {0, 10}}
food['rancid'] = L {trapezoid, {0, 0, 1, 3}}
food['delicious'] = L {trapezoid, {7,9, 10, 10}}

local tip = F {'tip', {0, 30}}
tip['cheap'] = L {triangle, {0, 5, 10}}
tip['average'] = L {triangle, {10, 15, 20}}
tip['generous'] = L {triangle, {20, 25, 30}}

-- IF service is poor OR food is rancid THEN tip is cheap
local rule1 = R()
rule1.premise = service['poor'] + food['rancid']
rule1.implication = tip['cheap']
-- IF service is good THEN tip is average
local rule2 = R()
rule2.premise = service['good']
rule2.implication = tip['average']
-- IF service is excellent OR food is delicious THEN tip is
generous
local rule3 = R()
rule3.premise = service['excellent'] + food['delicious']
rule3.implication = tip['generous']

local inputVariables = {
  service = 8.0,
  food = 6.5,
}
local result = FIS(inputVariable)
```

This example will result in a table with one output variable:

Output variable name	Value
tip	22.213269948097

This means you were most probably satisfied with the food and the overall service in the restaurant was great. Therefore, you can give a tip of around $22 from your budget of $30 for tips.

How it works...

The fuzzy inference system is the process of mapping input variables into output variables using fuzzy logic. There are two kinds of fuzzy inference systems: Mamdani and Sugeno. This recipe uses the Mamdani-type inference system as it's the most commonly used in this field and it's more intuitive than the Sugeno-type inference system.

The process of computing output variables in the Mamdani inference system can be briefly described in six steps:

1. Setting up and determination of fuzzy rules.
2. Fuzzification of input variables using membership functions.
3. Application of fuzzy rules on fuzzied input variables to obtain rule strength.
4. Computation of rule implication—consequences of using rule strength and the output membership function.
5. Combination of consequences in the output distribution function.
6. Defuzzification of the output distribution function into a crisp output variable.

First of all, you set mapping of crisp input variables into truth levels in a fuzzy set using the membership function. The following diagram shows a graphical representation of truth levels for service, food, and tip:

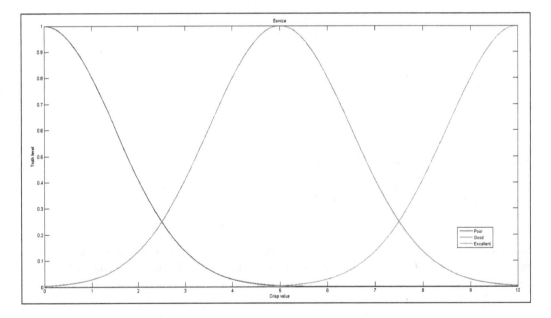

In the preceding diagram, the horizontal axis relates to the satisfaction level from 0 to 10 for the service. The vertical axis indicates the level of truth for all lexical terms that are used in this fuzzy set. As you can see, the lexical term *poor service* is the truest, around 0 level of satisfaction on the horizontal axis. Moving towards crisp value 5, the service is mostly regarded as a good one. This fuzzy set uses gauss curves to describe truth values for lexical terms.

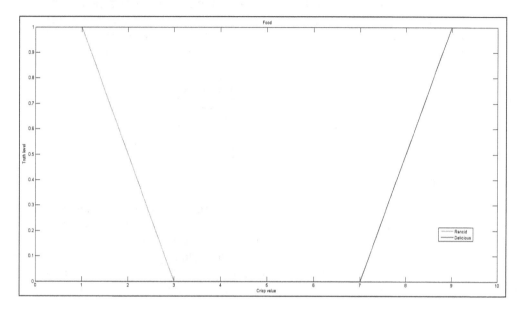

The second diagram contains a fuzzy set for food quality evaluation; it uses the trapezoid shape of truth values for both terms:

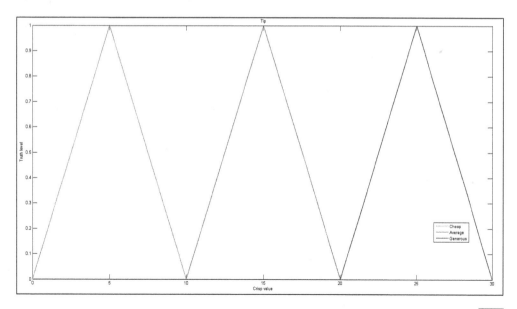

The preceding diagram contains a fuzzy set to determine what tip you should give to the waiter. Tips are divided into three levels: cheap, average, and generous. Notice that there's no exact result telling you how much you should give. Lexical terms use the triangular shape for truth values.

Input variable mapping can be interpreted as follows—if the crisp value for a service is 4, it means that the service is more likely good than poor, and even less likely excellent. The result of the input variable mapping are truth levels for each linguistic variable. For instance, if the crisp value of service is 4, truth levels would be as shown in the following table:

Lexical variable	Truth level
Poor	0.0286
Good	0.8007
Excellent	0.0003

This process is called **fuzzification**.

The next step applies fuzzied input variables in the premise part of all rules. Rules usually use one of the three fuzzy operators: AND, OR, and NOT. The AND operator uses a minimum value of input variables, the OR operator uses the maximum value, and the NOT operator negates the truth level of the input variable. The resulting value is used in the implication part of the rule. The implication process combines the premise result with the output variable in intermediate fuzzy sets using minimal values. The following diagram shows the computation of the first rule:

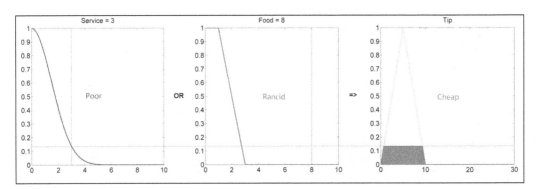

This process is repeated for all rules and output variables.

The second last step consists of fuzzy set aggregation into one output fuzzy set. Aggregation merges all the fuzzy sets that correspond to the same output variable by using the maximum value. The following diagram shows the aggregated output fuzzy set for the tip output variable:

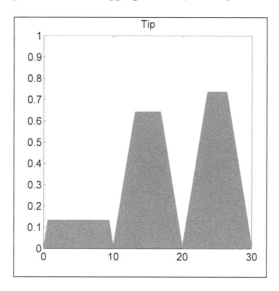

The last step of fuzzy inference is defuzzification to obtain a crisp value of the output variable. There are many defuzzification methods. This recipe uses an average of the weight function with approximation to speed up computation.

Note that aggregation and defuzzification is repeated for each output variable.

9
Sounds and Networking

This chapter will cover the following topics:

- ▶ Initializing the audio subsystem
- ▶ Playing sound samples
- ▶ Playing the background music
- ▶ Network communication with ZeroMQ
- ▶ Creating a basic client-server architecture
- ▶ Sending messages to many hosts at once
- ▶ Communication between threads

Introduction

In this chapter, you'll learn how to use the sound subsystem in LuaSDL and to communicate over the network or between the threads with the ZeroMQ library.

Sounds and music in games can enhance the overall atmosphere or make them even more memorable to players. The LibSDL library itself contains only the basic function to send raw data to your audio card. Fortunately, the LuaSDL library bundles the LibSDL library with the SDL_Mixer add-on, which extends a number of audio file decoders and adds simple audio effects, such as volume control, fade-in, and fade-out. You can load sound samples by using one of these file formats: WAV, MID, MOD, OGG, or MP3.

Whether or not you plan to use multiplayer, the ZeroMQ library can solve many common problems with network communication or multithreading.

This library provides a robust yet simple communication system. It supersedes classic socket connections with reliable message transport and automatic reconnection. Optionally, connections can be encrypted to ensure transport security. You can use the same networking code to send messages over the network or even between threads. It uses its own transport protocol—ZMTP, which is incompatible with most of the TCP-based network services. However, in special cases it can use the raw mode to communicate with other TCP services.

Initializing the audio subsystem

Before using your audio card, you'll need to initialize the sound playback parameters. These parameters are:

▶ Sampling frequency

▶ Output audio format

▶ Number of audio channels and buffer size

It's important to note that LuaSDL can play many sound samples at the same time, where each sound sample uses exactly one sound channel. This is often used for relatively short sounds. Longer sounds such as a game music can be played in the background. However, there's only one background channel, so there is no easy way to mix two songs together.

Getting ready

First, you'll need to initialize the LuaSDL library with its subsystems. It's common practice to just initialize all subsystems at the start.

You can achieve this with two lines of Lua code:

```
require 'LuaSDL'
assert(SDL.SDL_Init(SDL.SDL_INIT_EVERYTHING) >= 0)
```

This will prepare all subsystems to be fully operational.

How to do it...

To initialize the audio subsystem, follow these steps:

1. Normally, you would use the `SDL.SDL_OpenAudio` function to prepare your audio device for playback. Unfortunately, this would expect you to submit your audio callback function, which isn't very usable in the Lua language environment. You'd need to submit raw audio data as well as mix it up to play any sound at all.

2. You can use the `SDL.Mix_OpenAudio` function instead to get basic sound playback to work. This function accepts four parameters: sampling frequency, audio format, channels count and a size of audio buffer.

```
local frequency = 44100
local audioFormat = SDL.MIX_DEFAULT_FORMAT
local audioChannels = 2
local bufferSize = 4096

assert(SDL.Mix_OpenAudio(frequency, audioFormat,
audioChannels,
bufferSize) == 0)
```

3. After this step, you'll be able to play sound samples.

4. The audio device should always be closed after you finish playing sound samples. You can do this with the `SDL.Mix_CloseAudio` function without any parameters.

```
SDL.Mix_CloseAudio()
```

This function is usually used just before closing your application.

How it works...

The LibSDL library is divided into a set of subsystems that includes timers, audio, video, CD-ROM, and joystick. Each of these subsystems takes a small amount of computer memory and can be enabled when needed. Notably, the audio subsystem reserves internal memory for audio processing and audio buffers upon initialization. Without the SDL_Mixer extension, you will need to prepare your own audio mixing routine and do audio format decoding by yourself. The Lua language isn't very appropriate for such tasks, since it uses the garbage collector, which adds latention to code execution. This can be quite notable during audio playback. The SDL_Mixer extension handles this for you, so you can simply choose how many audio mixing channels you need and use the available audio decoding functions to play various audio formats.

The `SDL.Mix_OpenAudio` function will set up the correct audio format and prepares the audio mixing channels. By default, there are eight mixing channels. This means you can play eight sounds in parallel and this should be sufficient for simple games. One channel can be occupied by one sound at a time. More complex games can use up all eight channels quite quickly and would result in sound skipping. Many games today commonly use 32 mixing channels.

Another important thing is the sound buffer size. This will determine the minimal latency accompanied by sound mixing. A larger sound buffer can result in smoother playback; however, there's a price for that in the form of greater latency. So, the response to a quick change of sounds can be slower. This is especially true with **digital sound processing** (**DSP**), where the size of the sound buffer should be as small as possible. On the other hand, if the buffer is too small, your computer might not be fast enough to process all incoming data and can result in notable pops and clicks in the sound output. The usual size of the sound buffer is between 512 and 4,096 bytes.

The audio format can be left at its default value, `SDL.MIX_DEFAULT_FORMAT`, which means that each sound sample will be described by a 16-bit signed integer. A list of applicable sample formats can be found in the following table:

Sound format identifier	Description
SDL.AUDIO_U8	These are unsigned 8-bit samples
SDL.AUDIO_S8	These are signed 8-bit samples
SDL.AUDIO_U16LSB	These are unsigned 16-bit samples with little-endian byte order
SDL.AUDIO_S16LSB	These are signed 16-bit samples with little-endian byte order
SDL.AUDIO_U16MSB	These are unsigned 16-bit samples with big-endian byte order
SDL.AUDIO_S16MSB	These are signed 16-bit samples with big-endian byte order
SDL.AUDIO_U16	This is the same as SDL.AUDIO_U16LSB
SDL.AUDIO_S16	This is the same as SDL.AUDIO_S16LSB
SDL.AUDIO_U16SYS	These are unsigned 16-bit samples with system byte order
SDL.AUDIO_S16SYS	These are signed 16-bit samples with system byte order

The last important thing is the number of output channels. The `SDL.Mix_OpenAudio` function accepts one or two channels, so you can have mono or stereo output.

Playing sound samples

LuaSDL can play many sound samples at the same time by using mixing channels. This allows you to not only play more sounds simultaneously but also apply basic mixing functions to sound channels, such as volume control, panning, fade-in, and fade-out.

Getting ready

There are eight mixing channels by default, which is usually fine for simple games. You can increase the number of mixing channels by using the `SDL.Mix_AllocateChannels` function with one argument. The maximum number of channels is limited only by your memory.

Be extra careful when using a large number of mixing channels as you can easily slip into a segmentation fault and crash your application!

This can be used in three ways. If you submit a positive number of channels in the argument, it will allocate channels to match the desired channel count. If the submitted number is lower than a number of currently allocated channels, it'll free up the unnecessary channels. A negative number will only return a number of currently allocated mixing channels. Zero number will free up all mixing channels. However, the background music channel will still be available.

The following line of code will allocate 32 mixing channels, which should be enough even for action games:

```
SDL.Mix_AllocateChannels(32)
```

How to do it...

Now, you are ready to load and play sound samples:

1. In the first step, you'll need to load your sound file into the memory. This can be done with the `SDL.Mix_LoadWAV` function. Regardless of its name, it can load sound format files such as WAV, AIFF, RIFF, OGG, and VOC.

   ```
   local fileName = 'sound_file.WAV'
   local soundSample = SDL.Mix_LoadWAV(fileName)
   ```

   This will return a sound sample handle, which can be used later to play it. In case of failure or a nonexistent file, you'll get the `nil` value.

2. After you finish using the sound sample, you should always free it by using the `SDL.Mix_FreeChunk` function.

   ```
   SDL.Mix_FreeChunk(soundSample)
   ```

3. To play the desired sound sample, you can use the `SDL.Mix_PlayChannel` function. It accepts three arguments, namely, mixing channel number, sound sample handle, and a number of loops. Zero loops means that the sample will play only once:

   ```
   local channel = 0
   local loops = 0
   SDL.Mix_PlayChannel(channel, soundSample, loops)
   ```

4. You can pause or resume the mixing channel with functions `SDL.Mix_PauseChannel` and `SDL.Mix_ResumeChannel`.

   ```
   local channel = 0
   SDL.Mix_PauseChannel(channel)
   SD1.Mix_ResumeChannel(channel)
   ```

Channel can be stopped with the `SDL.Mix_HaltChannel` function, which accepts the channel number as the only argument. If you use -1 as the channel number, it'll stop all the available channels.

How it works...

All functions in this recipe are channel oriented, which means you can control the sound playback for a specific channel. The `SDL.Mix_LoadWAV` function incorporates decoders for various sound formats.

You can either implement your own mechanism of free channel selection for playback or you can use the channel number -1 in the `SDL.Mix_PlayChannel` function, so LuaSDL will pick one for you automatically.

Sound playback is done asynchronously in the background thread, so once you start playing a sound sample, you can go ahead and continue executing the other parts of your application.

There's more...

For more advanced uses there are two other functions to manage simple transitions between sound samples: `SDL.Mix_FadeInChannel`, `SDL.Mix_ExpireChannel`, and `SDL.Mix_FadeOutChannel`.

- The first one will start playing a sound sample while slowly increasing the sound volume from 0 up to full volume:

```
local channel = 0
local loops = 0
local time = 500 -- 500ms
SDL.Mix_FadeInChannel(channel, soundSample, loops, time)
```

- The second one will stop playing the sound sample after a specified amount of time in milliseconds:

```
local channel = 0
local time = 500 -- 500ms
SDL.Mix_ExpireChannel(channel, time)
```

- The last one will slowly fade out sound playback. This is used mostly for longer sound samples:

```
local channel = 0
local fadeOutTime = 500 -- 500ms
SDL.Mix_FadeOutChannel(channel, time)
```

You can query specific channels for their status with the functions `SDL.Mix_Playing`, `SDL.Mix_Paused`, and `SDL.Mix_FadingChannel`.

The first one will tell you whether the channel is occupied with sound playback at the moment. It will return 1 if the channel is currently playing, or 0 if there's nothing to play. However, it can also return a number of channels currently used in playback if you use -1 instead of the number of a channel:

```
local channel = -1
local status = SDL.Mix_Playing(channel)
```

The SDL.Mix_Paused function uses a similar mechanism to determine whether the channel is currently in a paused state:

```
local channel = -1
local status = SDL.Mix_Paused(channel)
```

The last one, SDL.Mix_FadingChannel, will tell you whether the channel is fading in or fading out.

```
local channel = 0
local status = SDL.Mix_FadingChannel(channel)
if status == SDL.MIX_NO_FADING then
   -- selected channel is not fading
elseif status == SDL.MIX_FADING_IN then
   -- selected channel is currently fading in
elseif status == SDL.MIX_FADING_OUT then
   -- selected channel is currently fading out
end
```

See also

▶ The *Initializing the audio subsystem* recipe

Playing background music

Music playback works similarly to the sound sample playback with one exception that there's only one music channel and it's controlled separately from the other mixing channels.

What's more, music playback can be moved into a specific position, so it can be used as a simple music player if that's your intention.

Getting ready

The music channel is allocated automatically, so there's no need to allocate more mixing channels to play music.

How to do it...

The first step in playing music is:

1. To load a sound file into memory with the `SDL.Mix_LoadMUS` function. In this case, you can use a different set of file formats, such as WAV, MOD, MIDI, OGG, MP3, or even FLAC. This function returns a handle upon success similar to sound samples. If there's a problem loading sound files, it returns the `nil` value:

```
local fileName = 'sound_file.MP3'
local musicHandle = SDL.Mix_LoadMUS(fileName)
```

2. From this moment, you can use various functions to control music. The first one, `SDL.Mix_PlayMusic`, is to start music playback. The following lines of code show how to play music twice.

```
local loops = 1
SDL.Mix_PlayMusic(musicHandle, loops)
```

3. You can pause and resume music playback by calling the `SDL.Mix_PauseMusic` or `SDL.Mix_ResumeMusic` function without any parameters.

```
SDL.Mix_PauseMusic()
SDL.Mix_ResumeMusic()
```

4. Music playback can be stopped in two ways. Either you stop the music immediately or slowly fade the volume down. For the first case, there is the `SDL.Mix_HaltMusic` function, and for the fade out effect, you can use the `SDL.Mix_FadeOutMusic` function:

```
local time = 500 -- 500ms
SDL.Mix_HaltMusic()
SD1.Mix_FadeOutMusic(time)
```

There is a fade-in effect for the music as well. This can be achieved with the `SDL.Mix_FadeInMusic` function:

```
local loops = 0
local time = 500 -- 500ms
SDL.Mix_FadeInMusic(musicHandle, loops, time)
```

5. The music position can be controlled with a set of two functions: `SDL.Mix_RewindMusic` and `SDL.Mix_SetMusicPosition`. You can either rewind the position to the beginning of the song or move to a specific time. The latter one can be tricky because `SDL.Mix_SetMusicPosition` will interpret the time value differently depending on the type of song. OGG files use the time value as a position from the beginning of the song in seconds. MP3 files use it as a relative position in seconds. And lastly, MOD files will cast the value into 16-bit unsigned integers that mark a pattern number.

```
local position = 1.5 -- 1.5s
SDL.Mix_RewindMusic(musicHandle)
SDL.Mix_SetMusicPosition(position)
```

6. Don't forget to free up the allocated resources after use with the `SDL.Mix_FreeMUS` function:

```
SDL.Mix_FreeMUS(musicHandle)
```

 Be careful not to use the sound sample handle in the music function by mistake as it could lead to an application crash!

How it works...

LuaSDL always reserves one special audio mixing channel for music playback. It's controlled by a separate set of functions, so it's guaranteed that sound samples won't disturb the music playback.

The `SDL.Mix_LoadMUS` function can decode other kinds of sound formats, such as MP3 and FLAC. You can't use these formats for sound playback because of the design decisions behind the SDL_Mixer library. These sound formats are better suited for streaming of audio data mainly because of the latency incorporated in audio decoding routines.

Handling of position change in music is not an easy problem to solve because you can easily disturb music playback by a sudden change in sound buffer content. Audio decoding works with chunks of sound data with various sizes depending on the used bit rate of the encoded audio file. That's one of the reasons why you can't use this feature with sound samples.

See also

▸   The *Playing sound samples* recipe

Network communication with ZeroMQ

The ZeroMQ library is written in the C/C++ programming language and it's not a part of the Lua language. Therefore, you'll have to use one of the Lua language bindings to expose its functions to Lua scripts. This chapter will use the LuaZMQ binding library as it tries to be up to date with the current ZeroMQ version. While it exposes all the available functions from the ZeroMQ API, it adds an object-oriented approach to make it easier to use.

Getting ready

Before you start using the LuaZMQ library, you'll have to compile it into binary form.

You'll need the following items:

- ► The Git versioning tool to get source files (optional)
- ► The C++11 compliant compiler
- ► The CMake build system
- ► Lua development files

Development files for the Lua language are available at the SourceForge.net page for the LuaBinaries project at `http://luabinaries.sourceforge.net/download.html`.

How to do it...

Let's see how to get started with the LuaZMQ library:

1. First, you'll have to download source files for the LuaZMQ library from the GitHub repository. This can be done using the Git tool to clone the repository. This will create a new directory called `luazmq`, where the source files will be stored:

   ```
   git clone git@github.com:soulik/luazmq.git --recursive
   ```

   Notice that there's a *recursive* parameter for the `git` command. It's used to download linked dependencies from GitHub as well. This will ensure that all the files that are necessary are there before building.

2. The next step will be to move into empty the `build` directory, where you can start building the project:

   ```
   cd luazmq/build/
   ```

3. Now, you can run the `cmake` command to prepare the project files. On the Windows platform, you'll probably need to set the correct paths for the Lua header and library files:

   ```
   cmake ..
   ```

   Alternatively, you can use the GUI frontend for `cmake`:

   ```
   cmake-gui ..
   ```

4. After you finish generating project files, depending on the platform used, you can start building either with the `make` command or with open project files in your favorite IDE.

5. After successful compilation, you should end up with two files: `luazmq.dll` (Windows) or `luazmq.so` (Unix-based OS) and `zmq.lua`.

6. These two files should be either in the same directory as your project or they should be placed in a directory where the Lua interpreter can find them. In the latter case, you can set search paths in the Lua language with the variables `package.path` and `package.cpath`.

7. On the Windows platform, you'll probably need to copy the `libzmq.dll` file into you project directory as well.

Now, you are ready to explore network communication with the ZeroMQ library using the Lua language.

How it works...

The LuaZMQ binding library consists of two files: the binary library and a Lua helper script to minimize the programming effort in use.

The LuaZMQ library handles differences between the C/C++ programming language and the Lua language. One of these differences is primarily memory management. The ZeroMQ library tries to minimize redundancy of message data duplication. This is mostly valid for C/C++ applications, where you can handle data access directly. However, the Lua programming language uses every string part as an atomic entity. Therefore, there are many redundant operations and allocations accompanied with simple message transfer. The LuaZMQ library tries to elevate these problems from the Lua language to specialized C/C++ functions. Such a problem can easily occur when you try to send very long messages over the network, for instance during file transfer.

Another thing that LuaZMQ handles quite well is thread management, so you can easily invoke other Lua states in parallel and connect them with ZeroMQ messaging.

This library introduces a set communication pattern that decides how the message transport will be handled. The following table shows valid combinations of socket types and it should be used as guidance for later recipes:

First side of the socket	Second side of the socket	Description
ZMQ_PUB	ZMQ_SUB	This pattern facilitates one-sided communication from one publisher to many subscribers.
ZMQ_REQ	ZMQ_REP	In this pattern, each message from the request side is paired with a message from the reply side.
ZMQ_REQ	ZMQ_ROUTER	The router prepends the identity information of the request side to the message and can send out the message to any of the peers. It consumes the first message to get the destination identity.

First side of the socket	Second side of the socket	Description
ZMQ_DEALER	ZMQ_REP	In this pattern, when the dealer is connected to more than one reply side, it sends messages in a round-robin fashion.
ZMQ_DEALER	ZMQ_ROUTER	This pattern can be viewed as a standard socket connection. You can send out as many requests as you want and you may receive more than one message from the router part. Be careful with the peer identifier message at the router side.
ZMQ_DEALER	ZMQ_DEALER	This pattern can be used to load-balance message transfer on both sides of the communication.
ZMQ_ROUTER	ZMQ_ROUTER	This combination is close to the peer-to-peer message sending pattern. Both sides can decide which peer will obtain the message.
ZMQ_PUSH	ZMQ_PULL	The push-pull combination represents the pipeline or pattern. You can connect many pull sides to one push side. All pull sides will receive messages in a round-robin fashion.
ZMQ_PAIR	ZMQ_PAIR	This combination is also called the exclusive pair pattern, where it can connect only one peer at each side. This is used mostly for interthread communication.

Creating a basic client-server architecture

If you have ever tried to make even a simple client-server application, you'll know that there are many issues for the programmer to solve. These problems are concurrency, flow control, reconnection, blocking, communication architecture, scalability, and much more. Even a simple demo application with a request-reply pattern can easily fail without proper precautions.

Fortunately, there's a ZeroMQ library that introduces a few network communication design patterns to make your application design much simpler.

In this recipe, you'll learn how to create simple request-reply applications, which you can later promote to simple HTTP web servers or file transferring applications. It all depends on your imagination.

Getting ready

One of the available communication patterns is called request-reply, which connects two nodes in a strict manner. You can send one message and you'll always get exactly one reply. After this, the whole process is repeated.

It might not seem obvious, but this design pattern is used fairly often even in applications you use today such as web browsers, FTP, network tool ping, and many others.

This pattern is easily adaptable in many applications because it emulates the most common form of communication between two people. First, you need to ask something. Eventually, you'll get your answer. The following diagram illustrates this design pattern:

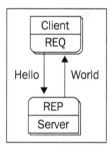

How to do it...

This recipe will be divided into server and client parts to make understanding a bit easier. Each part should be in its separate file so that you can run them at the same time. You can even run them from different computers. However, be sure to include all the necessary files on both sides along with the Lua language interpreter.

The server part

This part of the communication application will wait for a request and replies with a message.

1. First, you'll need to include the LuaZMQ library namespace with the following line of code:

```
local zmq = require 'zmq'
```

2. Now, you can initialize the context object for the ZeroMQ library and use it to define the kind of network socket you'll be using. In this case, the server path will use the zmq.ZMQ_REP constant that corresponds to the reply part.

```
local context = assert(zmq.context())
local socket = assert(context.socket(zmq.ZMQ_REP))
```

3. This will prepare the socket object that can be used to prepare one side of the network communication:

    ```
    assert(socket.bind('tcp://*:12345'))
    ```

4. After this step, your application will expect network communication over the TCP/IP protocol at the network service port **12345**. Of course, you can change the port number to suit your needs, but be sure to change the port number on the client side as well.

5. From this point, you can use the `socket.recv` function to actually receive a message but that would introduce blocking, so your server application would wait idly until the request arrives. This is not always desirable. Therefore, there's a poll object to handle situations like this.

6. First you need to create a poll object:

    ```
    local poll = zmq.poll()
    ```

7. Now you can assign a function to the poll, which will be used after you receive a message:

    ```
    poll.add(socket, zmq.ZMQ_POLLIN, function(socket)
       local result = assert(socket.recvAll())
       print('Received a message: '..result)
       assert(socket.send('This is a reply to: '..result))
    end)
    ```

8. This will print a received message and sends a reply to the **Request** side. For this to work, you'll have to start polling with the following lines:

    ```
    local timeout = 500 -- 500ms
    while (true) do
       poll.start(timeout)
    end
    ```

9. Notice that there's a timeout variable that contains a time in milliseconds to wait before doing other things. The whole process of waiting and replying is repeated indefinitely until you decide to break the cycle.

10. Lastly, you need to close a socket object after use with a single line of code:

    ```
    socket.close()
    ```

This concludes the server part of this recipe.

The client part

The client code is very similar to the server part. The only difference is in the type of socket and instead of using the bind function to listen for connection, you'll be using the `connect` function:

```lua
local zmq = require 'zmq'
local context = assert(zmq.context())
local socket = assert(context.socket(zmq.ZMQ_REQ))
assert(socket.connect("tcp://localhost:12345"))

local len = assert(socket.send("Test message"))
if len and len > 0 then
  local poll = zmq.poll()
  poll.add(socket, zmq.ZMQ_POLLIN, function(s)
    print(assert(socket.recvAll()))
  end)
  poll.start()
end
socket.disconnect()
```

There are a few more notable differences. A function to start polling, `poll.start()`, is used without parameters to define a timeout. This means that the client-side application will wait indefinitely until it gets a reply. After reply, it'll close the connection and quit.

How it works...

This recipe uses the request-reply pattern, where the communication starts with a request and it's followed with a single reply. Other operations regarding message transport are blocked. However, this communication pattern is bound only to a single pair of requests and reply peers. Therefore, you can connect the request side to many peers to send a request to all of them and get a reply from each one.

By using the `socket.bind` function, you'll create a listening part of the socket and it'll accept connections on your host. This function accepts an endpoint string that consists of three parts: a transport protocol, a host address, and a port number:

```
transport://address:port
```

A port number is omitted with interthread communication transports. Currently, ZeroMQ supports four types of transports, which are listed in the following table:

Transport names	Description
tcp	This is a unicast transport over TCP
ipc	This is an inter-process communication transport with socket files (Unix-like systems only)

Transport names	Description
`inproc`	This is an in-process or inter-thread communication transport over shared memory area
`pgm` or `egm`	This is a reliable multicast transport that uses PGM

Similarly, there's a `socket.connect` function to establish a network connection to the peer. Do note that the bind and connect functions are non-blocking. Therefore, code execution will continue until it reaches the `send` or `recv` functions. Connection and reconnection handling is processed in the background.

There are two functions used to send and receive messages. To send a message, just call a function `socket.send`, which accepts at least one argument as a string value. This string will be sent to the other side of the communication. A message can be received with the `socket.recv` or `socket.recvAll` function. The key difference between these two functions is that `socket.recv` will receive only one message. The other function, `socket.recvAll`, can receive even multiple parts of a message and glues them together into one string. This is useful mainly when transferring large data over a network. Sending multiple parts of one message can be done with the `socket.send` function, while adding a second argument with the `zmq.ZMQ_SNDMORE` flag. This flag signals the ZeroMQ library that there is more data to be sent. The following sample code shows the usage pattern for multipart messages:

```
socket.send('Part one', zmq.ZMQ_SNDMORE)
socket.send('Part two', zmq.ZMQ_SNDMORE)
socket.send('The last part of a message')
```

There's a more elegant solution to send multiple parts of a message. You can use the `socket.sendMultipart` function, where you can place all parts into a single table and send them in one shot.

```
socket.sendMultipart({
    'Part one',
    'Part two',
    'The last part of a message'
})
```

This is especially useful for the router socket type where the peer identifier is sent as a part at the beginning of a message.

The polling object helps to determine when the connection line is ready to receive or send data. Polling in general will effectively block code execution until the line is ready for specified I/O operation. When transferring a lot of messages, it's better to use polling even for sending data. You can achieve this by adding another polling function as follows:

```
poll.add(socket, zmq.ZMQ_POLLOUT, function(s)
    -- user code to send a message
end)
```

The polling function will always receive one parameter containing the socket object specific to the connection.

Polling must be started with the `poll.start` function, otherwise it will have no effect. You can set up a timeout value by adding a numerical argument to the `poll.start` function. The timeout value is expected to be in milliseconds.

You don't have to worry about the message queuing problem as the ZeroMQ library solves this in its separate thread.

Sending messages to many hosts at once

There might be a case when you'd like to send a single message to multiple hosts at the same time. A typical example of such a situation can be a chat application. The ZeroMQ library solves this problem with the Publisher-Subscriber model, which is similar to a well-known multicast. Multiple types of messages can be divided into topics identified by a simple string value.

Do note that with the Publisher-Subscriber model, you can send messages only from the publisher to the subscriber, not the other way round.

Getting ready

For this recipe, you'll be using one publisher part and at least one subscriber. You can run more subscriber instances to see the effect of this network model.

How to do it...

This recipe will be divided into two parts, one for the publisher and the other for the subscriber.

The publisher part

Let's take a look at the publisher recipe:

1. First you'll need to prepare the ZeroMQ socket for the publisher:

```
local zmq = require 'zmq'
local context = assert(zmq.context())
local socket = assert(context.socket(zmq.ZMQ_PUB))
assert(socket.bind("tcp://*:12345"))
```

2. Notice that now you're using a different type of socket identified by the `zmq.ZMQ_PUB` constant.

3. In the next step, you need to set up message polling for sending. In the publisher mode, you need to send the topic name first:

```
local poll = zmq.poll()
local topic = 'demo'
poll.add(socket, zmq.ZMQ_POLLOUT, function(socket)
  assert(socket.sendMultipart({topic, 'Hello everyone!'}))
end)
```

4. This time, you'll be using polling for the message output to keep up with your network bandwidth.

5. In the final part of the publisher, you'll be sending messages over and over in a loop. However, you'd be sending hundreds or thousands of messages per second. It's better to limit the message output to a reasonable one message per second.

```
local lastTime = os.clock()
while true do
  local newTime = os.clock()
  if (newTime-lastTime) >= 1 then
    lastTime = newTime
    poll.start()
  end
end
socket.close()
```

The subscriber part

In this part, you'll be using a socket with the `zmq.ZMQ_SUB` type identifier. Other code parts are almost identical to the previous code samples:

```
local zmq = require 'zmq'
local context = assert(zmq.context())
local socket = assert(context.socket(zmq.ZMQ_SUB))
assert(socket.connect("tcp://localhost:12345"))
```

1. The cool part starts with using socket options to subscribe to the specific topics:

```
local topic = 'demo'
socket.options.subscribe = topic
```

2. You can subscribe to additional topics by using the `subscribe` socket option multiple times. Refer to the following code, for instance:

```
socket.options.subscribe = 'topic1'
socket.options.subscribe = 'topic2'
```

3. There is an option to unsubscribe as well.

```
socket.options.unsubscribe = 'topic2'
```

4. If you subscribe to the topic with an empty string, it means you need to subscribe to all topics.

5. After this, you need to prepare polling functions to receive messages from all the subscribed topics:

```
local poll = zmq.poll()
poll.add(socket, zmq.ZMQ_POLLIN, function(s)
   local topic = assert(socket.recv())
   local result = assert(socket.recvAll())
   print(topic, result)
end)
```

 Do note that you need to use the `socket.recv` function to obtain only the topic name. Otherwise, the `socket.recvAll` function will merge the topic name and the message into one string. This way you can differentiate messages from different topics.

6. In the final step, you'll need to prepare a loop for message polling and cleanup.

```
while (true) do
poll.start()
end

socket.disconnect()
```

How it works...

This recipe uses the one-directional pattern that's very close to radio transmission. It can be viewed as if you were sending messages at different frequencies and people can tune-in to specific kinds of messages they like. Transmissions occur for connected peers only, so there's no wasted bandwidth. However, if you connect later to the publisher, you'll always miss the first few messages. It's just like a radio. You won't get your lottery winning numbers if you connect too late. Similarly, if there are too many messages in transmission, you'll miss some of them. This behavior is controlled by the so-called **high watermark** or **HWM** in short and it's interpreted as the maximum amount of messages. You can adjust HWM values for sending or receiving using the socket option, as shown in the following code:

```
socket.options.rcvhwm = 1000
socket.options.sndhwm = 1000
```

Each message sent from the publisher must contain a topic name, otherwise the subscriber will not get any message.

Similarly, the subscriber can be connected to many publishers with different topics. The topic name is received in the first part of a multipart message.

If you subscribe to the topic with an empty string value, it'll subscribe to all the available topics.

Communication between threads

Communication between threads can be tedious to get right. With a ZeroMQ library, you can easily reuse the previous code to move from the network to interprocess communication merely by changing the transport protocol in the connection string. The LuaZMQ library incorporates simple thread control capabilities but you're free to use any libraries to manage threads.

Note that the Lua language contains coroutines to achieve cooperative multitasking, except that everything is processed in a single thread relying on explicit scheduling. It means that only one CPU core is used by your application.

This recipe will give you basic insight in to parallel processing of information in the Lua language.

You'll be sending the well known filling text `Lorem ipsum` to the reply side and it'll append `dolor sit amet` in the end. The resulting text will be sent back to the request side and displayed on the screen.

Getting ready

You can view this recipe as a simple mashup of the request-reply model into one Lua script, while the request part is processed in parallel to the reply part.

How to do it...

In this case, the whole thread code for the request part will be stored in a string variable that will be processed in another thread:

```lua
local req = [[
  local name = unpack(arg)
  local socket,msg = assert(context.socket(zmq.ZMQ_REQ))
  local result, msg = assert(socket.connect("inproc://test1"))
  local poll = zmq.poll()

  poll.add(socket, zmq.ZMQ_POLLIN, function(socket)
    local result = socket.recvAll()
    if result then
      print(name, string.format("Recieved data: %q", result))
    end
  end)

  socket.send("Lorem ipsum")
  poll.start()
  socket.close()
]]
```

As you can see, there's not a single line that would explicitly say that this code will be processed in a thread.

1. You can move on to the **Reply** part. The following code will look incredibly similar to the code from previous recipes. This is a good example of the ZeroMQ library's versatility:

```
local zmq = require 'zmq'
local context, msg = assert(zmq.context())
local socket,msg = assert(context.socket(zmq.ZMQ_REP))
local result, msg = assert(socket.bind("inproc://test1"))
local poll = zmq.poll()

poll.add(socket, zmq.ZMQ_POLLIN, function(socket)
  local result = socket.recvAll()
  if result then
    print("Reply part",
      string.format("Recieved data: %q", result))
    socket.send(result.." dolor sit amet")
  end
end)
```

2. The only difference is the transport used. Instead of using the TCP transport protocol, there's an in-process communication transport.

3. The next steps will consist of starting a new thread with the Request part. The main thread with the reply part will wait until it gets a request to reply. You can create a new thread with the `context.thread` function, which expects at least one parameter with the thread code in a single string. You can add another parameter that will be added into the thread global argument list.

```
local thread = context.thread(req, 'Request part')
poll.start()
```

4. The last two lines will ensure that the main thread will wait until the thread closes properly. Without this, you'd get thread abortion, which is sometimes called `Parent thread kills its children`. It sounds horrible as it's a sign of bad application design.

```
thread.join()
socket.close()
```

How it works...

This recipe uses `inproc` or in-process transport to communicate with the request-reply pattern. Almost every aspect of communication remains the same except that the ZeroMQ library uses the shared memory region to transfer messages between threads. This works exceptionally well even without tedious synchronization routines. By using the push-pull socket types instead of request-reply, you can easily create a distributed processing system with a few lines of code or even combine it with the `pgm` transport protocol to achieve distributed computing on more than one computer.

Threads are created with the `context.thread` function, where the first argument is always a thread code. LuaZMQ will create a new independent Lua state that shares only the context object. The context object is thread-safe; therefore, it can be shared among all threads.

Optionally, you can add numerical or string variables, which will be available to the thread code via the global `arg` variable. This emulates a situation where you execute the Lua script with arguments.

The only tricky part is thread management. Before closing your main process, it should always wait for its threads to finish up using the `thread.join` function.

Index

Thank you for buying
Lua Game Development Cookbook

About Packt Publishing

Packt, pronounced 'packed', published its first book, *Mastering phpMyAdmin for Effective MySQL Management*, in April 2004, and subsequently continued to specialize in publishing highly focused books on specific technologies and solutions.

Our books and publications share the experiences of your fellow IT professionals in adapting and customizing today's systems, applications, and frameworks. Our solution-based books give you the knowledge and power to customize the software and technologies you're using to get the job done. Packt books are more specific and less general than the IT books you have seen in the past. Our unique business model allows us to bring you more focused information, giving you more of what you need to know, and less of what you don't.

Packt is a modern yet unique publishing company that focuses on producing quality, cutting-edge books for communities of developers, administrators, and newbies alike. For more information, please visit our website at www.packtpub.com.

About Packt Open Source

In 2010, Packt launched two new brands, Packt Open Source and Packt Enterprise, in order to continue its focus on specialization. This book is part of the Packt open source brand, home to books published on software built around open source licenses, and offering information to anybody from advanced developers to budding web designers. The Open Source brand also runs Packt's open source Royalty Scheme, by which Packt gives a royalty to each open source project about whose software a book is sold.

Writing for Packt

We welcome all inquiries from people who are interested in authoring. Book proposals should be sent to author@packtpub.com. If your book idea is still at an early stage and you would like to discuss it first before writing a formal book proposal, then please contact us; one of our commissioning editors will get in touch with you.

We're not just looking for published authors; if you have strong technical skills but no writing experience, our experienced editors can help you develop a writing career, or simply get some additional reward for your expertise.

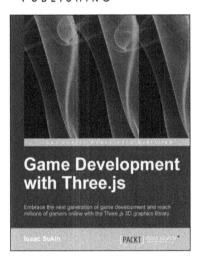
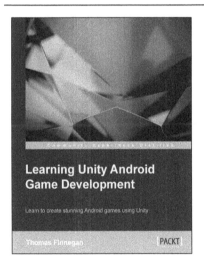

www.ingramcontent.com/pod-product-compliance
Lightning Source LLC
Chambersburg PA
CBHW080150060326
40689CB00018B/3926

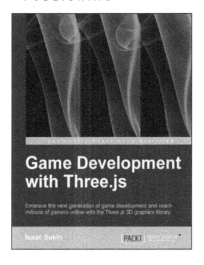

Game Development
with Three.js

ISBN: 978-1-78216-853-9   Paperback: 118 pages

Embrace the next generation of game development and reach millions of gamers online with the Three.js 3D graphics library

1.   Develop immersive 3D games that anyone can play on the Internet.

2.   Learn Three.js from a gaming perspective, including everything you need to build beautiful and high-performance worlds.

3.   A step-by-step guide filled with game-focused examples and tips.

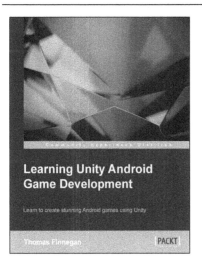

Learning Unity Android
Game Development

ISBN: 978-1-78439-469-1   Paperback: 338 pages

Learn to create stunning Android games using Unity

1.   Leverage the new features of Unity 5 for the Android mobile market with hands-on projects and real-world examples.

2.   Create comprehensive and robust games using various customizations and additions available in Unity such as camera, lighting, and sound effects.

3.   Precise instructions to use Unity to create an Android-based mobile game.

Please check **www.PacktPub.com** for information on our titles

www.ingramcontent.com/pod-product-compliance
Lightning Source LLC
Chambersburg PA
CBHW080150060326
40689CB00018B/3926